WATERLOO COUNTY

BOARD OF EDUCATION

W.C.I.   BOOK NO.

YEAR   FORM   NAME

2002 .1.R. Julie Button

2002 .1.C. Natasha Harinko

CIVICS

Participating in a Democratic Society

Senior Author

Alan Skeoch
Teacher, Parkdale Collegiate Institute (Retired)

Authors

Peter Flaherty
Teacher, Runnymede Collegiate Institute, Toronto, Ontario

D. Lynn Moore
Teacher, Forest Hill Collegiate Institute, Toronto, Ontario

McGraw-Hill Ryerson

Toronto Montréal New York Burr Ridge Bangkok Bogotá Caracas Lisbon London Madrid
Mexico City Milan New Delhi Seoul Singapore Sydney Taipei

McGraw-Hill
Ryerson Limited

A Subsidiary of The McGraw·Hill Companies

Canadian Cataloguing in Publication Data

Skeoch, Alan,
      Civics: participating in a democratic society

For use in grade 10.
Includes index.
ISBN 0-07-086389-X

Civics, Canadian. 2. Citizenship – Canada. I. Flaherty, Peter. II. Moore, D. Lynn. III. Title.

JL15.S58 2000   320.471   C00-930965-9

Publisher: Patty Pappas
Associate Editor: Dyanne Rivers
Supervising Editor: Crystal Shortt
Copy Editor: Gail Copeland
Permissions Editor: Ann Ludbrook
Production Supervisor: Yolanda Pigden
Production Co-ordinator: Jennifer Vassiliou
Editorial Assistant: Joanne Murray
Interior Design and Electronic Page Make-up: Greg Devitt
Interior Maps: Deborah Crowle
Cover Design: Greg Devitt

REVIEWERS

Angelo De Grazia
Social Science Chairperson, St. Patrick High School,
Thunder Bay, Ontario

Michael DeKay
Teacher, Thames Valley District School Board, Ontario

Roberta Fuller
Teacher, Clarke High School, Bethany, Ontario

Larry A. Glassford
Associate Professor, Faculty of Education,
University of Windsor

John Meyer
Faculty of Education, University of Windsor (Retired)

Marian B. Moon
Teacher, Prince Edward Collegiate Institute, Picton, Ontario

Pamela Spearns
Teacher, St. Paul Catholic Secondary School,
Mississauga, Ontario

James Terry
Head of History and Contemporary Studies, Wallaceburg
District Secondary School, Wallaceburg, Ontario

ACKNOWLEDGEMENTS

At the heart of citizenship is the recognition that we are not alone, that we do not want to be alone, and that we can join one another as informed, purposeful, and active citizens to blend individualism with the public good. Every citizen knows that the two seemingly contradictory human values, competition and co-operation, can be harmonized. Erasmus, a man nearly forgotten by history, was convinced in the turbulent 16th century that nearly all conflicts between peoples can be resolved happily with a little yielding by public-spirited citizens. This is the essence of democracy.

Authors get much credit for things they do not do. As the senior author of *Civics: Participating in a Democratic Society*, I am very much aware of this fact. As a result, I would like to thank the following people for their sung and unsung involvement in this project: Dr. Jim Langstaff, Patty Pappas, Dyanne Rivers, Mike Brillinger, my fellow authors Peter Flaherty and Lynn Moore, Dave Hopkins, Chris Delaney, Joanne Murray, Crystal Shortt, Gail Copeland, Greg Devitt, the Richmond Hill Historical Society, the teachers who contributed to the review process, the decision makers at McGraw-Hill Ryerson Ltd., and the great civic thinkers of human civilization. Most important, I would like to thank my wife Marjorie, who has embraced the fact that retirement does not mean the cessation of work, but rather the freedom to work at what is most enjoyable — cultural transfer. If anything has been transferred to our sons, Andrew and Kevin, and the thousands of students we have met along the way, we hope it is an awareness that our human journey cannot proceed without the help of others or without helping others.

— *Alan Skeoch*

I would like to thank Patty Pappas of McGraw-Hill Ryerson Ltd., who invited me to participate in the writing of *Civics: Participating in a Democratic Society* and gave me and the other authors great support and encouragement throughout. Dyanne Rivers, our editor, was incredibly energetic and creative in shaping my very rough chapter drafts into polished prose. She was also extremely patient and sympathetic in understanding the fact that textbook authors are often also teachers who must cope with great demands on their time. My fellow authors, Al Skeoch and Lynn Moore, were a pleasure to work with. We grew and developed as a team over the course of writing this book, and I learned a lot from both of them. Finally, I would like to thank my wife, Viviana Patroni, for her understanding on all those evenings when I arrived home from school and plunged straight into the writing of this book. It was well worth the effort!

— *Peter Flaherty*

I would like to thank Alan Skeoch, the senior author of this book, for his encouragement and mentorship. Peter Flaherty also provided friendly advice and encouragement. Many thanks to our editor, Dyanne Rivers, and publisher, Patty Pappas, for keeping us on track and providing valuable insight. I would also like to thank my colleagues in the history department at Forest Hill Collegiate Institute — David Hopkins, Robin Chan, Martin Sable, Stephan Spenceley, Jory Vernon, and Vincent Zambrano — for helping me through the writing process. Also thanks to James Whitaker for his support throughout my teaching career. Last, I would like to thank my friends and family for keeping sane through the time I spent working on this book and teaching.

— *Lynn Moore*

CONTENTS

The Active Citizen

McGraw-Hill Ryerson Ltd.

The Active Citizen

The Active Citizen

TOUR of the TEXTBOOK

Welcome to *Civics: Participating in a Democratic Society*. This textbook traces the development of democratic decision making, explains how decisions are made in Canada and other countries, and introduces a variety of themes and issues that will help you become an informed, purposeful, and active citizen — of Canada and the world.

Unit Opener

- *Civics: Participating in a Democratic Society* has two units, The Informed Citizen and The Purposeful Citizen. Integrated into both these units are activities designed to encourage you to become an Active Citizen.
- Each unit opener includes a large illustration that provides a visual introduction to the unit.
- An introduction sums up what the unit is about and helps you start thinking about what you will learn.
- Unit Expectations outline the things you will learn and the things you will do as the unit unfolds.

Chapter Opener

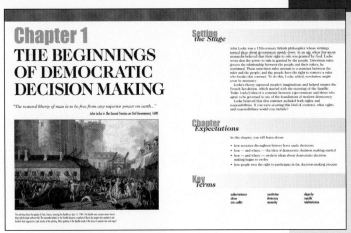

- Every chapter opens with a meaningful quotation drawn from literature, history, or recent speeches.
- An illustration accompanies the quotation and leads into the themes and issues that will be discussed in the chapter.
- Setting the Stage presents an overview of the chapter content.
- Chapter Expectations outline the specific topics you will learn about in the chapter.
- Key Terms is a list of important words that you will encounter in the chapter. The first time they appear in the text, the words are in boldface type and are defined. The words also appear in the glossary at the end of the book.

Think ... Discuss ... Act

- These features are placed at various points in the chapter and provide a brief scenario that expands on the themes and issues developed in the chapter. The scenario is followed by open-ended questions that will help you think about, discuss, and act upon the themes and issues.

McGraw-Hill Ryerson Ltd.

TOUR of the TEXTBOOK

Web Connection

- By following the directions given in these features, you can access the Internet at school or at home to find out more about what you have learned in the chapter.

FYI

- These features provide interesting tidbits "for your information." They relate to the themes and issues introduced in the chapter.

Case Study

- This full-page feature, which appears in every chapter, is designed to help you delve more deeply into the themes and issues of the chapter.
- Questions and activities help you focus your learning.

Citizens in Action

- Every chapter includes a full-page feature that tells the story of everyday citizens who have made a difference in their community, country, or the world.

TOUR of the TEXTBOOK

A Day in the Life ...

- Twice within each unit, these full-page features focus on people who have followed a political path to civic action.

Chapter Review

- At the end of each chapter, questions and activities appear under the headings Summing It Up, Getting the Facts, and Using the Facts. These questions and activities enable you to think more deeply about and put into practice what you have learned in the chapter.
- You and your teacher can choose which activities you wish to complete and whether you will complete them on your own, with a partner, or in a group.
- The activities take into account various learning styles.

Unit Review

- At the end of each unit are two pages of questions and activities titled Pulling It Together. The questions and activities appear under the headings Focus Your Learning, Apply Your Learning, and Reflect on Your Learning.
- You and your teacher can choose which activities you wish to complete and whether you will complete them on your own, with a partner, or in a group.
- These activities will enable you to apply your learning in a variety of ways that will help you become an informed, purposeful, and active citizen.

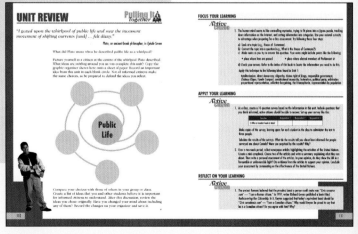

McGraw-Hill Ryerson Ltd.

ARE YOU BEING A GOOD CITIZEN?

"Dad, I got 99 percent in math on my report card," crowed Bruce Langstaff more than 40 years ago.

To this day, Bruce remembers his father's response: "That's great. But are you also being a good citizen?"

Are you being a good citizen? Bruce's father, Dr. Jim Langstaff, valued citizenship — the belief that our duty to society is as important as our duty to ourselves — as highly as personal achievement.

Dr. Langstaff practised medicine for decades in Richmond Hill, Ontario, as had his father before him and his grandfather before that. For all the Langstaffs, the medical practice meant responsibility. One example of what citizenship meant to Dr. Langstaff occurred on a stormy winter day in the 1930s. Word had reached him that a woman who lived on an isolated farm was about to give birth and needed help right away.

Dr. Langstaff warmed up the car, loaded his skis, checked his medical bag, wrapped himself up well, and set off into the blizzard. The roads became so bad that he could not continue driving. He abandoned the car and strapped on his skis.

Snowdrifts on the road made skiing difficult, so Dr. Langstaff took to the fields alongside the road. Going down one long slope, he gathered speed but failed to see the top wire of a farm fence that had been nearly buried by the deep snow. The tips of his skis caught the wire, and he tumbled head over heels into a tangle of fence wire and snow. He was so badly tangled that he thought he might freeze to death before he worked himself loose.

Eventually, he did manage to free himself. He reached the farmhouse, helped deliver the baby, and waited for the weather to clear. He was driven back to his car on a heavy sleigh hauled by a team of horses.

Dr. Langstaff took missions like this for granted. He was needed, and he went to help a fellow citizen. Payment was secondary. Sometimes in the 1930s, no payment was possible. Other times, payment was in kind, perhaps a chicken or a cut of beef.

This anecdote from the life of one person is echoed every day by thousands of Canadians who recognize that the privilege of citizenship includes responsibilities. Sometimes, their actions are dramatic. More often, though, their actions are simply small acts of citizenship that people take for granted, just as Dr. Langstaff did.

At the same time, thousands of other people do not take citizenship seriously at all. Many do not even understand the meaning of the word. It is to both these groups — the committed and the uncommitted, the active and the passive — that this book is dedicated.

Are you being a good citizen?

Alan Skeoch
May 2000

THE INFORMED CITIZEN

Parliament Hill in Ottawa, Ontario, is the home of Canada's national government. In the House of Commons, elected representatives make decisions that affect the lives of Canadians in many ways. But who gives elected representatives the power to do this? In a democracy like Canada, it is the people. Citizens have the right to choose who governs them.

Choosing who governs is not citizens' only responsibility, however. As Canada and the world move into a new millennium, people's lives are changing dramatically. New technologies such as computers and the Internet are changing the way people live. Dealing with these changes poses a huge challenge for both individual citizens and governments.

Since the birth of democracy in ancient Athens, it has been the duty of citizens to be informed about public affairs. Being informed means understanding how democratic decision making evolved; how democratic decision making works; what it means to be a citizen of a diverse, democratic society; and what it means to be a citizen of the global community. By exploring these issues, this unit will help you become an informed citizen.

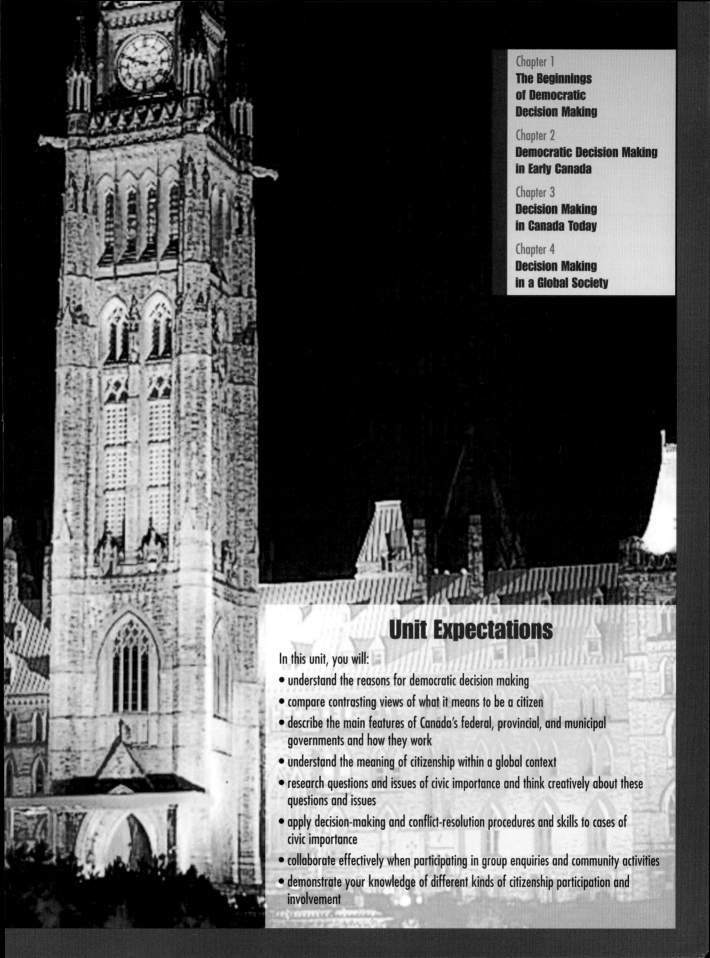

Unit Expectations

In this unit, you will:

- understand the reasons for democratic decision making
- compare contrasting views of what it means to be a citizen
- describe the main features of Canada's federal, provincial, and municipal governments and how they work
- understand the meaning of citizenship within a global context
- research questions and issues of civic importance and think creatively about these questions and issues
- apply decision-making and conflict-resolution procedures and skills to cases of civic importance
- collaborate effectively when participating in group enquiries and community activities
- demonstrate your knowledge of different kinds of citizenship participation and involvement

Chapter 1

THE BEGINNINGS OF DEMOCRATIC DECISION MAKING

"The natural liberty of man is to be free from any superior power on earth..."

John Locke in *The Second Treatise on Civil Government*, 1690

This painting shows the people of Paris, France, storming the Bastille on July 14, 1789. The Bastille was a prison where French kings jailed people without trial. The successful attack on the Bastille became a symbol of liberty for people who wanted to win freedom from oppression. Look closely at the painting. What qualities of the Bastille made it the focus of people's fear and anger?

John Locke was a 17th-century British philosopher whose writings turned ideas about government upside down. In an age when European monarchs believed that their right to rule was granted by God, Locke wrote that the power to rule is granted by the people. Unwritten rules govern the relationship between the people and their rulers, he continued. These unwritten rules amount to a contract between the ruler and the people, and the people have the right to remove a ruler who breaks this contract. To do this, Locke added, revolution might even be necessary.

Locke's theory captured people's imaginations and helped inspire the French Revolution, which started with the storming of the Bastille. Today Locke's idea of a contract between a government and those who agree to be governed is one of the foundations of modern democracy.

Locke believed that this contract included both rights and responsibilities. If you were creating this kind of contract, what rights and responsibilities would you include?

Chapter
Expectations

In this chapter, you will learn about:

- how societies throughout history have made decisions
- how — and where — the idea of democratic decision making started
- how — and where — modern ideas about democratic decision making began to evolve
- how people won the right to participate in the decision-making process

Key
Terms

authoritarianism	constitution	oligarchy
citizen	democracy	republic
civic conflict	monarchy	totalitarianism

THE RULES PEOPLE LIVE BY

Unwritten rules or customs govern the behaviour of people in every social community or society. Even in prehistoric hunting and gathering societies, people lived by unwritten rules. These rules governed things like the work the people did and the way they treated one another. Children learned the rules informally, by watching and listening to family members and other people around them. When they grew up, they in turn taught the rules to their own children.

Even today, this is often the way customs are passed from one generation to the next. What unwritten rules of behaviour have you learned from members of your family? What unwritten rules govern the way you behave when you get together with friends?

Societies need rules to help people live in harmony and decide what to do when a disagreement or conflict arises. And whenever people gather for any reason, disagreements or conflicts do arise. People might disagree about what they should do or how they should treat one another. In small social groups such as your family or class at school, disagreements and conflicts like these can usually be resolved through discussion.

Discussion is practical when only a few people are involved. It is not as practical when the society is larger. In societies that contain thousands or even millions of people, the potential for conflict is much greater because there are many more differing opinions. What is more, the conflicts may be very complicated — and resolving them may be difficult. In many respects, the history of government can be viewed as a history of making rules to help prevent and resolve conflicts and establish peace among people.

These students are waiting in line in the school cafeteria. Examine the picture and think about times you have waited in a line. What rules of behaviour are the students in this line observing? Why are they observing these rules?

Philosopher Robert Nisbet wrote about what he called the anticommunity. He said that it is "a world overwhelmingly characterized by strife, dissension and uncertainty."

We live in communities where human behaviour is governed by written and unwritten rules that make our lives safe and secure — most of the time. What would life be like in an anticommunity where there are no rules?

Writers have tried to imagine this. Futurists and science-fiction authors have written about what life would be like if a worldwide disaster occurred. Many believe that organized society would break down. It would be every person for him- or herself. There would be no communities of citizens.

1. Describe how your life might change if you suddenly found yourself living in an anticommunity. You might open with these sentences: "When I woke up this morning, everything I took for granted was gone. I noticed this first when I got out of bed ..."
2. Are rules necessary for communities to live in harmony? Choose examples from your school community to illustrate your point of view.
3. Some people believe that violence would be inevitable in a world without laws. Why do they think so? What do you believe? Why?

TWO WAYS OF MAKING DECISIONS

The Authoritarian Way

People have not always had the opportunity to make decisions about how they are governed. In fact, for most of human history, societies

Benito Mussolini marches at the head of his staff. Displays like this were common during the fascist dictator's 20-year rule of Italy, which started in 1922. His goal was to re-create the Roman Empire, which had existed 2000 years earlier. He did this by using his power ruthlessly.

were governed either by one person or by a small group who possessed complete power over the people they ruled.

For example, historians and archaeologists have found that ancient civilizations were ruled by a single person, usually a monarch such as a king, queen, or emperor. The monarch was often helped by a small group of hand-picked advisers, including priests or religious leaders who instructed people in the society's beliefs. These beliefs, of course, included absolute obedience to the will of the ruler.

Monarchies like these were — and are — authoritarian forms of government. Authoritarian governments require total obedience to the authority of a single person or small group. Individual freedom does not exist.

Totalitarianism is an extreme form of **authoritarianism**. It is a system in which the leader or party in power has total control over nearly every aspect of people's lives. Twentieth-century examples of totalitarian states include Nazi Germany under Adolf Hitler, Fascist Italy under Benito Mussolini, and the Union of Soviet Socialist Republics under the Communist dictator Joseph Stalin.

The Democratic Way

In a **democracy**, the people control the process of making the rules about how they are governed. In fact, the word "democracy" comes from the Greek words *demos*, meaning people, and *kratia*, meaning rule. "Democracy" means that the people rule.

Democratic forms of government are very different from authoritarian forms. The chart on this page shows some differences between the two systems. What are some other differences?

Some Differences between Authoritarian and Democratic Governments

Authoritarian Government	Democratic Government
Leaders are usually self-appointed.	Leaders are elected by citizens.
Leaders cannot usually be replaced.	Leaders' term in office is limited. Elections must be held at regular intervals.
Citizens cannot question or speak out against leaders' actions.	Citizens can question and speak out against leaders' actions.

In 1863, at the height of the American Civil War, President Abraham Lincoln defined democracy in a famous speech that became known as the Gettysburg Address. His speech was delivered at Gettysburg, Pennsylvania, where a terrible battle had been fought months earlier. Lincoln said that democracy is a system of government "of the people, by the people, and for the people."

Most people probably prefer to live in a democracy. Both democratic and authoritarian systems have benefits and drawbacks. In a democracy, for example, people have the right to criticize the government if they believe that its actions are wrong. This is usually considered a benefit, because citizens can express their views freely, though there are some people who regard this right as a drawback. What are some other benefits of living in a democracy?

People who regard freedom of expression as a drawback believe that it can lead to disturbances that upset public order. Authoritarian governments often claim that their countries, where freedom of expression is non-existent or limited, are peaceful, orderly places. They say this because strikes and protests rarely occur. Do you agree with this claim? Why?

THE ROOTS OF DEMOCRATIC CITIZENSHIP

When people lived in small, nomadic groups, on farms, or in villages, they knew nearly everyone around them. In some cases, they were even related to many of them. They did not need written rules because their society was small and their customs were similar. Everyone understood the unwritten rules they lived by.

Ancient Governments

Things started to change as villages grew into towns and towns grew into cities. When people began to share the same space with many others whom they did not know, they found that their customs were sometimes very different. This led to **civic conflicts** — disagreements among people who live in the same community.

These civic conflicts arose over issues such as land and property, the purchase and sale of goods, and things that disturbed the public peace. As a result, people had to work out formal ways of preventing and resolving conflicts. To make sure that everyone understood the rules, they were recorded in writing as laws.

Hammurabi, who ruled Bab-Ilu from about 1792 to 1750 BCE, created some of the earliest written laws. Called Hammurabi's Code, the 282 laws were carved into this column of rock. The laws covered things such as murder, theft, divorce, adoption, military service, interest rates, tenant farming, and wages for labourers.

The rulers of these ancient city states often waged war against their neighbours. When their wars were successful, the city states took over neighbouring territory and sometimes became the hub of vast empires.

Bab-Ilu, also known as Babylon, was one ancient city state that grew into an empire. It was located on the Euphrates River in present-day Iraq. As the rulers of Bab-Ilu captured more and more territory, they became even more powerful. Eventually, these rulers dominated the lives of thousands — and even millions — of people.

When a state was ruled by a monarch, the right to rule was usually hereditary. When the monarch died, the eldest child — usually the eldest son — inherited the throne. This system, known as **monarchy**, continues in some countries today,

Emperor T'ai Tsung is often called China's greatest ruler. Though he was an absolute monarch, he was also a well-educated, thoughtful person who introduced many reforms. For example, he chose military leaders and civil servants for their loyalty and ability, not because they were from powerful families.

though most modern monarchs have far less power than in the past.

How did monarchs stay in power? Often, they were able to persuade the people that their right to rule had been granted by their god or gods. In ancient China, for example, the emperors insisted that their right to rule came from what they called the Mandate of Heaven. The people believed that Heaven, their chief god, was the husband of Earth and that their emperors were the Sons of Heaven. The duty of the emperor was to carry out the will of Heaven, not the will of the people.

This idea of government persisted for thousands of years. Rulers like Emperor T'ai Tsung, who ruled China from 626 to 649 CE, and King Louis XIV, who ruled France from 1643 to 1715, were absolute monarchs.

Like other European monarchs of the time, Louis XIV claimed that he ruled by "divine right." He believed that his right to rule had been granted by God and was, therefore, divine. As a result, he also believed that he had a right to tax people heavily to pay for his extravagant lifestyle.

Louis XIV once said, *"L'état, c'est moi"* — "I am the state." What do you think he meant?

The most extravagant monument built by King Louis XIV of France was the Palace of Versailles. The palace, which took 47 years to build, was surrounded by huge formal gardens. It housed Louis XIV and his family as well as 5000 nobles, who lived there permanently so that they could better serve their king. Another 5000 servants lived nearby.

Think ... Discuss ... Act

Early in his rule of China, Emperor T'ai Tsung said:

> *The first principle in kingship is to preserve the people. A king who exploits the people for his personal gains is like a man who cuts his own thighs to feed himself. He quenches his hunger for the time being but will die eventually ... As there is no such thing as a crooked shadow following a straight object, it is inconceivable that the people can be disloyal when their rulers are virtuous ...*

1. What did T'ai Tsung mean when he said that a "king who exploits his people ... is like a man who cuts his own thighs to feed himself"?
2. T'ai Tsung and France under Louis XIV were authoritarian regimes. How were the beliefs of these two rulers similar? How were they different?
3. Substitute the word "leadership" for "kingship" in the first sentence of T'ai Tsung's statement and discuss why this new statement is — or is not — true today. Illustrate your position with examples from your school or a team or group you belong to.

Ancient Athens

The first city states of ancient Greece were much like those that existed in other parts of the world. They were governed by a single ruler or ruling clique. Later some of them began to evolve very differently. Between about 700 and 350 BCE, the people who lived in some Greek city states gradually won the right to share in decision making.

To the ancient Greeks, a city and a state were the same thing. As a result, they used a single word, *polis*, to mean both. From *polis* came the word *politics*, which referred to the public affairs of the city. In English, this meaning has been expanded to include the affairs of government in general. The word *polis* continues to exist in English words like "metropolis" and "megalopolis." What other English words come from *polis*?

The ancient Greek *polis* of Athens is often called the cradle of democracy. It is where the idea of democracy first took root. In Athens, all **citizens** were expected to participate actively in the city's affairs.

The mountainous geography of Greece contributed to the growth of independent city states such as Athens, Sparta, Corinth, and Thebes. The mountains protected the cities from attack — and made it hard for one city to launch an attack against another. As a result, Greek city states usually stayed small. This made it easy for citizens to participate in public affairs.

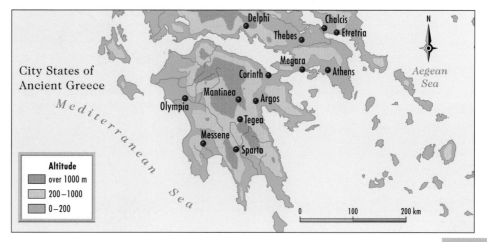

City States of Ancient Greece

Altitude	
	over 1000 m
	200 – 1000
	0 – 200

Pericles, an Athenian who lived between about 495 and 429 BCE, believed firmly in his city's democratic form of government. When Athens went to war with its rival, the city of Sparta, in 430 BCE, Pericles was elected *strategos* — military leader — by the citizens. Unlike Athens, Sparta was not a democracy. Spartans had little say in their city's affairs. Because of this, winning the war against Sparta was very important to the Athenians.

Early in the war, Pericles spoke at the funeral of some Athenian soldiers who had been killed in battle. In his speech, he explained what was at stake: the survival of Athenian democracy. His "Funeral Oration" is still considered to be a statement of classical democratic values. Here is an excerpt from his speech:

> Our constitution is called a democracy because power is in the hands not of a minority but of the whole people. When it is a question of settling private disputes, everyone is equal before the law; when it is a question of putting one person before another in positions of public responsibility, what counts is not membership of a particular class, but the actual ability which the man possesses. No one, so long as he has it in him to be of service to the state, is kept in political obscurity because of poverty ...

> [In Athens] each individual is interested not only in his own affairs but in the affairs of the state as well: even those who are mostly occupied with their own business are extremely well informed on general politics — this is a peculiarity of ours: we do not say that a man who takes no interest in politics is a man who minds his own business; we say that he has no business here at all ...

This marble bust of Pericles was made centuries after he died. As a result, no one knows for sure if this is what he really looked like. People are more certain about the words of his "Funeral Oration," though. They were written down by an eyewitness: the historian Thucydides, who included the speech in his account of the war between Athens and Sparta.

When the time came to discuss and vote on important issues, Athenian citizens assembled at the Pnyx, their equivalent of Canada's Parliament Hill. This is what the Pnyx looks like today. In the distance — on another hilltop called the Acropolis — is the Parthenon, a beautiful temple dedicated to Athena Parthenos, the patron goddess of Athens.

Every citizen had the right to vote on decisions affecting the way the city was governed. As a result, the system of government that existed in ancient Athens is called a direct democracy.

The ancient Athenians' idea of democracy was different from ours, though. Only citizens were allowed to participate in the city's public affairs — and only free male adults who had been born in Athens could call themselves citizens. Slaves, women, children, and anyone not born in the city were protected by the law, but they had no political rights at all. This meant that most people who lived in the city had no say in their government.

www.school.mcgrawhill.ca/resources

To find out more about citizenship in ancient Athens, go to History Resources, then to *Civics: Participating in a Democratic Society* to see where to go next.

Ancient Rome

At about the same time as a form of democracy was flourishing in Athens, people were starting to settle in a city state on the Italian peninsula. This city was Rome.

Like the citizens of Athens, the people of Rome waged a long struggle to win the right to participate in their own government. At first, the city was ruled by kings. In 509 BCE, the king was driven out and Rome became a **republic**, a state that is not ruled by a hereditary monarch. People from rich and powerful families took over governing. They were called patricians.

Although power was now shared among more people, this change in the form of government made little difference to the *plebs*. These were the ordinary people — the plebeians — who made up most of the city's population. Though they greatly outnumbered the patricians, the plebeians had little say in the government.

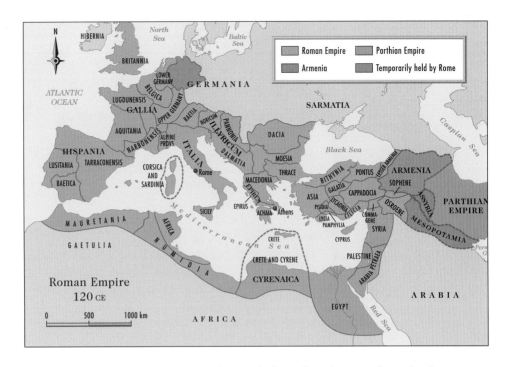

This map shows the Roman Empire in about 120 CE. The Romans called the Mediterranean Sea *Mare Nostrum* — Our Sea. Why did this name make sense to them?

Roman Empire
120 CE

Legend:
- Roman Empire
- Armenia
- Parthian Empire
- Temporarily held by Rome

Fed up with strict laws that limited their freedom and made their lives miserable, the plebeians staged what amounted to a general strike in 494 BCE. Vowing to found a new city where they would have a voice in governing themselves, they packed up their belongings and walked out of Rome.

The strategy worked. The patricians gave in to the demands of the plebeians. Over the next few centuries, the plebeians gradually won more rights, including the right to have a voice in making laws.

Though the plebeians won the right to form assemblies and contribute to making laws, these assemblies were unlike the assembly of Athens, which included all citizens of the city. The real law-making power in Rome belonged to a separate assembly called the Senate — and only patricians could be members of the Senate.

Traffic was a big concern in ancient Rome, just as it is in modern cities. The city's busy streets were often jammed with carts, wagons, and coaches of all descriptions. To ease the gridlock, the Romans passed a law barring nearly all traffic from the city during the day.

As Rome waged wars against its neighbours and expanded its territory, its borders were extended. The Romans granted many of the rights of citizenship to the male residents of the lands they had conquered.

The English word "citizen" comes from Latin, the language spoken in the city state of Rome. A *civis* was an individual citizen of the territory controlled by Rome, and each *civis* was part of the *civitas*, the citizenry as a whole. Citizenship was a highly prized status, one that not everyone was able to attain. *"Civis romanus sum"* — "I am a Roman citizen" — was the proudest claim an ancient Roman could make.

As in Athens, however, only men were entitled to call themselves citizens. Women, children, and the slaves who did the work that supported Rome's power and prosperity were not considered citizens.

Our word "city" also comes from the Latin word *civis*. The Romans, like the Greeks before them, believed that only city-dwellers could truly belong to a body of citizens and share in decision making. The ancient Greeks and Romans also believed that only city-dwellers could be truly "civilized" — able to enjoy and participate in the things cities had to offer. What other English words come from *civis*?

Though the Roman Republic lasted for centuries, it was eventually taken over by a dictator. When this happened, the Roman government had come full circle — from authoritarianism, to democracy of sorts, and back to authoritarianism.

Think ... Discuss ... Act

Justinian was an emperor who ruled Rome between 527 and 565 CE. He ordered his lawyers to gather all the Roman laws into one legal code called the *Corpus Juris Civilis*. This code later became the basis of modern European — and, therefore, Canadian — law.

Here are some of the ideas that guided the creation of Justinian's legal code:

- Something that is wrong in the beginning does not become right as time goes on.
- Someone who knows about a crime that will be committed but cannot stop it cannot be blamed for the crime.
- It is better for the crime of a guilty person to go unpunished than for an innocent person to be condemned.
- No one must suffer a penalty because of what she or he thinks.
- When a punishment is imposed by the court, the age and inexperience of the guilty party must be taken into account.

1. Form groups and choose one of these ideas. Discuss what the idea means and come up with at least one case that illustrates it. The case may be imaginary or from real life. Present your case to the class.

THE BIRTH OF MODERN DEMOCRATIC CITIZENSHIP

The end of the Roman Republic marked the beginning of a long period in which the idea of democracy seemed to have been nearly snuffed out. It was not revived till the late Middle Ages in Europe, when independent city states started to emerge again. At various times, forms of democracy existed in cities such as Venice, Genoa, Florence, Milan, Cologne, Amsterdam, and Hamburg. Like Athens and Rome, though, these city states were oligarchies. The power to make decisions was limited to a small number of people.

Though many of these medieval city states were eventually absorbed into larger nation states that were ruled by monarchs, the idea of democracy never disappeared completely. People in various countries thought and talked about the meaning of citizenship and took action to try to win citizenship rights. Their actions ultimately affected the way ideas about citizenship developed in other countries, including Canada.

The island-nation of Singapore is the only independent, self-governing city state in the modern world. This thriving metropolis in Southeast Asia is one of the world's busiest seaports and is home to about three million people.

Magna Carta

At the beginning of the 13th century, England was an absolute monarchy. Its kings believed that they ruled by divine right. In 1215, however, a group of nobles forced King John, the tyrannical reigning monarch, to sign a document that placed important limits on his power. This document was known as the Magna Carta — the Great Charter. It required the king to respect certain rights of his subjects and exercise power fairly.

The Magna Carta said that no free man could be imprisoned "except by the lawful judgment of his peers and by the law of the land." It also forced King John and his noble supporters to stop

- forcing widows to remarry
- forcing villagers to build bridges over rivers
- forcing knights to pay money to excuse themselves from guarding castles
- confiscating the horses or carts of freemen
- helping themselves to firewood that did not belong to them

Early Parliaments

Soon after the Magna Carta was signed, the kings of England started calling together representatives of the people to discuss important matters. These matters included making laws and raising taxes. The gatherings became known as parliaments, from the French word *parler*, which means to talk or speak. Eventually, the English Parliament was split into two parts. The House of Lords included people who had inherited titles, such as earls, dukes, and barons. The House of Commons was made up of commoners, people who did not have inherited titles.

These early parliaments were different from the Parliament that exists today in Canada in several important ways. Members of the House of Lords inherited their seats along with their noble titles. Members of the House of Commons were not elected by the people as a whole. They were chosen by a small number of wealthy and influential landowners, the only people allowed to vote.

However, most people living in England at the time were serfs or peasants who owned no land. As a result, they had no political rights, and no one spoke for them in Parliament.

Over time, members of Parliament gained more influence over decision making and sometimes criticized and even opposed royal policies. Still, the monarch could convene and dissolve Parliament at will. How would this power have affected decisions made by members of Parliament?

In November 1999, Queen Elizabeth II, with the Duke of Edinburgh, opened a new session of the British Parliament by delivering the Speech from the Throne in the House of Lords. For the first time in centuries, though, none of the members listening to the speech were there simply because they had inherited their seats in this House. Earlier in 1999, the British Parliament had introduced reforms that did away with the inherited seats in the House of Lords.

The Beginnings of Democratic Decision Making

England's Century of Revolution

The 1600s was a time of change in England. The tradition of calling together Parliament had become well established. Now members of Parliament wanted more say in making decisions. King Charles I, however, believed in the divine right of kings and refused to give up any of his powers. Finally, in 1642, this struggle exploded into a civil war that pitted those who supported a strong king against those who supported a strong Parliament.

The parliamentary supporters, led by Oliver Cromwell, raised an army to challenge the rule of King Charles I and his Royalist supporters. The war raged for years, until Cromwell's forces finally defeated the Royalists. Charles was put on trial, convicted of treason, and beheaded in 1649. For the next 11 years, England had no king. Cromwell and his supporters ruled the country.

This cartoon was drawn while England was controlled by Oliver Cromwell and his advisers. It shows them sitting around a council table. Read the caption and the list of those present at the table. Who is the first "person" named? Was the cartoonist a Royalist or Roundhead?

The monarchy was restored in 1660 when Charles II, son of Charles I, took the throne. This did not end the struggle over who should make political decisions, however. In 1688, the English Parliament again took action against a king whose policies it opposed.

This time, the king was James II. James had succeeded his brother, Charles II, to the throne in 1685. Like his father, Charles I, James believed that kings ruled by divine right. He wanted to limit the decision-making power of Parliament.

Many people believed that James, a Roman Catholic, was planning to declare Catholicism the official religion of England. This did not sit well with most people, who were Protestants.

As a result, many Protestant members of the House of Lords joined Protestant members of the House of Commons in a movement to force James to abdicate, or give up the throne. They wanted to replace him with a Protestant monarch. They chose James's daughter Mary, who had been raised a Protestant and was married to Prince William of Orange, the Protestant ruler of the Netherlands. When William and Mary landed in England in 1689, James fled quietly and lived the rest of his life in exile.

Case Study

John Locke (1632–1704), believed that all men — kings and commoners — are born equal and possess certain "natural rights" at birth. These rights include the right to life, liberty, and property.

What is more, said Locke, governments exist *only* to protect and promote people's rights. In Locke's view, governing is a two-way street: rulers can expect obedience from the people they rule only if they respect and uphold the people's rights. Locke said that this amounted to a contract. He said that if their natural rights are threatened, people have the "right of revolution" — the right to rebel and choose a new ruler.

These were radical ideas at a time when much of the world was ruled by absolute monarchs. Though Locke's ideas were forward-thinking, he was not a democrat in the modern sense. Men might be born equal, he said, but they do not remain equal. He also said that poor people, women, children, and non-Europeans do not have the time, education, or common sense to make informed decisions about how they should be governed.

Locke's writings were first published in 1690. They were used to justify the Glorious Revolution that had taken place in England two years earlier. They also inspired the leaders of the American and French Revolutions that took place after Locke's death.

Here is an excerpt from Locke's *The Second Treatise on Civil Government*:

Using force upon the people without authority, and contrary to the trust put in the person who does so, is a state of war with the people who have a right to reinstate their [elected leaders] in the exercise of their power: for having [elected leaders] with an intent they should exercise the power of making laws ... when they are hindered by any force from what is so necessary to the society ... the people have the right to remove it by force. In all states and conditions, the true remedy of force without authority is to oppose force to it.

John Locke was a teenager when his father joined the Cromwell's forces in their fight against the Royalists under King Charles I. The war, which pitted neighbour against neighbour, helped shape the trend-setting ideas that later made Locke famous.

The Active Citizen

1. Locke wrote these sentences more than 300 years ago. Rewrite what he said in your own words.

2. Do you agree with Locke's belief that a ruler who uses force against the people is at war with the people? Why?

3. Do you agree that the people have the right to rebel against a ruler who does not uphold the contract? Why?

4. These early discussions of human equality usually focused only on the rights of men. Women were not part of the discussion. Research the role played by one of the following women in ensuring that women won equal rights:

   - Olympe de Gouges
   - Ho Hsiang-ning
   - Catherine Booth
   - Emily Murphy
   - Mary Wollstonecraft
   - Emmeline Pankhurst

Before King William III and Queen Mary II came to power, they agreed to abide by the English Bill of Rights, which had been passed by Parliament early in 1689. Some of the rights guaranteed in this document were:

- free speech
- free election of members of Parliament
- freedom to petition the monarch without fear of punishment

The Bill of Rights also required the monarch to be a Protestant and to get the approval of Parliament before making laws and levying taxes. It made Parliament and the monarch partners in government.

These events became known as the Glorious — or Bloodless — Revolution because power was transferred peacefully. It also served notice that British monarchs would be wise to recognize that Parliament was an important part of the decision-making process.

American Revolution

By 1775, many people who had settled in the British colonies along the eastern seaboard of North America were angry with King George III and the British Parliament. Among other things, the colonists resented paying taxes when the members of Parliament who approved the taxes were elected in Britain. The colonists had no vote and, therefore, no voice in Parliament. Their slogan "No taxation without representation!" became a familiar cry throughout the colonies.

Things came to a head in 1775. Many colonists were so angry that they decided that the only solution was to break away from Britain. To signal their intentions, Thomas Jefferson, one of the revolutionary leaders, wrote the famous Declaration of Independence in 1776. The colonists' action sparked years of bitter warfare. The war ended only when the British government agreed in 1782 to grant independence to the 13 rebellious colonies. A new nation was founded — the United States of America.

In 1787, the founders of the United States decided that their new country needed a written **constitution**.

Among other things, the Declaration of Independence stated: "We hold these truths to be self-evident, that all men are created equal, that they are endowed by their Creator with certain unalienable rights, that among these are Life, Liberty, and the pursuit of Happiness. — That to secure these rights, Governments are instituted among Men, deriving their just powers from the consent of the governed, — That whenever any Form of Government becomes destructive of these ends, it is the Right of the People to alter or to abolish it, and to institute new Government ..."

This wooden staff listed the members of the Great Council when the Iroquois Confederacy consisted of five nations — the Mohawk, Oneida, Onondaga, Cayuga, and Seneca. Each of the five sections of the staff represents one nation. Within each section, each peg represents the name of a council member.

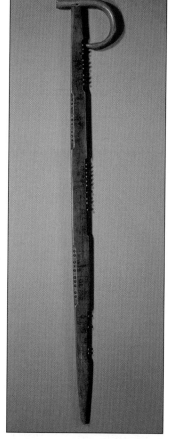

A constitution is a document or series of unwritten guidelines that set out the rules for governing a nation. The American Constitution established the United States as a republic with an elected president. It defined how the country's federal and state governments were to work and set out the powers of each. It also provided for a justice system and explained how courts of law would work.

The politicians who created the American Constitution drew heavily on British ideas and constitutional traditions. They also borrowed ideas from the Iroquois and their unwritten constitution, called the Great Law of Peace. The Great Law of Peace had been created several hundred years earlier when the Iroquois nations united to form the Iroquois Confederacy. Its terms were passed down orally from generation to generation.

The Great Law of Peace established an elaborate system to ensure that the Confederacy's member nations were represented at its annual decision-making gathering, which was called the Great Council. It also clearly set out the separate powers of various government leaders, or chiefs, and how these powers should be exercised. Reaching consensus — general agreement — before taking action was important to the Iroquois. Decisions were made only after each council member had been given a chance to contribute to the discussion.

Web Connection

www.school.mcgrawhill.ca/resources
To find out more about the Great Law of Peace, go to History Resources, then to *Civics: Participating in a Democratic Society* to see where to go next.

Though the American Constitution explained how the government of the United States would work, it did not define the rights of the citizens of the new republic. Many people, including Jefferson, feared that the new government might whittle away the rights the people had fought so hard to win. They wanted their rights recorded in writing and included in the Constitution.

As a result, the first 10 amendments, or changes, to the Constitution were passed in 1791. Together, these amendments became known as the American Bill of Rights. Among the rights guaranteed in the Bill of Rights are freedom of speech, freedom of the press, and freedom of religion.

FYI

In recent years, the second amendment to the American Constitution, which is part of the Bill of Rights, has sparked bitter controversy. It states: "A well regulated militia, being necessary to the security of a free State, the right of the people to keep and bear Arms, shall not be infringed." Today, people who are against gun control use this to argue that it is unconstitutional for the American government to limit the right of citizens to own and carry guns.

Like the democracies it was modelled on, the new American republic was an oligarchy. Only prosperous male landowners were eligible to vote. Poor people who did not own land, slaves, women, and Aboriginal people were left out of the decision-making process. It was only later that the Constitution was amended and citizenship rights were gradually extended to people in these groups.

Think ... Discuss ... Act

Though he died more than 70 years before the American Revolution began, John Locke is sometimes called the spiritual leader of the Revolution. This is a tribute to his strong influence on Thomas Jefferson, author of the Declaration of Independence.

1. What beliefs did Locke and Jefferson share? How were their ideas different?
2. What does "pursuit of happiness" mean?
3. In their writings, do Locke and Jefferson provide a recipe for chaos or a recipe for justice? Explain your opinion.

French Revolution

By 1789, King Louis XVI, grandson of Louis XIV, had ruled France for 15 years. The world had changed since his grandfather's time, however. The country's finances were reeling from expensive wars with Britain. In one of these wars, France had lost its North American colonies to Britain.

Many people in France had fallen under the spell of ideas expressed by political thinkers such as Jean-Jacques Rousseau, a French writer and philosopher who had been influenced by John Locke. French people knew that the British had won certain civil rights a hundred years earlier. They had also watched the American Revolution unfold. The former American colonies presented a model of a different kind of government.

This cartoon shows a French peasant staggering under the weight of a religious official and a nobleman on his back. In the late 18th century, ordinary people in France were heavily taxed. Nobles and clergy, on the other hand, paid few taxes. Many people, including the cartoonist who drew this picture, believed that nobles and the clergy were getting a free ride.

The rights of women were rarely mentioned when people discussed citizens' rights. Mary Wollstonecraft, pictured here, was a British writer who believed that this was unfair. In response, she wrote a book titled *A Vindication of the Rights of Woman*. In it, she argued that women, too, deserved equal rights — and earned herself a place in history as one of the first British feminists.

In 1787 and 1788 poor harvests in France led to food shortages. The price of food rose. People did not have enough money to buy food and pay their heavy taxes.

Many people faced starvation, yet King Louis XVI and the nobles who ran the government still lived in luxury. The nobles not only refused to pay taxes, but they also tried to grab more money for themselves. They attempted to revive the long-forgotten dues peasants had been forced to pay under the feudal system. All these factors led to a violent showdown that erupted first in Paris but soon spread to other parts of the country.

The cry "*Liberté, Egalité, Fraternité*" — "Liberty, Equality, Fraternity" — rang out across France as leaders of the Revolution issued the Declaration of the Rights of Man and of the Citizen. This document, which was modelled on the American Declaration of Independence, proclaimed that men are born free and remain free and equal. It said that men have the right to liberty, property, and safety, as well as the right to resist oppression.

The French Revolution sparked political instability and conflict across Europe. In other countries, supporters of the revolutionary ideals called on their own people to follow the example set by the French. The French Revolution became a beacon that inspired people in other countries to work toward gaining the right to make democratic decisions for themselves.

King Louis XVI was beheaded in the violence and turmoil that gripped France for many years after 1789, a period known as the Reign of Terror. The king's execution by guillotine is depicted in this painting. Many nobles, as well as anyone who even whispered criticism of the new republican government, were also sent to the guillotine. In the end, thousands of people were executed during the Reign of Terror.

CHAPTER REVIEW

SUMMING IT UP

The path to the kind of democracy that exists in Canada and other countries today has not been short — or smooth. In fact, it has taken more than 1500 years for modern democracies to evolve. Along the way, many hurdles had to be overcome by people who wanted a say in making decisions about the way they were governed.

1. Before you start to read the next chapter, sum up what you have learned in this chapter. Here is an easy way to do this. Skim the headings and subheadings. Then, write a sentence or two explaining what each means to you.

   For example, start with the unit title — "The Informed Citizen." In a sentence or two, explain the difference between an informed and an uninformed citizen.

GETTING THE FACTS

1. Why did direct democracy work in ancient Athens? Why would it not work in Canada today?

2. Create a chart that summarizes the differences between early democracies, such as those of Athens and Rome, and the kind of democracy that exists in Canada today.

3. Winston Churchill, prime minister of the United Kingdom during World War II, said that democracy is the worst form of government — "except for all those other forms that have been tried from time to time." List the terms for some other forms of government that have been tried from time to time.

4. Many English words were borrowed from other languages. Some of these, such as "civic" and "politics," are found in this chapter. In your notebook or journal, set up a section titled "New Words with Special Meaning." List these words and write a definition of each. Write a sentence that shows the meaning. Add to this list as you read farther in the book.

5. Garbage was a concern in ancient Athens, just as it is in most communities today. Reducing the amount of garbage by recycling is a common practice. Form groups to talk about the issue of garbage in your school. Could more be done? What actions could you take as an individual, or as part of the group, the class, or the school?

USING THE FACTS

1. Citizens have responsibilities as well as rights. What are some responsibilities and rights of citizens today? List these under the headings "Responsibilities" and "Rights."

Responsibilities	Rights

2. Civic conflicts occur when people disagree over how to resolve issues. Brainstorm to create a list of conflicts or disagreements that are occurring in your school or community right now. Choose one of these and summarize it under the following headings:

   Reasons for the Conflict
   Groups or Individuals Involved
   Points of View of Groups or Individuals
   Main Events to Date
   How the Conflict Might Be Resolved

3. Imagine that you are a citizen of the oligarchy of ancient Athens (or ancient Rome, 17th-century England, or 18th-century France or the United States). You believe that more people should have a say in making decisions about the way your government works. Write one or two paragraphs designed to persuade other people to agree with your point of view.

4. "Power tends to corrupt and absolute power corrupts absolutely." These words were written in 1887 by Lord Acton, a British politician and writer. What do they mean? Can citizens do anything to control corruption in their government? How?

5. Form groups and organize a debate on this issue: Democracies are unstable and prone to become dictatorships.

Chapter 2

DEMOCRATIC DECISION MAKING IN EARLY CANADA

"Canadians! Do you love freedom? I know you do. Do you hate oppression? Who dare deny it? ... Then buckle on your armour, and put down the villains who oppress and enslave our country ... The prize is a splendid one. A country larger than France or England; natural resources equal to our most boundless wishes ... Up, then brave Canadians! Get ready your rifles, and make short work of it!"

William Lyon Mackenzie, Upper Canadian reformer, on the eve of the Rebellion of 1837

Chanting and waving placards, the people in this photograph are urging the Canadian government to introduce laws to protect endangered species. What citizenship rights are the protesters exercising?

When William Lyon Mackenzie issued his call to arms quoted on the previous page, his goal was to overthrow the British colonial government that ruled Upper Canada. He wanted to establish a republic, similar to the one in the United States. Mackenzie was frustrated by the refusal of the British governor and his hand-picked advisers to give the people more say in making decisions affecting the colony.

Faced with a government that was violating the social contract, Mackenzie believed that violent revolution was justified. Do you agree with him? Would other methods of resolving this conflict have worked?

Modern democracies have developed methods to ensure that citizens have ways of resolving conflicts without resorting to violence. The protesters shown in the photograph are trying to resolve a conflict in a peaceful way. Do you think that governments listen to peaceful protesters like these? Why?

Chapter
Expectations

In this chapter, you will learn about:

- the values that guide democratic decision making
- how democratic decision making evolved in Canada
- how Canada achieved self-government
- how — and why — Canada became a constitutional monarchy, a federal state, and a parliamentary democracy

Key
Terms

civil law	legislature	representative government
constituency	parliamentary democracy	residual powers
federal	representation by population	responsible government

DEMOCRATIC VALUES

Modern democracies such as Canada are very different from those that existed in ancient times — and even those that existed as little as a hundred years ago. Today, Canada is a democratic country governed by an elected parliament that operates according to rules set out in a written constitution.

In Canada, people have a voice in making decisions. Laws protect people from harm and ensure that the needs of both individuals and the community are met. This system has changed a great deal since Canada's early days — and is likely to keep changing to meet the needs of citizens in the 21st century.

The values of a society are one force that drives change. Values are the beliefs that govern the behaviour and choices of the citizens who belong to a society. Four important values that guide the government of a democratic society such as Canada's are

- rule of law
- common good
- majority rule
- minority rights

Canada's system of government is designed to promote and uphold these values.

One way people in Canada participate in government is by electing members of Parliament to represent them. In this photograph, Heritage Minister Sheila Copps is responding to questions in the House of Commons. When Parliament is in session, a special time is set aside every day for questions. This time, called Question Period, gives MPs a chance to question the government about important issues.

Rule of Law

Canadians abide by the rule of law. This means that everyone is governed by laws that apply to all people. These laws protect and improve citizens' rights. No one — not even the most important or powerful leader — is above the law. No one can say, "I am so important that I can ignore the law and do whatever I want."

In Canada, laws are made by the elected representatives of the people. Laws can be changed, but only after the changes are discussed and voted on by the elected representatives.

Common Good

The common good refers to the best interests of all the people living in a community or society such as Canada. These interests include peace, justice, safety, and economic stability. What other interests might be included in the common good?

It is the responsibility of elected representatives to keep the common good in mind when they make political decisions. Of course, in a country as large and diverse as Canada, it is often hard to define the common good. Political decisions often please some people while angering others. As a rule, however, governments try to make decisions that are likely to benefit the most people.

Majority Rule

The idea that the will of the majority — what most people want — should prevail is a basic principle of democratic decision making. It means that the view shared by the largest number of people in a community is the one that rules when decisions are made.

In Canada, however, the idea of majority rule does not mean that those who are in a minority have no rights at all. Majority rule is balanced by the idea of minority rights.

Minority Rights

In democratic societies, the rights of minority groups are recognized and protected by the majority. This means that members of groups

This stop sign in Iqaluit, Nunavut, displays both English and Inuktitut, two of the three official languages of this Canadian territory. French is the third official language. Though speakers of Inuktitut are a small minority in Canada, they form a majority in Nunavut. Their right to conduct the business of Nunavut in their first language is protected by law.

who do not share the views of the majority enjoy the same rights to legal, economic, and social equality as members of the majority.

In Canada, for example, the language rights of linguistic minorities such as English-speaking people in Québec and French-speaking people in other parts of Canada are guaranteed in the Constitution. The rights of other minorities such as Aboriginal Peoples and religious groups are also protected.

DECISION MAKING UNDER FRENCH RULE

The rights Canadian citizens enjoy today, and sometimes even take for granted, were not won all at once. The struggle for political, legal, social, and economic rights is an important part of our country's history. It is a struggle that many say is still not finished. The Aboriginal Peoples who inhabited Canada when the Europeans arrived had their own systems of government and ways of making decisions. Some of these, like the

Beaver pelts were the foundation of the fur trade. This drawing, titled "View of the Industry of the Beavers of Canada," shows how wildly inaccurate European views of New France could be. Still, the beaver has become Canada's national emblem. Is it a good choice?

system developed by the Iroquois Confederacy, were more democratic than the systems that were transferred from Europe by the first settlers. Aboriginal forms of decision making were largely ignored, however, by the settlers, who introduced their own government systems when they arrived in what they called the New World.

In the early 1600s, the French and British were the first Europeans to start settling in Canada. At the time, both countries were monarchies — and this is the system that was transferred to the New World by the settlers. A few British people established settlements in Newfoundland, while the French settled in present-day Nova Scotia and along the St. Lawrence River, in what they came to call New France.

In these early days, the French monarchs were not interested in governing New France directly. They viewed the colonies as business ventures — a source of money for the royal treasury. As a result, they were content to place control of the colonies in the hands of merchants. The monarch granted groups of merchants monopolies on the rich fur trade. In return, the merchants were supposed to bring settlers to the area.

Many of the people who settled in New France were called *habitants*. Though this word means "inhabitant," in New France it referred to the tenant farmers who rented their land from *seigneurs*. The *seigneurs* had been granted ownership of large tracts called *seigneuries*, where they organized villages and rented farms to *habitants*. The *habitants* were also called *canadiens*, a term that was later used to refer to any French-speaking inhabitant of Canada.

By 1663, however, it was clear that this plan was not working. The population of New France was not growing, and the Iroquois had launched an all-out war against the French and their Aboriginal allies. The Iroquois wanted to drive out the invaders who were moving onto their traditional hunting grounds.

As a result, King Louis XIV decided to change the way New France was governed. He declared the colony a royal province and decreed that it be governed by a sovereign council, the system used in many other French provinces. The council was made up of a governor, an intendant, a Roman Catholic bishop, and five councillors.

Though this system handed decision-making power to more people, it did little for the *habitants* of New France. They had little say in choosing the members of the sovereign council or in the decisions made by the council. For the most part though, they did not object to this way of doing things. The system was familiar because it was like the one they had known in France.

THE BRITISH CONQUEST

During the 1700s, France and Britain became embroiled in a series of wars against each other. For New France, the most important of these was the Seven Years' War, which started in Europe in 1756. The fighting soon spread to the North American colonies. In 1759, a British force captured Québec City, marking the beginning of the end of New France.

Four years later, in 1763, the colony's fate was made official when Britain and France signed the Treaty of Paris. Under its terms, New France was handed to the British. The colony was now part of the British Empire.

DECISION MAKING UNDER BRITISH RULE

In 1759, the famous French writer Voltaire wrote that Britain and France "have been at war over a few acres of snow near Canada, and ... they are spending on this fine struggle more than Canada is worth." What do Voltaire's words reveal about European attitudes toward Canada?

The takeover of New France by Britain was a defining moment in the history of Canada. It set the country on a completely different course. Though France was an absolute monarchy, Britain had been inching toward constitutional monarchy for hundreds of years. The differences between these two forms of government were felt immediately by the people of Québec, the name bestowed on Britain's newest colony.

Soon after the signing of the Treaty of Paris, King George III of Britain issued the Royal Proclamation of 1763. The proclamation imposed British institutions and laws on the former French colonies of East Florida, West Florida, Grenada, and Québec and made them British provinces. Each province was ruled by a governor appointed by the British Parliament, though each was also to have an elected legislative assembly to look after local issues.

In Québec, the new government arrangement presented problems. British law allowed only Protestant men to be elected to colonial assemblies or to be appointed to public office. The same law applied in Britain, where Roman Catholics and non-Christians were barred from holding public office until 1829.

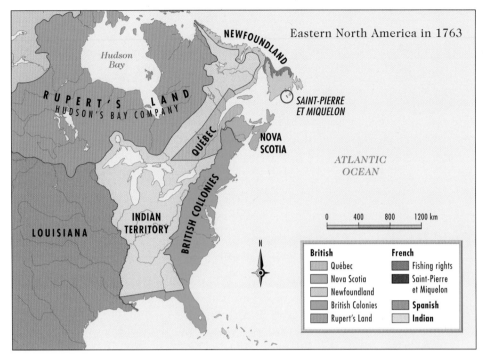

Eastern North America in 1763

Most people in Québec were French-speaking Roman Catholics. If they were not eligible to hold public office, decision making in the colony would be dominated by the few hundred English-speaking Protestants who had arrived after the British takeover.

James Murray, the first British-appointed governor of Québec, sympathized with the *canadiens*. He understood that an elected assembly that did not represent their interests would not work. As a result, he wisely decided against establishing one. Instead, he managed the business of the colony with the help of a 12-member appointed council.

In 1774, the British Parliament solved this problem by passing the Quebec Act. This was one of the most important pieces of legislation ever introduced in Canada.

The Quebec Act recognized the distinctiveness of French-speaking canadiens. It affirmed their religious and land rights. It also cleared the way for Catholics to play a role in government by taking a special oath of loyalty to the British crown. What is more, it restored the canadien system of civil law, though it kept the British system of criminal law. It did not, however, give the people more say in government. They were still governed by an appointed governor and his hand-picked council.

Sympathy with the *canadiens* was not the only reason the British decided to give them certain rights. By 1774, unrest was growing in the British-ruled colonies along the Atlantic seaboard of the present-day United States. The British government wanted to ensure that Québec stayed loyal to the king.

The strategy worked. When the American Revolution erupted a year later, the generous terms of the Quebec Act did much to prevent the idea of independence from spreading northward. The people of Québec refused to join the American colonists' fight for independence.

Think ... Discuss ... Act

As officials of Britain and France negotiated to end the Seven Years' War, a ferocious debate raged in Britain. Which of the conquered French colonies should the British keep? It boiled down to a choice between New France and Guadeloupe. Some people wanted to keep Guadeloupe, a rich, sugar-producing island in the Caribbean Sea. Others wanted to keep New France, to strengthen their country's grip on North America. In the end, Britain chose New France. Guadeloupe was handed back to France.

1. If you had lived in Britain in 1763, which colony would you have chosen? Why?
2. Within 30 years of the fall of Québec, two great revolutions had occurred. One happened in North America, the other in France. If New France had remained in French hands, how might Canada's system of government be different today?
3. Create a chart comparing Canada today with Guadeloupe today. Use the following headings:

> Size   Population
> Location   Economy

Did the British make the right decision? Why?

British North America Expands

The influx of Loyalists during and after the American Revolution sparked great changes in British North America. The first of these was the creation of two new British provinces, New Brunswick and Cape Breton, in 1784. Then, in 1791, after a large number of Loyalists had moved into present-day southern Ontario, the British Parliament decided to reorganize the province of Québec.

The Constitutional Act of 1791 split the province into two parts: Upper Canada and Lower Canada. Upper Canada was the area west of the Ottawa River where many English-speaking Loyalists were making new homes. Lower Canada, to the east, was home to the French-speaking *canadiens* and a small number of recently arrived British settlers.

Under the terms of the Constitutional Act, each province had its own governor, who was appointed by the British Parliament. Each province also had an executive council modelled on the British House of Lords. Members of the executive council were appointed by the governor. Though each

During the American Revolution — and afterward — people in the 13 colonies who remained loyal to Britain were branded traitors and often ill-treated. This drawing shows a Loyalist being tarred and feathered by Americans. Many of these Loyalists fled northward to British North America, the name given to the British colonies of Québec, Nova Scotia, and Newfoundland.

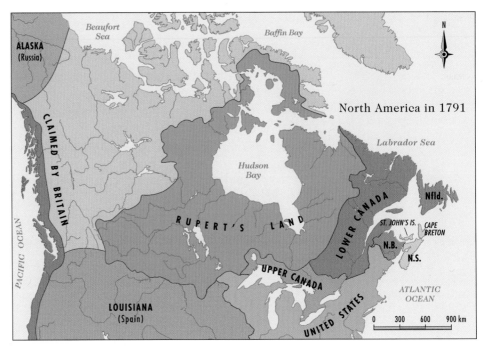

North America in 1791

province also had an elected assembly with the right to levy taxes, the power to make important decisions remained in the hands of the governor and the executive council.

Although the Constitutional Act gave Upper and Lower Canada a form of **representative government**, it did not give them **responsible government**. This meant that the governor was not bound by the decisions of the elected assembly. The provincial governors could veto, or strike down, laws passed by the assembly and dissolve the assembly whenever they saw fit. In this way, the Constitutional Act set the stage for the violent conflicts that were to erupt decades later.

REBELLION IN UPPER AND LOWER CANADA

The American and French Revolutions captured the imagination of many people in the British North American colonies. Though they remained loyal to Great Britain, people started thinking and talking about citizenship rights.

Because the governors and executive councils of the British North American provinces were not required to answer to the assembly of their provinces, decision making was in the hands of a few people. This small group answered neither to the elected assembly nor to the people as a whole. This system virtually guaranteed that ruling cliques would develop.

In Nova Scotia, the ruling clique was called the Council of Twelve. In Upper Canada, it became known as the Family Compact, because many of its members came from wealthy families and were related to one another.

Colonel Robert Moodie, a well-known government loyalist, was shot when he tried to ride past rebels who were gathering on Yonge Street north of Toronto in 1837. Moodie, who later died of his wound, wanted to warn the governor that the rebels were arming to fight.

FYI

By 1837, Black people were fleeing to Upper Canada to escape slavery in the United States. Many of these former slaves were suspicious of Mackenzie's ideas, and some joined the Canadian militia to fight the rebels. Why did these Black people oppose the rebellion?

In Lower Canada, an elite called the *Château Clique* had the ear of the British-appointed governor and wielded great influence. Nearly all the members of the *Château Clique* were English-speakers while most of the colony's residents spoke French. The *canadiens'* resentment of the *Château Clique* contributed to the tensions that already existed between the British and French in Québec.

By the 1830s, two men had become vocal critics of the way the colonies were ruled. They were Louis-Joseph Papineau in Lower Canada and William Lyon Mackenzie in Upper Canada. Each had sat as a member of the elected assembly in his province, and each had been frustrated when the assembly's decisions were ignored by the governor and his hand-picked elite.

At first, Mackenzie and Papineau wanted responsible government. Each wanted the executive council of his province to be made up of people supported by a majority of the members of the elected assembly. This would give voters more influence in the decisions that affected their lives.

The pleas of the reformers fell on deaf ears, however. The British government and the ruling elites stubbornly refused to discuss change. This response pushed both Mackenzie and Papineau to embrace the idea of creating an independent republic, an idea that horrified moderates in both parts of the colony.

By 1837, Mackenzie, Papineau, and their more radical supporters had decided that armed revolution was the only way to get what they wanted. Rebellions broke out in both Upper and Lower Canada.

Fighting erupted first in Lower Canada where many pitched battles were fought before British troops restored order. In Upper Canada, the rebellion amounted to a handful of armed skirmishes that were easily quelled by Canadian militia.

William Lyon Mackenzie (left) and Louis-Joseph Papineau led the push for reform in Canada.

Mackenzie and Papineau, along with some of their supporters, fled to the United States as political refugees. Many of those who did not flee were imprisoned or expelled from Canada. Some were even convicted of treason and hanged. To the defeated and discouraged supporters of reform, it seemed as if the rebellions had failed. But had they?

Web Connection

www.school.mcgrawhill.ca/resources
To find out more about the rebellion in Upper Canada, go to History Resources. Then go to *Civics: Participating in a Democratic Society* to see where to go next.

The Active Citizen

Think … Discuss … Act

The people of British North America were certainly intrigued by ideas about citizens' rights and responsibilities. At the same time, though, they were fearful of violent revolution. Memories of the mistreatment of Loyalists by American revolutionaries remained vivid. People were also shocked by the killings that had taken place in France during the Reign of Terror. These events made them suspicious of democracy.

1. Put yourself in the place of a resident of Upper or Lower Canada in the 1830s. Create a graphic organizer showing the pros and cons of democracy.
2. One of the thorny issues of citizenship is the treatment of people who disagree with the opinion of the majority. Should the rights of these people be protected? Why?
3. "The end justifies the means." Can this saying be used to justify the Rebellions of 1837–1838? Choose a partner and try to convince him or her that it can. Does the saying apply today? Cite at least one example to support your opinion.

Navy Island is located in the middle of the Niagara River about five kilometres above Niagara Falls. The island is uninhabited today, but it was a hive of activity for a few weeks during the winter of 1837–1838. William Lyon Mackenzie, leader of the rebel forces in Upper Canada, and some of his supporters took refuge there after their rebellion failed.

Undaunted by the reluctance of the people of Upper Canada to rally to his cause, Mackenzie raised a flag and declared Navy Island the independent Republic of Canada. From the island, he prepared to invade Upper Canada and urged others to join his rag-tag band. Though a few Americans responded to his call to arms, Mackenzie managed to raise a force of only about 200.

In the meantime, British loyalists were making plans to crush this last spark of rebellion. Under cover of darkness on December 29, 1837, 60 Canadian volunteers slipped across the Niagara River to the United States. There, they boarded the *Caroline*, an American paddlewheel steamer that was being used to ferry recruits and supplies to the island. Chasing passengers and crew off the boat, the Canadians set fire to the *Caroline*. The blazing boat drifted toward the Falls and sank.

In the scuffle over the *Caroline*, a passenger was killed. He had been felled by a musketball, though no one ever knew who had fired the fatal shot.

Soon after the sinking of the *Caroline*, Canadian militia began firing on Navy Island from the north shore of the Niagara River. After suffering this bombardment for two weeks, Mackenzie and his band fled to the United States. The short life of the Republic of Canada was over.

William Lyon Mackenzie used this painting of the *Caroline* plunging over Niagara Falls to arouse anti-British feelings in the United States. He even tried to make people believe that passengers were on board. He wanted to goad the United States into attacking Canada. Some people accused him of spreading propaganda. Do you agree with them?

The Active Citizen

1. In 509 BCE, the plebeians of Rome staged a strike to win a greater say in decision making. More than 2000 years later, William Lyon Mackenzie tried a different strategy — armed rebellion — to achieve the same end. Which strategy do you think was the most successful? Why do you think so?

2. If Mackenzie and his followers had achieved their goal of creating a Canadian republic, how would the government of Canada be different today?

3. Write the text (about 100 words) of a historical marker commemorating the events on Navy Island in 1837–1838. Will your marker appear on the Canadian or American side of the Niagara River? Did this decision make a difference in what you wrote? How?

THE BATTLE FOR RESPONSIBLE GOVERNMENT

The violent conflicts in what had always been peaceful colonies startled the British government — and spurred it to action. The government sent John Lambton, Earl of Durham, to the Canadas on a mission. He was to look into the causes of the rebellions and propose solutions.

Early in 1839, Lord Durham issued his report. Titled *Report on the Affairs of British North America*, it proposed two important reforms in the way the colonies were governed. The first was to reunite Upper and Lower Canada into one province with a single elected assembly. The second was to introduce responsible government, which would give the colonists more say in making decisions about their own affairs.

Both these proposals sparked controversy. In Lower Canada, *canadiens* were outraged by Durham's negative comments about them — and their future in Canada. He suggested that the conflict in Lower Canada was caused by tension between English and French. "I expected to find a contest between a government and a people," he wrote. "I found two nations warring in the bosom of a single state: I found a struggle, not of principles, but of races."

Durham's solution? Assimilation. He believed that the conflict would be resolved only when the *canadiens* were absorbed into English-speaking society. Though French-speakers were still a majority in Lower Canada, the English-speaking population of the two colonies was growing. In Durham's view, uniting the two provinces would speed the assimilation of the *canadiens* by ensuring that English-speaking members formed a majority in a single legislative assembly.

The *canadiens* were not the only ones unhappy with Durham's recommendations, however. The British Parliament dismissed his proposal calling for responsible government. The idea was far too radical.

Lord Durham, whose nickname was Radical Jack, spent the summer of 1838 gathering information in Upper and Lower Canada. In his travels, he was influenced deeply by the views of the moderate reformers of Upper Canada. They had supported Mackenzie's call for responsible government but not his violent method of achieving it.

The British did not reject Durham's entire report, however. In 1840, the British Parliament passed the Act of Union, uniting Upper and Lower Canada into the Province of Canada. Upper Canada was renamed Canada West, while Lower Canada became Canada East. A governor appointed by the British Parliament would oversee the province, and a single elected assembly would include an equal number of representatives from Canada West and Canada East. The act also declared English the official language of the colony.

In the end, the Act of Union pleased few people. Already angered by Durham's report,

When Lord Durham's report was published in 1839, Louis-Hippolyte LaFontaine was torn. He felt hope — but he also felt deep anger.

The veteran French-speaking politician from Canada East had spent his entire career working to win government reform. He was please by Durham's call for responsible government in Canada. As a *canadien*, though, he was angered by Durham's attack on his culture.

And when it seemed that the battle for responsible government might be won, the British Parliament passed the Act of Union. Not only did this act stop short of granting responsible government to Canada, but it also outlawed the French language in the House of Assembly.

No longer could LaFontaine and his fellow *canadiens* feel comfortable about engaging in debate.

Rather than crushing LaFontaine, however, this turn of events increased his determination to win reforms. Furthermore, the union of the two Canadas provided him with an unexpected ally: Robert Baldwin, a reform leader from Canada West. When the two met in the new legislative assembly, they quickly realized that they had much in common, despite their language and cultural differences. They soon joined forces to unite English- and French-speaking reformers.

It was not until 1842, however, that LaFontaine really made his mark. He rose in the legislature and, defying the law, gave a speech in French. This action eventually led to the repeal of the clause in the Act of Union that prohibited debate in French.

Here is some of what LaFontaine said in this famous speech:

I distrust my abilities to speak in English, yet I must inform the honourable members that, even should I have as proficient a knowledge of English as I have of French, I would still give my first speech in the language of my French-Canadian compatriots, if only as an act of solemn protest against this cruel injustice of the Union Act, which outlaws the mother tongue of half the population of Canada. I owe it to my compatriots. I owe it to myself.

By refusing to give in to an unfair British law, Louis-Hippolyte LaFontaine set the stage for the recognition of French as one of Canada's official languages. People sometimes call this man the first prime minister of Canada because he was the first leader of the country after responsible government was achieved.

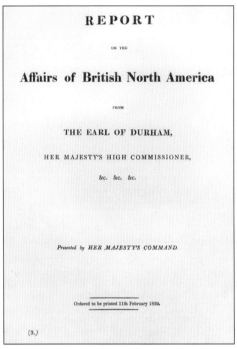

REPORT

ON THE

Affairs of British North America

FROM

THE EARL OF DURHAM,

HER MAJESTY'S HIGH COMMISSIONER,

&c. &c. &c.

Presented by HER MAJESTY'S COMMAND.

Ordered to be printed 11th February 1839.

(3.)

canadiens were outraged by the act's anti-French measures. Because the population of Canada East was greater than that of Canada West, the *canadiens* believed that they should have more representatives in the assembly.

At the same time, many people in both parts of the province were upset by Great Britain's refusal to grant responsible government. In practice, however, this refusal did not make much difference. For the next several years, the governors appointed by the British government wisely tried to follow the wishes of the assembly even though they were not obliged to do this.

At the same time, political reformers such as Joseph Howe of Nova Scotia, Louis-Hippolyte LaFontaine of Canada East, and Robert Baldwin of Canada West were using peaceful, constitutional means to persuade the British Parliament to grant responsible government to its North American provinces. Their efforts were helped by changing attitudes in Great Britain. Politicians there were starting to realize that maintaining colonies was costly. To reduce costs, they wanted the colonies to become more self-supporting. If the colonies were to start paying their own way, though, they would need more control over their own affairs.

Gradually, Canadian reformers and the British Parliament came to agree that responsible government was a goal that they both wanted to achieve in British North America — though their reasons for setting this goal were different. By 1848, responsible government was a reality in Great Britain's North American provinces.

This victory marked an important step forward in the struggle to win democratic political rights in Canada. From 1848 until Confederation in 1867, no appointed British governor acted against the wishes of the elected assembly.

This political cartoon shows Lord Elgin, the British-appointed governor general at the time, dressed as a nanny. He is babysitting "Young Canada," which has just achieved responsible government. What is the cartoonist saying about Canada's ability to handle responsible government?

YOUNG CANADA
DELIGHTED WITH RESPONSIBLE GOVERNMENT.

Louis-Hippolyte LaFontaine, a *canadien* political leader, angrily denounced the Act of Union in the House of Assembly. He said:

> *The purpose of the Union, as conceived by its author, has been to wipe out the French population. Be not deceived. The means brought to bear will not achieve that result. Without our active co-operation, without our involvement in power, the government cannot function in a way that will lead to peace and trust, both of which are essential for the success of any administration.*

1. What did LaFontaine mean when he said this?
2. LaFontaine uttered these words more than 150 years ago. At the heart of his argument was the issue of minority rights. Do his words hold true today? Why?
3. Borrow LaFontaine's ideas to create a slogan for a placard urging the government to recognize minority rights today. How could you put your slogan into effect?

THE NEXT STEP: CONFEDERATION

By the 1850s, the Province of Canada faced serious political problems. A wave of immigration from Great Britain and Ireland had boosted the population of Canada West during the 1840s. Its population was now greater than that of Canada East — and growing. As a result, the English-speaking majority in Canada West began demanding changes to reflect the new reality.

One of the changes many people wanted was **representation by population**. They wanted every elected member of the legislature to represent about the same number of voters. Though "rep by pop" was

This cartoon makes fun of some of the British immigrants who were arriving ill-equipped to face the harsh conditions in Canada.

John A. Macdonald, seated on the steps in the centre, and George-Étienne Cartier, standing to Macdonald's right, led the seven Canadian delegates who attended the Charlottetown Conference on 1864. They wanted to persuade the Atlantic colonies to join a union of all Great Britain's North American colonies.

a popular idea in Canada West, it was not in Canada East. Many *canadiens* resisted the idea because it would make them a minority in the assembly.

Between 1858 and 1864, Canada was in a state of flux. Uncertainty ruled as the government changed 12 times! People agreed that their government was no longer working, but they could not agree about how to fix it.

In the end, it took an outside threat to spur British North American political leaders to find a solution to Canada's problems. When civil war broke out in the United States in 1861, many Americans in the North believed that Great Britain and the British North American colonies favoured the South. As the bloody conflict was drawing to a close, some Northerners even started talking about annexing, or taking over, Canada. They believed that their army, which was well-armed, well-trained and, by now, well-experienced, would have no trouble subduing the British colonies.

Faced with this threat, many people in Canada and the Atlantic colonies came to believe that uniting would be the best defence against an American invasion. Union would also strengthen the economic links among the provinces.

Leaders of the Atlantic colonies of Nova Scotia, New Brunswick, Prince Edward Island, and Newfoundland planned to meet in September 1864 at Charlottetown, P.E.I., to discuss a Maritime union. They were surprised, however, when political leaders from

The Latin inscription on Canada's coat of arms reads *"A mari usque ad mare"* — "From sea to sea." It was inspired by a verse in the Bible that says, "[God's] Dominion shall be from sea to sea ..."

the Province of Canada asked to attend the conference. The Canadian delegates wanted to place an even bigger proposal on the table: a union of all Great Britain's North American colonies.

www.school.mcgrawhill.ca/resources

To find out more about the Charlottetown Conference, go to History Resources. Then go to *Civics: Participating in a Democratic Society* to see where to go next.

Once the British North American colonies agreed to unite, they faced an enormous task: figuring out how Confederation would work. A month after the Charlottetown Conference, another meeting was held in Québec City. Here, the delegates agreed on a plan to unite the colonies into one self-governing unit. In 1866, at a final conference in London, England, the last details of the new country's system of government were worked out.

Called the Dominion of Canada, the new nation would include New Brunswick, Nova Scotia, and the Province of Canada, which would be split into two separate provinces. Canada West would become Ontario, and Canada East would become Québec. The country's capital would be Ottawa.

Though Prince Edward Island and Newfoundland were involved in early discussions of Confederation, both rejected the invitation to join the new union in 1867. Eventually, of course, both did join, as did other British North American colonies.

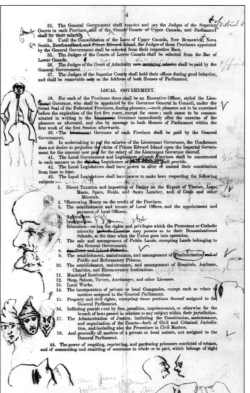

When the debate over the precise wording of the BNA Act became too dull, John A. Macdonald sometimes passed the time by doodling on his copy of the Act. This page, with his notes about changes — and his doodles — has been preserved.

Gradually, the representatives of the colonies worked out their differences and drafted the document — called the British North America (BNA) Act — that would create the new country and form an important part of its constitution. To become official, however, this document required the approval of the British Parliament. This was granted on March 29, 1867. On July 1, 1867, Canada officially came into being.

Confederation did not give Canada total independence from Great Britain. In fact, the British North America Act ensured that the British government would continue to exercise considerable control over the country's affairs for decades to come.

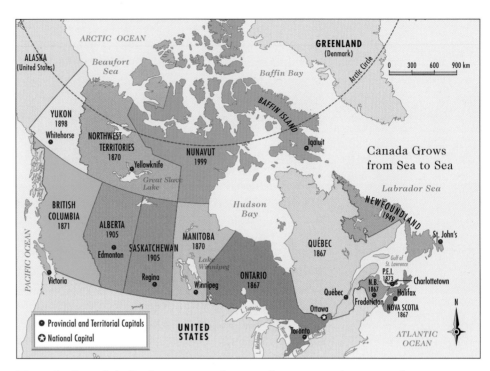

This map shows how Canada expanded after 1867.

Though Canada's Parliament took over the country's internal matters, relations with other countries were still Great Britain's responsibility.

Still, passing the BNA Act was a major step forward on Canada's long road to independence.

THE COUNTRY CREATED BY THE BRITISH NORTH AMERICA ACT

From the outset, the debate over the kind of country that would be created by Confederation required compromise. John A. Macdonald, a Canada West politician who would become the first prime minister of the new country, played a prominent role in this debate.

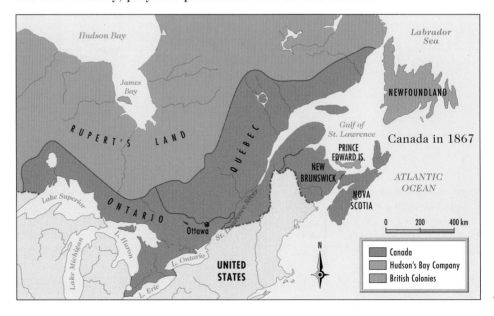

The brown areas show the extent of Canada in 1867. At the time, British Columbia, Prince Edward Island, Newfoundland, and the North-Western Territory remained British colonies. Rupert's Land was controlled by the Hudson's Bay Company.

A Federal State

Macdonald and some of the other architects of Confederation wanted a strong national government. They believed that the American Civil War, which ended in 1865, had occurred because the American Constitution granted too much power to the states and not enough to the central government. They did not want to make the same mistake in Canada.

As a result, Macdonald suggested a single national assembly. This idea, called unitary government, was opposed by representatives of the Atlantic colonies, who refused to give up their local assemblies. Representatives from Québec did not like the idea either. They feared that French-speaking Canadians would be outvoted in a single assembly dominated by English-speakers.

Instead, delegates to the conferences agreed that Canada would have a **federal** system of government. This meant that there would be two levels of decision making — one at the national level and another at the provincial level. A federal legislature would be responsible for making decisions about issues affecting the whole country. In addition, each province would have its own legislature. The provincial legislatures would be responsible for making decisions about issues affecting the people living in the province.

In addition, a key clause of the BNA Act grants to the federal government the power "to make laws for the peace, order and good government of Canada" in all matters that are not assigned to the provinces. This means that it is the federal legislature's responsibility to ensure that all laws passed in Canada uphold the principles of "peace, order and good government." To guarantee that it can do this, the federal legislature has the right to overrule any provincial law that oversteps provincial powers or challenges federal responsibilities.

The architects of Confederation wanted to create a strong central government to guard against a civil war such as the one that had divided the people of the United States. Early photographs such as this, showing the dead after the Battle of Gettysburg, were stark reminders of the horrors of civil war.

The decision to grant these residual, or leftover, powers to the federal government contrasts with the situation in the United States, where the Constitution assigns these powers to the states. Macdonald and the other Fathers of Confederation believed that the disputes that sparked the American Civil War could have been resolved peacefully if the American federal government had been stronger. As a result, they wanted residual powers to rest with the federal government rather than the provincial governments.

The British North America Act set out the law-making powers of the federal and provincial legislatures. The responsibilities assigned to each level of government are shown on the chart. Some responsibilities, known as concurrent responsibilities, are shared between the two levels.

Some Powers of the Federal and Provincial Governments

Federal Government Responsibilities	Provincial Government Responsibilities
Taxes	Taxes for provincial purposes
National defence	Education
Trade	Property and civil rights
Banks and money	Municipalities
Criminal law and penitentiaries	Civil law
Postal service	Local public works projects
Aboriginal Peoples	Hospitals, asylums, and charities
Navigation and shipping	
Sea coast and inland fisheries	
Citizenship	
Trade and commerce	

Concurrent Responsibilities
Agriculture
Immigration

A Constitutional Monarchy

By the time of Confederation in 1867, Great Britain had become a constitutional monarchy. A constitutional monarchy is a system of government in which the power of the monarch is limited by a constitution. The same form of government was adopted in Canada under the terms of the British North America Act. As a result, the British monarch is Canada's head of state. In constitutional monarchies, the title "head of state" is largely ceremonial. In Canada, the governor general represents the monarch.

A Parliamentary Democracy

In addition to creating a constitutional monarchy, the British North America Act established a **parliamentary democracy**, which is a kind of representative or indirect democracy. In parliamentary systems such as those of Canada and the United Kingdom, the leader is usually called a prime minister and must be an elected member of the national legislature. In republics, such as those of the United States and France, the president is not an elected member of the national legislature. The president is elected separately.

Under the terms of the BNA Act, Canada's federal Parliament is a bicameral legislature — an assembly made up of two houses. The House of Commons is the elected house. Each of its members represents an electoral district known as a **constituency** or riding. In 1867, each province was divided into ridings based on its population. In this way, those who had been demanding "rep by pop" finally achieved their goal.

"Rep by pop" was not popular in provinces with smaller populations, however. At the time of Confederation, Ontario's population was growing rapidly and the other provinces feared that the voices of their members of Parliament would be drowned out in the House of Commons by representatives of Ontario.

To ensure that this did not happen, the BNA Act established a second house called the Senate. Members of the Senate, called senators, were appointed by the governor general to represent the regions of Canada. Each region was represented by the same number of senators. In 1867, the three regions were Ontario, Québec, and the Maritimes.

The Fathers of Confederation also hoped the Senate would be a moderating influence on what they feared might be radical or extreme laws passed by the elected members of the House of Commons.

This 1953 cartoon shows the difference between a parliamentary democracy and a republic. Dwight D. Eisenhower, nicknamed Ike, was elected president of the United States — but his party did not win a majority in Congress. Louis St. Laurent became prime minister of Canada because his party won a majority in the House of Commons. What comment is the cartoonist making about the power of the two leaders?

CHAPTER REVIEW

SUMMING IT UP

The people of Canada have lived through many different forms of government. The people of the Aboriginal nations governed themselves in a variety of ways that suited their circumstances. The first European settlers lived under monarchies. When Britain took over New France, Canada joined the British who were travelling down the road toward constitutional monarchy. During the 1800s at least some people won a greater say in decision making when the country achieved responsible government. Then, with Confederation in 1867, Canada became a parliamentary democracy with a measure of independence from Great Britain — and prepared to continue its journey toward independence.

1. Write each of the following words or phrases on a sheet of paper. Beside each, write a sentence that sums up your recollection of the term — without looking back through the chapter. When you finish, skim the chapter to see whether your memory was correct. Briefly note your corrections.

common good	rule of law
majority rule	minority rights
Quebec Act, 1774	Constitutional Act, 1791
Act of Union, 1840	British North America Act, 1867
federal responsibilities	provincial responsibilities

2. With a partner, design a time line for the period from 1600 to 1867. Tie events that affected the governing of Canada to events that happened outside Canada.

3. Skim the chapter and add to your list of New Words with Special Meaning.

GETTING THE FACTS

1. Create a graphic organizer showing the stages of Canada's evolution from monarchy to parliamentary democracy.

2. In the late 1700s, many Aboriginal people regarded King George III of Britain as a champion of their interests. Why? Many people in the colony of Québec were also grateful to this king. Why?

3. In the colonies along the Atlantic seaboard of the present-day United States, King George III was regarded as an authoritarian figure who ruled with an iron fist. Find out more about this king and why people either loved or hated him.

4. Provincial boundaries have changed since 1867. Compare a map of Canada in 1867 with a map of Canada today. How have the boundaries of your province changed over the years? What implications do the changes have for Canada?

USING THE FACTS

1. In 1837–1838, some reformers in Upper and Lower Canada tried to use violence to achieve their goals. In 1842, Louis-Hippolyte LaFontaine tried a different method. Which method was more successful? Why?

2. Just as they were in the time of Louis-Hippolyte LaFontaine, French language rights are an issue in Canada today. This issue is so divisive that some Québécois, called separatists, want Québec to separate from Canada and become an independent republic. Other Québécois, called federalists, want to stay in Canada. The issue is debated often in daily newspapers. What arguments are used by separatists and federalists? Start collecting news clippings that can be used later for a project.

3. Do you agree with the architects of Confederation who created a strong federal government? Review the list of federal and provincial responsibilities on page 46. Choose one federal responsibility and explain why it should now be transferred to the provincial governments. Choose one provincial responsibility and explain why it should now be transferred to the federal government.

   The clippings you choose should conform to the three rules of evidence:

   - Good evidence must be relevant.
   - Good evidence must have weight (i.e., it should be important).
   - Good evidence must come from a reliable source.

4. In area, Canada is the second-largest country in the world. Is this an argument for creating provinces? Do boundary lines that divide territory also divide citizens? Do provincial boundaries create more problems than they solve? Why? Do you identify most strongly with your province or your country? How?

Chapter 3

DECISION MAKING IN CANADA TODAY

A Vancouver girl enjoys Canada Day celebrations on Parliament Hill in Ottawa. Why are Canadians proud of their country and system of government? How do you think this system of government might be made even better?

"Balanced budgets are only the means to the real purposes of government: to provide services such as health and education; create a climate for economic growth and job creation; protect those in need of protection; and ensure that citizens can participate in the decisions affecting their lives."

Saskatchewan Premier Roy Romanow in
The Globe and Mail, February 17, 1995

Setting *the Stage*

For more than a hundred years before Confederation in 1867, Canada was a British colony. It is not surprising, then, that the architects of Confederation copied the British model when they created Canada's system of government.

Even after Confederation, decision making in Canada was closely linked to Great Britain. In fact, many decisions that affected Canadians were still made by the British Parliament.

As the 20th century unfolded, though, the Canadian government gradually took more control of its own affairs. It was not until 1982, however, that the British Parliament passed an act affecting Canada for the last time. Called the Canada Act, this law said that no future act of the British Parliament would apply to Canada.

Although Canada's system of government is modelled on British parliamentary traditions, Canadian society is rooted in British, French, and Aboriginal traditions. It has also been enriched by the arrival of immigrants from around the globe. Together Canadian citizens share certain beliefs and values, which include fairness, equality, and respect for human dignity. What other beliefs and values are important to Canada and Canadians? Why?

Chapter *Expectations*

In this chapter, you will learn about:

- how Canada's system of government works
- the role of political parties in government decision making
- how lobbyists influence government decision making
- how Canada's judicial system works
- arbitration as another method of resolving conflicts
- how the Constitution evolved
- the rights and freedoms enjoyed by Canadian citizens

Key *Terms*

amending formula
arbitration
balance of power
collective bargaining

co-operative federalism
head of state
head of government
lobby

majority government
minority government
political party
referendum

The terms of the British North America Act of 1867 set up a parliamentary government in Canada that was like the system in Great Britain. Canada's government had three branches: the executive branch, the legislative branch, and the judicial branch.

This chart shows the three branches of the Canadian government. What elements make up each of the three branches?

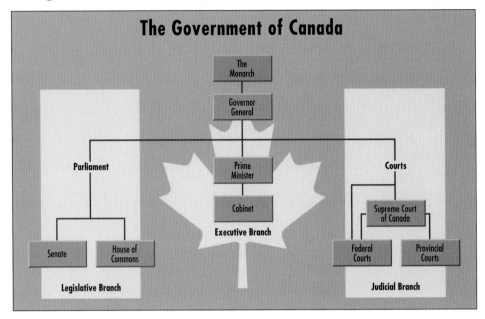

The Government of Canada

- The Monarch
  - Governor General
    - Prime Minister
    - Cabinet
    - **Executive Branch**
- Parliament
  - Senate
  - House of Commons
  - **Legislative Branch**
- Courts
  - Supreme Court of Canada
    - Federal Courts
    - Provincial Courts
  - **Judicial Branch**

http://www.school.mcgrawhill.ca/resources

To find out more about Canada's system of government, go to History Resources. Then go to *Civics: Participating in a Democratic Society* to see where to go next.

The Monarch

The BNA Act recognized the British monarch as Canada's official **head of state** and commander-in-chief of the country's armed forces.

An onlooker reaches over a barricade to hand Queen Elizabeth a basket of flowers during the queen's visit to Canada in 1997. Whenever the queen visits the country, large crowds turn out to greet her.

In 1867, the monarch was Queen Victoria. Today, Queen Victoria's great-great-granddaughter, Queen Elizabeth II, holds these positions.

The British monarch's role as official head of state is, in reality, only ceremonial. Since Confederation, no reigning British king or queen has played an important role in Canada's decision-making process.

Because the monarch does not live in Canada, she or he is represented here by the governor general. The governor general is appointed by the monarch on the advice of Canada's prime minister.

The Governor General

At Confederation, the governor general represented both the British government and the monarch. At the time, the governor general was expected to co-operate with Canada's elected prime minister in managing the internal affairs of the new dominion.

Because the British Parliament still controlled Canada's relations with other countries, the governor general took orders about external affairs directly from the Colonial Office in London, England. This continued until 1931, when the Statute of Westminster was enacted. This law changed the governor general's status. From then on, the governor general represented only the monarch, not the British government. As a result, the governor general's role became merely ceremonial.

Canada's system of government distinguishes clearly between the unelected head of state and the elected **head of government**. The head of state is the British monarch, who is represented in Canada by the governor general. The head of state is supposed to stand apart from political debates and conflicts. The head of government is the prime minister.

The governor general holds office for five years. This term can be renewed once. Unlike the prime minister, who speaks as a political figure representing the party that has formed the government, the governor general is supposed to act as a unifying symbol who speaks for all Canadians. As the monarch's representative, his or her duties include making public appearances, signing bills passed by Parliament, and receiving foreign ambassadors, heads of state, and other dignitaries when they visit Canada.

The governor general also plays a ceremonial role in summoning, opening, and ending sessions of Parliament.

Vincent Massey became the first Canadian-born governor general in 1952. Until then, Canada's governors general had always been British lords.

In 1984, Jeanne Sauvé (left) became the first woman appointed governor general. This was just one of many firsts for Sauvé, who had also been the first woman speaker of the House of Commons and the first woman MP from Québec to be a Cabinet minister.

Governor General Adrienne Clarkson (right) speaks with a war veteran during Remembrance Day ceremonies on November 11, 1999. When Clarkson was appointed governor general earlier in 1999, she became only the second woman to hold this post.

Decision Making in Canada Today

When the prime minister decides to call an election, for example, tradition calls for him or her to ask the governor general to dissolve — or end — a sitting of Parliament by declaring it closed.

Visitors cycle up to the main entrance of Rideau Hall, the 35-hectare Ottawa estate that is one of the governor general's official residences. The other is the Citadel in Québec City, original home of the French governors.

The governor general also opens each new sitting of Parliament by delivering the Speech from the Throne. This tradition is strictly ceremonial, however. The Speech from the Throne, which describes the goals of the new sitting of Parliament, is actually written by members of the prime minister's staff.

The Prime Minister and Cabinet

The prime minister is Canada's head of government. He or she is usually the leader of the **political party** that won the most seats in the House of Commons in a general election. As the most powerful person in the government, the prime minister controls his or her party, speaks for the government in power, chooses the members of the Cabinet, and sets the agenda for Cabinet meetings. The prime minister is the only person who can ask the governor general to dissolve Parliament and call an election.

Sir Wilfrid Laurier, Canada's first French-speaking prime minister, served from 1896 to 1911. This was the longest unbroken term of any prime minister.

The Cabinet is a group of government ministers chosen by the prime minister to help carry out the day-to-day business of government. Together, the prime minister and Cabinet form the core of the government's executive branch.

A Cabinet member is usually assigned responsibility for a specific area of government. This area is known as a portfolio or department. The departments of the federal government include environment, fisheries and oceans, national defence, citizenship and immigration, and human resources. Though most Cabinet ministers are chosen from among the members of the House of Commons, senators may also be appointed to the Cabinet.

William Lyon Mackenzie King (left) was prime minister from 1921 to June 28, 1926, from September 25, 1926, to 1930, and again from 1935 to 1948. King spent more years as prime minister than anyone else.

Pierre Elliott Trudeau (right), who was prime minister from 1968 to 1979 and from 1980 to 1984, received the Albert Einstein Peace Prize in 1984 for his efforts to make the world more peaceful by ridding it of nuclear weapons.

As the responsibilities of the federal government have increased since Confederation, the size of the Cabinet has also grown. New roles have been created for Cabinet ministers. Today, Cabinet ministers fall into five categories:

- department ministers, who run one or more government departments
- ministers with special responsibilities in Parliament
- ministers without portfolio, who do not run a specific department, but who are appointed to Cabinet to ensure that it includes members from all regions of Canada
- ministers of state who develop new policies outside normal departmental responsibilities
- other ministers of state, who may help department ministers

The Senate

The Senate is the so-called upper house of Canada's bicameral legislature. Since Confederation, however, the Senate's role as a chamber of "sober second thought" has not been as important as the architects of Confederation thought it might be. The unelected senators usually rubber stamp bills passed by the elected members of the House of Commons.

This is not always the case, though. In 1990, the Liberal majority in the Senate, supported by many Canadians, refused to pass a law that had been approved by the House of Commons. The law, which was created by Prime Minister Brian Mulroney's Conservative government, introduced the Goods and Services Tax, also known as the GST.

To overcome the Senate's opposition to the GST, Mulroney turned to a little-known clause of the British North America Act. The clause permits the prime minister to appoint new senators for a limited term. Mulroney chose eight new Conservative senators. This was enough to give his party a majority in the Senate. As a result, the GST Act passed. Mulroney's action sparked an outcry from Canadians who view the unelected Senate as an old-fashioned, undemocratic body that should be either reformed or eliminated.

Many people object to the fact that senators are often appointed to reward their loyal service to

Prime Minister Brian Mulroney rises in the House of Commons to answer a question about his decision to appoint extra senators and force passage of the GST Act through the Senate.

the party in power, rather than to recognize their service to Canada. In 1965, one minor reform of the Senate was introduced. Until then, Senate appointments were for life. Senators appointed since 1965 have been required to retire when they turn 75.

In recent years, many people have demanded more sweeping Senate reform. One proposal calls for a triple-E Senate — elected, equal, and effective. Strongly supported by the Reform Party which is now known as the Canadian Alliance, this proposal is very popular in Western Canada. It says that senators should be elected, with equal representation from each province, so that they can play an effective role in government.

So far, however, attempts to reform the Senate have failed. Despite its unpopularity with many Canadians, the upper house of the federal Parliament continues to exist much as it did at Confederation.

Many Canadians believe that Senate reform is long overdue. What does this cartoon say about the reforms that have been carried out so far?

Think ... Discuss ... Act

In humans, vestigial organs are body parts that no longer seem to serve a useful purpose. Some people, for example, say that the tonsils and appendix are vestigial.

In the same way, some people believe that the Senate is a vestigial part of the decision-making process and should be abolished. Others argue that it plays an important role as a body of "sober second thought," but does need to be changed. Still others think that it is just fine as is. Though the debate over Senate reform has been going on for decades, little has been done except to abolish the life terms of senators.

1. What do you think should be done about the Senate? Why? Record your thoughts in a sentence or two. Then discuss what you think with a group or the whole class.
2. Conduct a sample survey of 10 people chosen at random. Ask this question: What does the Senate mean to you? Record their answers and present them to the class.
3. Organize a class debate on abolishing the Senate.
4. Think about the points that were made during the class discussion, the survey, and the debate. Write a persuasive argument setting out your proposals for reforming the Senate.

The House of Commons

The House of Commons is the elected house of Parliament. Though it is sometimes called the lower house, it has always been the more important of the two houses. No new law can come into effect unless it has been debated in the House of Commons and approved by a majority of members of the House.

Members of the House of Commons are called members of Parliament, or MPs. Each MP represents a geographical area of the country. This area is called a riding, constituency, or electoral district. Because each riding is supposed to include roughly the same number of voters, their geographic area varies widely. The area of rural ridings is much larger than that of urban ridings.

As the population of Canada grew after 1867 and new provinces joined Confederation, the number of seats in the House of Commons increased. At Confederation, 181 MPs sat in the House. Today, there are 301 seats. Because Ontario and Québec are the two provinces with the highest population, most MPs come from these provinces.

The House of Commons is composed of

- the prime minister and elected members of the governing party;
- elected members of the opposition parties, as well as elected independent MPs who do not belong to a political party; and
- the speaker of the House, an MP chosen to supervise debates in the House of Commons. In fact, the job of the speaker is not to speak. Instead, the speaker, who is usually a member of the party that has formed the government, decides which MP has "the floor" — the right to speak. The speaker serves as a kind of umpire or referee who keeps order during debates. The speaker does not vote on bills brought before Parliament, except to break a tie.

People outside Ontario and Québec often complain that MPs from these two provinces dominate debates in the House of Commons. This map shows the number of MPs from each province and territory. Examine the map and explain why you think this complaint is — or is not — justified.

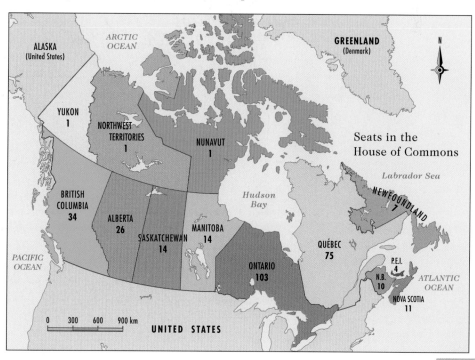

Seats in the House of Commons

Members of Parliament have the right to speak freely during debates. They cannot be sued for what they say in the House of Commons. Still, they do not have the right to use "unparliamentary language," such as calling another MP a liar. MPs who "breach parliamentary privilege" by breaking the rules of parliamentary procedure are "named" by the speaker and must withdraw from the House for the rest of the day's sitting.

In the House, MPs must address all their remarks to the speaker, who refers to them not by name but as "the honourable member from (name of the riding they represent)."

Gilbert Parent, the Speaker of the House of Commons, stands in front of his ornately carved chair. From this chair, Parent referees the debates in the House.

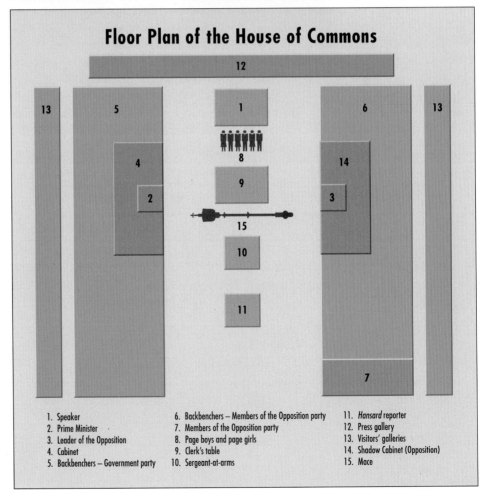

Floor Plan of the House of Commons

1. Speaker
2. Prime Minister
3. Leader of the Opposition
4. Cabinet
5. Backbenchers – Government party
6. Backbenchers – Members of the Opposition party
7. Members of the Opposition party
8. Page boys and page girls
9. Clerk's table
10. Sergeant-at-arms
11. *Hansard* reporter
12. Press gallery
13. Visitors' galleries
14. Shadow Cabinet (Opposition)
15. Mace

The House of Commons meets in a chamber in the west end of the Centre Block of the Parliament Buildings in Ottawa. This diagram shows where the various members sit. MPs who are not Cabinet ministers or who do not play an important role as opposition critics sit in the back rows. This has given rise to their nickname: backbenchers.

A word-for-word record of parliamentary debates is recorded by a reporter and published every day while Parliament is in session. This publication is called *Hansard*, the name of the printer who first published the debates of the British Parliament.

Both the House of Commons and the Senate appoint standing and special committees to examine issues and proposed legislation in detail. Many of these committees also appoint sub-committees to look into certain issues. Some of the standing committees of the House of Commons are Aboriginal Affairs and Northern Development, Finance, Foreign Affairs and International Trade, Health, and Justice and Human Rights.

In Parliament, proposed laws are called bills and assigned a number, such as C-17. The C in the bill number stands for Commons. Though most bills are introduced in the House of Commons, they can also be introduced in the Senate and move from there to the House of Commons. When bills are introduced in the Senate, they are identified with an S.

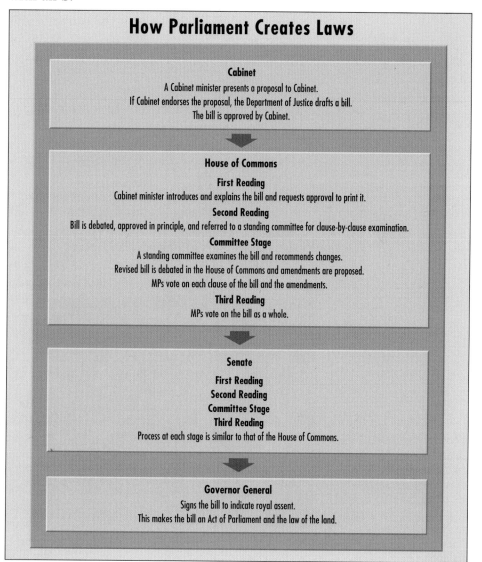

How Parliament Creates Laws

Cabinet
A Cabinet minister presents a proposal to Cabinet.
If Cabinet endorses the proposal, the Department of Justice drafts a bill.
The bill is approved by Cabinet.

House of Commons

First Reading
Cabinet minister introduces and explains the bill and requests approval to print it.

Second Reading
Bill is debated, approved in principle, and referred to a standing committee for clause-by-clause examination.

Committee Stage
A standing committee examines the bill and recommends changes.
Revised bill is debated in the House of Commons and amendments are proposed.
MPs vote on each clause of the bill and the amendments.

Third Reading
MPs vote on the bill as a whole.

Senate

First Reading
Second Reading
Committee Stage
Third Reading
Process at each stage is similar to that of the House of Commons.

Governor General
Signs the bill to indicate royal assent.
This makes the bill an Act of Parliament and the law of the land.

Before becoming law, bills pass through several stages. This chart shows the main steps of this process.

PROVINCIAL GOVERNMENTS

FYI

In all provinces but Ontario, Québec, and Newfoundland, elected members of provincial legislatures are called MLAs — members of the Legislative Assembly. In Ontario, they are called MPPs — members of the Provincial Parliament. In Québec, they are called MNAs, members of the National Assembly. In Newfoundland, they are called MHAs — members of the House of Assembly.

Like the federal government, the government in each of Canada's 10 provinces is a parliamentary system. The provincial premier is the leader of the political party that holds the most seats in the provincial legislature. Representation in the legislature is based on population, as it is in the federal house. Unlike the federal Parliament, however, provincial legislatures are unicameral. They have no unelected upper house like the Senate.

In each province, a lieutenant-governor acts as the monarch's representative, just as the governor general does at the federal level. The lieutenant-governor is appointed by the governor general on the advice of the provincial premier.

The goal of the architects of Confederation was to create a strong federal government. Since Confederation, however, the provincial governments and their premiers have become more powerful — at the expense of the federal government. One reason for this is that the British North America Act gave the provinces control of education and health care. In 1867, these were considered minor responsibilities. Since then, however, their importance has increased dramatically. Education and health care now account for about 50 percent of the budget of each province.

To give the federal government a say in social programs such as health care, an amendment to the BNA Act was required. In return for sharing their responsibility for social programs, the provinces received federal money to help to pay for these programs. In return for helping the provinces pay for social programs, the federal government gained the power to set rules governing social programs in all the provinces.

Though the provinces administer many social programs such as health care, they must follow the rules set by the federal government if they are to continue receiving federal funds. This sharing of responsibilities is called **co-operative federalism**.

The BNA Act also handed the provinces responsibility for municipalities. In 1867, when Canada's population was largely rural, this too was considered a minor responsibility. Throughout the 20th century, however, cities grew larger and became more important. The population of large cities such as Toronto and Vancouver is now greater than that of many provinces. As a result, their municipal politicians have a great deal of influence.

Ujjal Dosanjh, shown with his wife Raminder, made history in February 2000 as the first Canadian of Indian heritage to become a provincial premier.

A Day in the Life

ALVIN CURLING AN ONTARIO MPP

"I'm Black, as you can see," Alvin Curling often tells students during his frequent school visits. "People may say you can't achieve this or that because you're Black, or because you're female, or whatever. But you can!"

Curling loves to encourage young people. First elected to the Ontario Legislature to represent the riding of Scarborough-Rouge River in 1985, he served as minister of housing and minister of skills development in the Liberal government of Premier David Peterson. Even when the Liberals were defeated in 1990, Curling held on to his seat. Today, he is the youth advocate for the Official Opposition. His job is to examine and propose changes to the Progressive Conservative government's youth-related policies.

On days when the provincial legislature is not sitting, Curling looks after the business of his constituency. On a typical morning, he leaves home at about 8 A.M. for an 8:30 school visit. On these visits, he talks to students about various aspects of government, such as how laws are made. He also encourages students to set goals and make a difference in their communities.

After speaking to the students, Curling often meets their teachers to listen to their concerns and ideas.

By 10 or 10:30, he is in his constituency office for prearranged half-hour meetings with constituents. Some bring him personal problems: "I need a job" or "My mother is overseas and I would like to bring her to Canada." Some bring organizational problems: "How can we operate our business?" or "What can our minority group do about discrimination?" An attentive listener, Curling helps them explore solutions.

After eating lunch whenever there is time, Curling meets his staff at about 2 or 3 P.M. They discuss new requests from constituents and prepare for the next session of the legislature, which meets at Queen's Park in Toronto. After the staff meeting, the busy MPP often visits a senior citizens' home, a boys' club, or another organization in his constituency.

At 4 or 5 P.M., Curling goes home briefly. He often uses this break to answer some of the 20 or more phone calls he receives every day.

In the evenings, Curling is often invited to events in his constituency. These events may have been organized by members of Caribbean, Asian, African, Scottish, Chinese, or other communities. Curling tries to give equal attention to all groups in his culturally diverse riding.

By about 10 P.M., Curling's day is finally over. He is often tired, but he is also energized by his contact with constituents. A strong defender of democracy, he says, "I need [constituents'] input more than they think. I really don't have all the answers."

When the Ontario Legislature is not sitting, MPP Alvin Curling often speaks to groups of constituents or meets constituents in his constituency office.

Municipal Governments

Canada has about 5000 municipal governments. The population of municipalities varies greatly. They range in size from the megacity of Toronto, to metropolitan areas such as Montréal, to smaller cities such as Fredericton, New Brunswick, and Saskatoon, Saskatchewan, to towns, villages, counties, and rural municipalities.

Because municipal government is a provincial responsibility, each provincial government decides what powers municipal governments will have and how they will operate. Most municipalities are headed by an elected mayor or reeve. The mayor or reeve is helped by an elected council. Council members are usually called councillors or alderpersons.

Because municipal government is local, it is the government level closest to most Canadians. It has a big influence on people's daily lives.

Though the responsibilities of municipal governments vary, the following list shows some of the services municipalities may provide:

- maintaining local streets and roads, including ploughing snow, regulating parking, and locating stop signs and traffic lights
- maintaining the community water and electricity supply
- collecting garbage and managing waste, including sewage
- building and maintaining community parks, swimming pools, and ice rinks
- operating community libraries and art galleries
- operating a police department, fire department, and ambulance services
- administering welfare services
- regulating where industries, businesses, and homes may locate by enacting zoning bylaws and issuing building permits
- operating a public transportation system
- operating a public health department that regulates such things as restaurant cleanliness and housing for the elderly

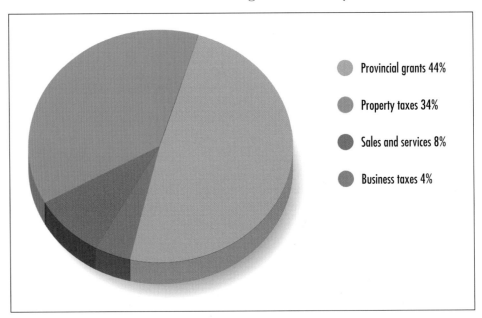

- Provincial grants 44%
- Property taxes 34%
- Sales and services 8%
- Business taxes 4%

The chart on this page shows how municipalities raise the money to fund the services they provide. Property taxes are taxes levied on the value of the property owned by homeowners and businesses.

Though provincial governments have often demanded — and won — more powers from Ottawa, they have steadfastly resisted requests to give more control to municipal governments. A familiar complaint of municipal councillors in large cities such as Toronto is that provincial politicians demand that they provide more and more services — but do not give them the money needed to do this.

http://www.school.mcgrawhill.ca/resources

To find out more about Canada's provincial, territorial, and municipal governments, go to History Resources. Then go to *Civics: Participating in a Democratic Society* to see where to go next.

With a population of 2.4 million, Toronto is Canada's largest city. Population does not equal popularity, however. Former Ontario Premier David Peterson once joked, "One of the things that keeps this country together is that everybody hates Ontario, and what keeps Ontario together is that everybody hates Toronto, and what keeps Toronto together is that everybody hates Bay Street [location of the Toronto Stock Exchange and the head offices of many large corporations]."

THE ROLE OF POLITICAL PARTIES

As in other democratic countries, political parties play a central role in the Canadian political system. Political parties are organized groups that compete with one another for the support of voters during federal and provincial elections. The goal of parties is to win enough seats to gain control of Parliament or a provincial legislature and form the government. Political parties differ over policies — ideas about the best way to run the country or province.

After an election, the political party that has won the most seats forms the government. Its leader becomes the prime minister or the provincial premier. The party winning the second-greatest number of seats forms the Official Opposition. Its leader becomes the leader of the Official Opposition.

When the party that forms the government holds more seats than all the opposition parties combined, it forms a **majority government**. Sometimes, a party wins the most seats, but these do not add up to more seats than the all the opposition parties combined. This means that none of the parties has a majority. When this happens, one of the parties forms a minority government.

The party that forms a minority government is not always the one that holds the most seats. In the 1985 Ontario election, for example, the Progressive Conservatives won four more seats than the Liberals. Neither party had enough seats to form a majority government, however.

The New Democratic Party, or NDP, also won seats — enough to ensure that this party held the **balance of power**. The balance of power is the power held by a small group when larger groups are of roughly equal strength. The NDP decided to throw its support behind the Liberals. As a result, this party formed a minority government. Its leader, David Peterson, became premier of Ontario.

From 1867 to 1921, every federal government elected in Canada was a majority government. This was because only two political parties — the Liberals and Conservatives — had enough voter support to elect MPs to the House of Commons. Since 1921, though, every Parliament has included MPs from more than two political parties.

In recent years, five main political parties have been represented in the House of Commons. They are the Liberal Party, the Bloc Québécois, the New Democratic Party, the Progressive Conservative Party, and the Canadian Alliance, which was formerly known as the Reform Party. A number of smaller parties also contest elections but do not usually win enough votes to win seats in Parliament.

As in the United Kingdom, Canada's system is called a first-past-the-post system. In each riding, political parties nominate a candidate to contest the election. The winner is the candidate who receives the most votes on election day. This means that there can be a big difference between the percentage of the popular vote a party receives and the number of seats it actually wins. The popular vote refers to the total number of ballots cast in an election.

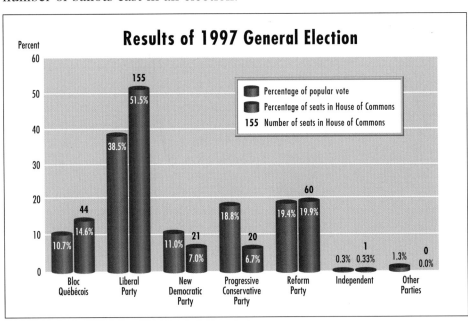

Results of 1997 General Election

Percent

Legend:
- Percentage of popular vote
- Percentage of seats in House of Commons
- 155 Number of seats in House of Commons

Party	Seats	% popular vote	% seats
Bloc Québécois	44	10.7%	14.6%
Liberal Party	155	38.5%	51.5%
New Democratic Party	21	11.0%	7.0%
Progressive Conservative Party	20	18.8%	6.7%
Reform Party	60	19.4%	19.9%
Independent	1	0.3%	0.33%
Other Parties	0	1.3%	0.0%

This graph shows the results of the 1997 federal election. Compare the percentage of the popular vote won by the various parties with the number and percentage of seats the parties actually won in the House of Commons.

FYI

In this age of high-tech mass communication, some people have suggested that it might be possible to re-create the kind of direct democracy that existed in ancient Athens. People could be linked by the Internet to a number of political chat-rooms, where they could discuss an issue and eventually vote on it. Is this is a good idea? Why? How do you think it could work?

In the 1985 Ontario election, for example, 38 percent of all those who voted cast ballots for the Liberals, while 37 percent voted for the Progressive Conservatives. Still, the Progressive Conservatives ended up with four more seats than the Liberals because of the way the vote split in various ridings.

The first-past-the-post system benefits parties whose support is concentrated in one area of the country. The Bloc Québécois, whose support is concentrated in Québec, and the Canadian Alliance, whose support is concentrated in Western Canada, are able to win a large number of seats because they have many supporters in certain ridings.

The system places parties such as the NDP at a disadvantage, however. NDP supporters are distributed more or less equally across the country. As a result, they form a majority in only a few ridings. Critics complain that this system gives people who voted for smaller parties little or no voice in Parliament.

Some people want to make Canada's electoral system reflect the popular vote more closely. One idea calls for "proportional representation." Instead of voting for a single candidate in one riding, people in a specified area would vote for several candidates on a list. The names on the list would be put forward by the various parties. Seats in Parliament would be assigned according to the percentage of the popular vote won by the candidates of a particular party. A party that received 30 percent of the vote in a particular area, for example, would receive 30 percent of the parliamentary seats assigned to that area.

Most Western democracies except Canada, the United Kingdom, and the United States practise some form of proportional representation. Supporters believe that this system is fairer. Critics argue, however, that it can lead to political instability. It sometimes makes it difficult, if not impossible, for one party to win a majority in Parliament.

On election day, qualified voters go to their polling station. A polling station official ensures their name is on the voters' list and hands them a ballot.

They enter a voting booth and mark their ballot in secret.

They mark an X in the circle after the name of the candidate they prefer.

They fold their ballot and hand it to a polling station official who inserts it in the ballot box.

AND THE RESULTS OF THE ELECTION...

After the polls close, polling station officials count the ballots and send in the results. The results are announced to the public.

Think … Discuss … Act

Governments in Canada are often elected by a minority of people because many parties split the vote in each riding. Refer to the chart on page 62, which shows how this split affected the composition of the House of Commons after the 1997 federal general election.

1. Calculate the number of seats each party would have won if a system of proportional representation had been in place.
2. If proportional representation had been in place, which party might have formed the government? Are there alternatives? Analyze these alternatives and explain the political alliances that might have been necessary to make each work.
3. The current system makes it possible for Canada to have strong governments even when the government does not represent a majority of voters. Would a system that truly reflects the will of the people be better? Why?
4. How do student government elections work in your school? Invite a student council representative to explain the system to your class.

LOBBYING AS A MEANS OF INFLUENCING GOVERNMENT

Suppose you want the government to lower taxes, reduce student violence in schools, or add a traffic light on a street corner in your community. In Canada, citizens do not always need to wait until the next election to make their wishes known. Between elections, individual citizens and like-minded groups of citizens often **lobby** — try to persuade — elected representatives to do things.

Lobbying takes many forms. It can include things like writing, e-mailing, and telephoning government officials, conducting a survey to find out how other people feel about an issue and presenting the results to government officials, preparing and presenting a petition, and organizing a conference and inviting government officials to attend. Are there lobby groups within your school? If so, how do they work?

On what local issue are Satch and his group lobbying their municipal government? What community issues concern you?

Get Fuzzy reprinted with permission of United Features Syndicate, Inc.

Pressure Groups

Pressure groups are organizations that try to advance certain causes, issues, or interests. Examples include the Urban Alliance on Race Relations and the Black Action Defence Committee (race issues), Pollution Probe and Greenpeace (environmental causes), the Canadian Cancer Society and the Thyroid Foundation of Canada (health issues), and the Canadian Manufacturers' Association and the Canadian Labour Congress (economic interests).

Pressure groups often hire consultants to lobby on their behalf. Paid lobbyists use many of the same tactics as individual citizens. They also try to influence governments through advertising campaigns and mass mailings. Some even offer expert advice to government officials in areas where these officials lack expertise, a tactic that can be very effective.

Some Canadians worry about the influence of pressure groups, which sometimes spend a great deal of money to advance their views. The tactics of some pressure groups raise questions about their influence on governments. What about citizens who do not have as much money to spend? Are their voices heard clearly enough? When governments comply with the wishes of small groups, does this mean that the interests of the majority are ignored? These are questions that political representatives at every level must deal with.

When fuel prices rose in early 2000, truckers across Canada staged protests to pressure governments and oil companies to control costs. The truckers also started talking about creating a formal organization to lobby for base salaries and other financial guarantees.

COURTS AND THE LAW

Canada has a civil law system and a criminal law system. Civil law deals with civil conflicts — disputes between people. In a civil suit, one person or group takes a complaint about another person or group to court and asks a judge to rule on the issue. The case might involve someone trespassing on someone else's property, a dispute between employers and employees, false advertising, a contract or mortgage, a separation or divorce, or any other matter involving private rights.

Because the federal and provincial governments share responsibility for civil law, civil laws differ from province to province. Every province has its own code of civil law. In Québec, this code dates to the Quebec Act of 1774, which guaranteed the province of Québec the right to retain the French civil code. The civil codes of other provinces are based on British common law, which has evolved over the centuries based on precedents — first-time decisions — set in various court cases.

Criminal law deals with actions that are considered crimes against society. Though individual people are usually the victims, these crimes are regarded as a threat to society as a whole. As a result, they are prosecuted by the federal government on behalf of the people.

Because the federal government is responsible for criminal law, the law is the same across Canada. These laws evolved from British common law and are recorded in the Criminal Code. The federal government, through the crown attorney, lays the charge and takes a person or group to court for offences such as theft, disorderly conduct, assault, murder, kidnapping, and hijacking.

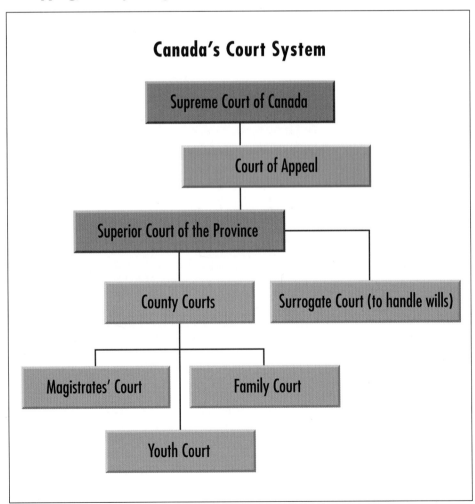

Canada's Court System

- Supreme Court of Canada
- Court of Appeal
- Superior Court of the Province
- County Courts
- Surrogate Court (to handle wills)
- Magistrates' Court
- Family Court
- Youth Court

This diagram shows how Canada's court system works — in general. The names of provincial courts vary from province to province.

THE INFORMED CITIZEN

Citizens in Action

MARY ELLEN TURPEL-LAFOND
JUSTICE FOR ABORIGINAL PEOPLE

When 13-year-old Mary Ellen Turpel-Lafond came down with a serious illness, her life changed forever. The illness kept her out of school for nearly a year. The bored teenager passed the time by reading. The books she chose awakened her to possibilities that she had never imagined. They inspired her to take charge of her life — and getting an education became her first step toward achieving this goal.

Born in Manitoba, Turpel-Lafond was the youngest child in a troubled family. Drinking and fighting were routine in her home. Turpel-Lafond's Cree father and Scottish mother never had enough money, and the teenager watched her older sisters make mistakes that she became determined not to repeat.

After finishing high school, Turpel-Lafond enrolled in university. Then she went on to study law and graduated from Osgoode Hall Law School at the top of her class. This did not end her education, though. She went on to earn a master's degree in international law at Cambridge University in England, then a doctorate of law at Harvard University in the United States. After that, she taught law at several universities.

Turpel-Lafond's mixed heritage had given her some unwelcome insights into the discrimination experienced by Aboriginal people. When the opportunity presented itself, she used her expertise in international law to throw herself into the battle to win self-government for Aboriginal Peoples. She spent several years advising Aboriginal groups on constitutional issues.

During this time, Turpel-Lafond moved to Saskatchewan. She continued advising Aboriginal groups and opened a private practice. In 1998, she was named a Saskatchewan Provincial Court judge. She was the first Aboriginal woman appointed to this post.

As a judge, Turpel-Lafond deals with many different cases and has vowed to work hard for everyone in Saskatchewan. Still, she is very concerned about the way the courts treat Aboriginal people. Too many are sent to jail for minor crimes, she says. She believes strongly in alternative forms of sentencing that help people turn their lives around.

"People must be treated fairly," Turpel-Lafond told Jacqueline Hennessy of *Chatelaine*. "Historically, Aboriginal people have been left out of everything — the legal system, elections, the school system. Equality has to be applied across the board. That's worth getting up in the morning and working hard for."

When Mary Ellen Turpel-Lafond was sworn in as Saskatchewan's first Aboriginal woman Provincial Court judge, the ceremony combined Aboriginal rituals with Canadian legal traditions.

The Supreme Court

As its name suggests, the Supreme Court of Canada is the highest court in the country. It is the court of last resort for everyone in Canada, whether the case is criminal or civil and whether it involves individual citizens, groups, or governments.

One of the Supreme Court's most important responsibilities is to rule on disputes between the federal government and the provinces. It received this power in 1949 from the Judicial Committee of the Privy Council in London, England. Until then, legal appeals from Canada had been heard in the United Kingdom.

The Supreme Court also interprets the Constitution and the meaning of the rights and freedoms granted to Canadians in the Charter of Rights and Freedoms. It has the power to declare certain federal and provincial laws unconstitutional if the judges believe that they violate the Constitution.

Nine judges sit on the Supreme Court. One of these is the chief justice, the leading judge. Three of the nine judges come from Québec. This guarantees the continuation of that province's civil law tradition. Of the six remaining judges, three usually come from Ontario, two from Western Canada, and one from Atlantic Canada.

Judges are appointed by the prime minister and must be lawyers with at least 10 years' experience.

All arguments before the Supreme Court of Canada take place in this building (left), which is located in Ottawa. The court hears about 100 cases a year.

When Beverley McLachlin (right) was sworn in as chief justice of the Supreme Court of Canada in January 2000, she became the first woman to hold the position. Born in Pincher Creek, Alberta, McLachlin has sat on the Supreme Court since 1989.

RESOLVING LABOUR DISPUTES

About one out of every three people in the Canadian workforce belongs to a labour union. Unions in Canada include the Canadian Union of Public Employees, the Canadian Auto Workers, and the Canadian Paperworkers Union.

Unions concern themselves with matters of interest to workers, such as wages, working conditions, benefits, pensions, and job security. On behalf of their members, unions negotiate with employers over work-related issues. The process, called **collective bargaining**, is recognized

In March 1999, the minister of justice introduced the proposed Youth Criminal Justice Act to the House of Commons. This act, known as Bill C-68, passed first reading and is before the House of Commons Standing Committee on Justice and Human Rights. The new act is designed to replace the Young Offenders Act, which has been in effect since 1984.

The proposed Youth Criminal Justice Act is the federal government's response to criticism that the Young Offenders Act is too easy on adolescent lawbreakers. Like the Young Offenders Act, the Youth Criminal Justice Act emphasizes rehabilitation and the need for young people to take responsibility for their criminal actions. At the same time, it gets tougher on youth who commit violent crimes.

The new act includes provisions that would enable the courts to

- impose adult sentences on youth 14 and older who are convicted of a serious offence
- allow publication of the names of all young people who receive adult sentences
- impose adult sentences on young offenders whose convictions show a pattern of serious violent crimes
- create a special sentence for serious violent offenders who suffer from mental illness, a psychological disorder, or emotional disturbance that includes a plan for treatment, control, and supervision
- help young offenders reintegrate into the community by requiring controlled supervision after they are released from custody
- impose tougher penalties on adults who wilfully fail to comply with court undertakings to supervise youth who have been denied bail and placed in their care
- use a full range of community-based and alternative sentences for young people who commit non-violent crimes
- recognize the principles of the United Nations Convention on the Rights of the Child

What comment is the cartoonist making about the proposed Youth Criminal Justice Act? Do you agree with what he says? Why?

The Active Citizen

1. Should young offenders — teens between the ages of 12 and 17 — be treated more leniently than adult offenders? Why?

2. The Young Offenders Act prohibits the publication of the names of adolescents convicted of crimes, except in special circumstances. The Youth Criminal Justice Act would change this. Do you think this change is a good idea? Why?

3. Should the courts be tougher on adolescents who commit violent crimes? Why?

4. Find out more about the Youth Criminal Justice Act and track its progress through Parliament. Write a letter or send an e-mail message to the minister of justice or your member of Parliament expressing your reaction to the act's proposals.

and regulated by law. The law requires both employers and unions to bargain in good faith; in other words, they must bargain with truthful and honourable intentions.

If the parties cannot reach agreement, the dispute-resolution process moves to the next stage. An arbitrator — a person who is a skilled negotiator — is asked to step in. Sometimes the law requires this kind of third-party intervention. The arbitrator calls together negotiators for both sides and helps them resolve the dispute.

When the dispute is resolved through **arbitration**, the union and employer sign a collective agreement. When the dispute is not resolved, the law enables most workers to go on strike, unless they provide "essential services" such as firefighting and policing. At the same time, employers may legally lock out employees, preventing them from entering their workplace. The strike or lockout continues until an agreement is reached.

THE CANADIAN CONSTITUTION AND CITIZENS' RIGHTS

In countries such as the United States, the Constitution is a formal written document that has been in effect for a long time. The constitutions of other countries, such as the United Kingdom, are largely unwritten. They are based on a series of political and legal decisions and traditional practices, called conventions, that have shaped the system of government over centuries.

The Evolution of Canada's Constitution

In 1981, the Supreme Court ruled that Canada's Constitution is made up of both unwritten conventions and written documents. Many of the

conventions and documents that form part of Canada's Constitution originated in British constitutional traditions. They include the Magna Carta of 1215 (see Chapter 1, page 14) and the English Bill of Rights of 1689 (see Chapter 1, page 16).

Other documents included in Canada's Constitution are acts or decisions of the British government

Harper's Weekly, an American magazine, published this artist's sketch of the opening of the first Parliament of the new Dominion of Canada in 1867.

that applied to Canada when it was a colony. These include the Royal Proclamation of 1763 (see Chapter 2, page 29), the Quebec Act of 1774 (see Chapter 2, page 30), and the Act of Union of 1840 (see Chapter 2, page 36).

When the British North America Act was passed by the British Parliament in 1867, it became the cornerstone of Canada's Constitution for more than 100 years.

In addition, the Supreme Court ruled that the Constitution included

- decisions of the Supreme Court of Canada since its creation in 1875;
- acts creating new provinces that were not part of Canada at the time of Confederation in 1867. These include the Manitoba Act of 1870 and the Alberta and Saskatchewan Act of 1905; and
- the Statute of Westminster, which was passed by the British Parliament in 1931. This act said that future laws passed by the British Parliament would apply to Canada only at the specific request of the Canadian government.

Bringing Home the Constitution

For 115 years after Confederation, the Constitution could be amended only by the British Parliament. By 1980, however, British officials had made it clear that they no longer wanted this power.

Despite this, no Canadian government had patriated, or brought the Constitution home, so that changes would be made in Canada. The obstacle was always that the federal and provincial governments could not agree on an **amending formula** — a procedure for changing the Constitution in Canada.

Then, in 1980, the Parti Québécois government of Québec held a provincial **referendum**, a special vote on a single issue. Residents of the province were asked whether they wanted to separate from Canada. Prime Minister Pierre Trudeau, himself a Quebecker, promised Québécois that if they voted to stay in Canada, he would patriate the Constitution. When 60 percent of French-speaking Quebeckers said NO to independence, Trudeau began the patriation process.

In the months after the Québec referendum, Trudeau called together the 10 provincial premiers to

Québec Premier René Lévesque concedes defeat after 60 percent of Quebeckers voted NO to separation in a 1980 referendum.

work out Canada's new constitutional arrangements. When these talks broke down, Trudeau announced that the federal government would proceed unilaterally — on its own.

Trudeau's plan outraged the provincial leaders, who asked the Supreme Court to rule on whether the federal government had the right to proceed unilaterally. The ruling said that the federal government did have the right — technically. However, the decision also said that an unwritten convention required the federal government to seek the agreement of the provinces.

This ruling sparked another round of talks between federal and provincial leaders. Finally, in late 1981, an agreement was reached. This was called the "kitchen compromise" because it was worked out in a hotel kitchen pantry during a private meeting involving Jean Chrétien of the federal government, Roy McMurtry of Ontario, and Roy Romanow of Saskatchewan. At the time, Chrétien was the federal attorney general. McMurtry and Romanow were the attorneys general of their provinces. The compromise gave the provinces the right to veto certain constitutional amendments, but not others.

The federal government and nine of the 10 provinces accepted the compromise. However, Premier René Lévesque of Québec angrily rejected it. Lévesque wanted every province to have the right to veto all constitutional amendments. He also wanted a national referendum on the proposed changes.

Trudeau decided to go ahead despite Lévesque's objections. Before Trudeau could officially patriate the Constitution, however, the British Parliament needed to pass one last act affecting Canada. This was the

At a colourful ceremony in front of the Parliament Buildings in Ottawa on April 17, 1982, Prime Minister Pierre Trudeau and Queen Elizabeth II signed the new Canadian Constitution. This made it the supreme law of the land.

Canada Act of 1982. The Canada Act said that no future act of the British Parliament would apply to Canada under any circumstances. It also cleared the way for the Canadian Parliament to pass the Constitution Act of 1982. This ensured that all future constitutional decisions would be made in Canada.

Trudeau's action left a legacy of bitterness in Québec, however. It ensured that wrangling over the Constitution would continue for years to come.

The Canadian Charter of Rights and Freedoms

By far the most important part of the Constitution Act of 1982 is the Canadian Charter of Rights and Freedoms. The Charter contains 34 clauses that identify the rights to which all Canadian citizens are entitled. The Charter also ensures that these rights are protected against the power of the state, or government.

Because the Charter is entrenched in the Constitution, neither the federal Parliament nor any provincial legislature can change or abolish people's rights by simply changing the law. Instead, a constitutional amendment is required. The process of amending the Constitution is much more complicated and difficult than the process of changing the law. How does this protect citizens' rights and freedoms?

The Charter is open to interpretation, however, and the courts have been assigned responsibility for making these interpretations. By 1984, two years after the Canadian Charter of Rights and Freedoms was entrenched in the Constitution, more than 1000 Charter-related challenges had been brought before the courts. Many of these cases made their way to the Supreme Court of Canada.

The Charter guarantees a variety of basic rights. These include freedom of expression, religion, and association. As a result, Canadian citizens are free to speak their minds on public issues, even if what they say criticizes the government. They may also practise any religion they choose — or no religion at all — without fear. And they may meet in groups for any purpose within the law.

The Charter also guarantees Canadians certain democratic rights, including the right to vote in elections. What is more, the Charter requires governments to hold elections every five years, except in certain circumstances. Canadians also enjoy "mobility rights" — the right to enter, remain in, or leave Canada, and move to and earn a living in any part of Canada.

Many legal rights are also set out in the Charter. For example, Canadians have the right to "life, liberty, and security." These rights may be suspended if a person is found guilty of a crime, however. Canadians also have the right to be secure against unreasonable search and seizure of their property by the police, and the right not to be imprisoned without knowing what charges have been brought

FYI

Governments did not always willingly grant people the right to vote. Many women could not vote in federal elections until 1918, and women in Québec did not win the right to vote in provincial elections until 1940. Aboriginal people who lived on reserves could not vote in federal elections until 1960. In 1971, the voting age was reduced to 18 from 21, extending this important democratic right to many more young people. Do you think the voting age should be lowered even more? Why?

against them. Anyone arrested and charged with committing a crime is also guaranteed certain legal protections, including the right to a reasonably quick and fair trial.

According to the section of the Charter dealing with equality rights, Canadians must be treated equally under the law. This means that no one can be discriminated against on the grounds of race, colour, national or ethnic origin, religion, sex, age, or mental or physical disability.

Canadians are also entitled to use either English or French, Canada's two official languages, when dealing with governments and the courts.

Some of the clauses of the Charter are shown on the opposite page.

http://www.school.mcgrawhill.ca/resources
To find out more about the Canadian Charter of Rights and Freedoms, go to History Resources. Then go to *Civics: Participating in a Democratic Society* to see where to go next.

Think … Discuss … Act

Section 15 (1) of the Canadian Charter of Rights and Freedoms prohibits discrimination on the basis of age and sex. At the same time, Section 1 states that all the rights and freedoms set out in the Charter are "subject only to such reasonable limits prescribed by law as can be demonstrably justified in a free and democratic society."

1. Choose a panel of students to act as judges. Form groups and choose one of the following statements. Prepare arguments explaining why the limits described in each statement are — or are not — reasonable. Present the arguments before the judges, who must hand down a ruling on the issue.

   • It is discriminatory under the Canadian Charter of Rights and Freedoms to require licensed drivers to be 16 years old.

   • It is discriminatory under the Canadian Charter of Rights and Freedoms to bar people younger than 18 from buying cigarettes or alcohol.

   • It is discriminatory under the Canadian Charter of Rights and Freedoms to require workers to retire at the age of 65.

   • It is discriminatory under the Canadian Charter of Rights and Freedoms to require drivers older than 80 to pass a special driving test.

Canadian Charter of Rights and Freedoms

Whereas Canada is founded on principles that recognize the supremacy of God and the rule of law:

Guarantee of Rights and Freedoms

1. The Canadian Charter of Rights and Freedoms guarantees the rights and freedoms set out in it subject only to such reasonable limits prescribed by law as can be demonstrably justified in a free and democratic society.

Fundamental Freedoms

2. Everyone has the following fundamental freedoms:
   a) freedom of conscience and religion;
   b) freedom of thought, belief, opinion and expression, including freedom of the press and other media of communication;
   c) freedom of peaceful assembly; and
   d) freedom of association.

Democratic Rights

3. Every citizen of Canada has the right to vote in an election of members of the House of Commons or of a legislative assembly and to be qualified for membership therein.

Legal Rights

7. Everyone has the right to life, liberty and security of the person and the right not to be deprived thereof except in accordance with the principles of fundamental justice.
8. Everyone has the right to be secure against unreasonable search or seizure.
9. Everyone has the right not to be arbitrarily detained or imprisoned.
10. Everyone has the right on arrest or detention
    a) to be informed promptly of the reasons therefor;
    b) to retain and instruct counsel without delay and to be informed of that right; and
    c) to have the validity of the detention determined by way of *habeas corpus* and to be released if the detention is not lawful.

12. Everyone has the right not to be subjected to any cruel and unusual treatment or punishment.

Equality Rights

15. (1) Every individual is equal before and under the law and has the right to the equal protection and equal benefit of the law without discrimination and, in particular, without discrimination based on race, national or ethnic origin, colour, religion, sex, age or mental or physical disability.

Official Languages of Canada

16. (1) English and French are the official languages of Canada and have equality of status and equal rights and privileges as to their use in all institutions of the Parliament and government of Canada.

General

28. Notwithstanding anything in this Charter, the rights and freedoms referred to in it are guaranteed equally to male and female persons.

CHAPTER REVIEW

SUMMING IT UP

Processes are very important in Canadian society. Canada has processes for choosing political representatives and governments, for making the laws that govern society, for dealing with disputes between people and organizations, for dealing with people accused of crimes, and for protecting the rights of citizens. These processes help guide decision making and ensure that the voices of citizens are heard in the decision-making process.

1. List the people who make the decisions that affect the daily lives of Canadians.

2. Create a time line showing the changes in the Canadian Constitution.

3. Add terms from this chapter to your list of New Words with Special Meaning.

GETTING THE FACTS

1. Create a graphic organizer that shows how Canada's system of government works.

2. What is the role of political parties in the Canadian system?

3. Explain how the justice system works.

4. Disputes among Canadians can be resolved in a variety of ways. Explain this statement by referring to the information in this chapter.

5. What are the rights of Canadian citizens?

6. The British Constitution is largely unwritten. The American Constitution, on the other hand, is completely written. The Canadian Constitution is said to be somewhere in between these two. Why this is so?

USING THE FACTS

The **Active Citizen**

1. Once elected, politicians must represent all their constituents, including those who voted for different candidates. If you were a politician, would you find it difficult to represent people who voted against you? Why?

   How can people who voted for different candidates ensure that their voices are heard?

2. Create a graphic organizer showing whose interests members of Parliament must represent.

3. Invite a politician from your community to visit your class to explain the process of getting elected.

   If the person you invite is a federal or provincial politician, prepare for the visit by finding out where his or her party stands on some current issues.

   If the person is a municipal politician, prepare for the visit by finding out about local issues.

   Create a list of questions you would like to ask.

4. Explain how each step in the evolution of the Canadian Constitution made decision making more democratic. To help you do this, refer to the time line created earlier.

Chapter 4

DECISION MAKING IN A GLOBAL SOCIETY

"Let us recognize that our neighbours in this global village are our fellow human beings — with hopes and dreams just as we have, and problems and faults just as we have."

Mary Robinson, United Nations High Commissioner for Human Rights, on Human Rights Day, December 10, 1999

Two Red Cross volunteers collect stones near the famous lighthouse at Peggy's Cove in Nova Scotia. The stones were given as mementoes to the families of the victims of Swissair Flight 111, which plunged into the Atlantic Ocean near Peggy's Cove in September 1998. The 229 victims of the crash included only one Canadian. Still, these volunteers believed that it was important to collect the stones to give to the families of people from other countries. What message did their action send?

Setting
the Stage

Today's world has been called a global village. This means that all people are neighbours. Everyone is linked. International trade provides one of these links. The clothes Canadians wear, the CDs Canadians listen to, and much of the food Canadians eat may have been made by workers in distant lands. By buying the goods produced by these workers, Canadians affect their lives.

Television and other media are another link. Whether it's a famine or an epidemic, a flood or an earthquake, a civil war or a war between nations, or a terrible plane crash, people around the world learn about events like these almost instantly through the mass media, such as television, radio, and newspapers. As the media flash news of these events to every corner of the earth, people everywhere reach out to help their neighbours in the global community.

Simply being a citizen of Canada also links Canadians to the global village. This is because the Canadian government works with the governments of other countries through organizations such as the United Nations, the North Atlantic Treaty Organization, the Commonwealth, and the Francophonie.

The Red Cross volunteers who collected the stones at Peggy's Cove, Nova Scotia, did so in response to an extraordinary event. How do the everyday things you do affect your neighbours in the global community? Have you, your friends, or family members — like the Red Cross volunteers in the photograph — ever responded to an extraordinary event in an extraordinary way?

Chapter
Expectations

In this chapter, you will learn about:

- how decision making takes place in other countries of the world
- how the denial of human rights in Germany led to the Holocaust, or Sho'ah, during World War II
- how democracy helped resolve a deadly conflict in South Africa
- how Canada participates in international organizations
- how the United Nations helped define the rights and responsibilities of citizens in the global context

Key
Terms

anarchy	Communist Party	means of production
apartheid	Holocaust	political prisoner
Cold War	junta	veto

DECISION MAKING IN OTHER COUNTRIES

In Canada, the head of government is the prime minister. The prime minister chooses ministers who help to run the country. But who chooses the prime minister? In parliamentary democracies like Canada, the prime minister is usually the leader of the political party that controls the most seats in the House of Commons. This means that the prime minister is actually selected by the members of his or her political party, and only indirectly by the voters at large.

Not all democracies are parliamentary democracies, however. The United States, for example, is a republican democracy. In a republican democracy, the executive branch of the government is made up of the president and vice-president. The president and vice-president are elected separately from the legislative branch of the government. In the United States, the legislative branch is made up of members of the Senate and the House of Representatives. In a republic, the president is both the head of state and the head of government.

In the United States, each political party chooses a candidate for president, just as Canadian parties choose their leaders. This ends the similarity between the two systems, however. Americans vote for their president and vice-president in a separate election.

In the United States, elections are held at specific intervals. Presidential elections are held every four years. Senators run for election every six years, and members of the House of Representatives are elected to a four-year term. Even judges are elected in the United States.

In Canada, the government is elected for a maximum term of five years, but the prime minister can call a new election whenever she or he decides the time is right. And if the governing party is defeated in certain votes in the House of Commons, an election must be called.

The American system of electing a president separately can create political problems. For example, a president whose party does not hold a majority of seats in Congress may be unable to do much.

What is more, the process of removing a president from office in the United States is so complicated that it can interfere with the business of government. In 1999, for example, American President Bill Clinton was brought before the Senate on charges that he had committed "high

Prime Minister Jean Chrétien speaks to a news conference after the 1997 federal election. When the Liberals won the most seats in the House of Commons, Chrétien became prime minister for a second term because he was the leader of the Liberal party.

crimes and misdemeanours." During his trial, the normal affairs of the U.S. government ground to a near-halt for months. In the end, Clinton was acquitted and his presidency continued.

The term "republic" has been associated with democracy since the 18th-century revolutions that created the United States and turned France into a republic. Still, a republic is not necessarily a democracy. A republic is simply a country that is not governed by a monarch. As a result, many non-democratic countries also call themselves republics. The People's Republic of China, which is a one-party state, is an example.

In some countries, the system of government combines parliamentary and republican institutions. France and Russia, for example, have both a president, who is the head of state, and a prime minister, who is the

American President Bill Clinton speaks to reporters in 1999 after the Senate voted to acquit him on charges of perjury and obstruction of justice. In Canada, getting rid of a prime minister or provincial premier is much easier. Why?

head of government. Voters elect the president directly. The legislature, however, operates like a parliament. The leader of the party that holds the most seats becomes the prime minister. The president and prime minister work together. They split the leadership duties.

Within both republican and parliamentary systems, there is a creative tension between the leader and the elected representatives. The elected representatives keep a close eye on the leader. The relationship between the leader — the executive branch of a government — and the representatives — the legislative branch of a government — are set out in a country's constitution.

Think ... Discuss ... Act

The citizen is the basis of the decision-making process in Canada, the United Kingdom, the United States, and France. By exercising their voting rights, citizens choose who will make decisions on their behalf. Citizens do not, however, make decisions directly. Their authority is indirect.

1. Create a diagram showing how decisions are made in Canada, the United Kingdom, the United States, and France. Which system of decision making gives the voter the most power? Why?
2. a) Do you think changes should be made in Canada's decision-making process or do you support the status quo — the existing situation? Why?
   b) What process do you follow when making decisions?

How Countries Become Democracies

In every country, the nature of government changes constantly. At one time, many countries did not even have their own government. They were colonies of other countries.

Both Canada and the United States, for example, were colonies at one time. In 1900, most African countries and many of the countries of Asia and Central and South America were colonies of European powers. Many of these countries, such as India and South Africa, did not achieve independence until after World War II.

Until about a hundred years ago, many nations were also absolute monarchies. Today, only a few countries, such as Saudi Arabia, are ruled by an absolute monarch.

The fact that a country has a monarch does not mean that it cannot be a democracy. In constitutional monarchies such as the United Kingdom, Canada, Sweden, Spain, and Thailand, kings or queens serve as the head of state or symbolic leader. The power of the monarch is limited by the constitution, however, and the day-to-day operation of the government is in the hands of elected officials.

The United States and France are among the few nations in which democratic decision making was established by revolutions that got rid of monarchs. In most countries, democracy evolved over a long period. Most of today's democracies started out as oligarchies, then evolved into full-fledged democracies. The kind of democratic decision making practised a hundred years ago was very different from the kind of democracy that is practised today. What are some of the differences?

Many non-democratic countries have leaders who seized power by force. Libya and Iraq, for example, are ruled by dictators. Countries such as Zaire and Egypt are ruled by a single political party, though the leader of the party may change. Still other countries such as Myanmar and Nigeria are ruled by a **junta**, a group of military officers who took over the government by force.

The Kingdom of Saudi Arabia is one of the few countries that are still ruled by an absolute monarch. Here, Saudi subjects sit under portraits of some of the country's kings. Why does democracy fail to develop in some countries?

Most non-democratic governments rule by decree. A decree is an order that must be obeyed. The leader or leaders issue their decrees without consulting the country's citizens. People and groups who object are often treated brutally.

Communist governments, such as the People's Republic of China, North Korea, Vietnam, and Cuba, operate much the same way. In Communist countries, leaders are members of the Communist Party, which is the only official party. The government plans the country's economy and owns the **means of production**. This means that things such as factories and farms are owned by the government.

When a civil war causes a breakdown of law and order, it creates **anarchy**. Anarchy is a situation in which the government is either ineffective or non-existent. Countries like Bosnia and Herzegovina, Somalia, and Rwanda have recently experienced the terrors of anarchy. Often, an outside force such as the United Nations must step in to restore order and separate the warring sides.

In many countries, democracy has become stronger over time. In Canada, for example, democracy became stronger during the 20th century as more people won the right to vote. What other changes have made democracy stronger in Canada?

The opposite may also happen. Democracy can become weaker. If citizens are not vigilant, their democratic rights may be eroded. This is what happened in Germany in the 1930s.

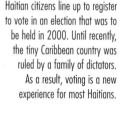

Haitian citizens line up to register to vote in an election that was to be held in 2000. Until recently, the tiny Caribbean country was ruled by a family of dictators. As a result, voting is a new experience for most Haitians.

A DEMOCRACY DIES

On a cold evening in February 1933, a fire broke out in a big, old public building in Berlin, Germany. The blaze was started by people who wanted to turn back the clock and govern without restraint. They wanted a free hand to "exterminate" Communists, Jews, homosexuals, Roma, and anyone else who did not agree with their ideas.

The building was the Reichstag, the German parliament. Though the fire in the Reichstag was soon put out, the flames of hatred that had started it kept burning until they had affected most of the world. By the time World War II ended in 1945, more than 50 million people had lost their lives.

Out of the ashes of the fire would grow a new resolve, however. With one voice, the nations of the world would say, "Never again." For the first time, human rights would be protected by international laws.

After its defeat in World War I, Germany was forced to pay the victors for some of the damages caused by the war. As a result, the country went deeply into debt.

The National Socialist German Workers' Party — nicknamed the Nazis — took advantage of this situation. The Nazis blamed Jews for Germany's troubles. More than 600 000 Jews lived in Germany. Many Jewish families had lived there for generations.

Some Jews were among the élite in German business, finance, and culture. These Jews became a special target of Nazi hatred. In 1923, for example, publisher Julius Streicher wrote in the first issue of a violently anti-Semitic newspaper *Der Stürmer (The Storm)*: "As long as the Jew is in the German household, we will be Jewish slaves. Therefore he must go. Who? The Jew!"

Adolf Hitler became the leader of the Nazis in 1921, when he was 32. In 1924, he published a book titled *Mein Kampf*, which means "my struggle." In the pages of *Mein Kampf*, Hitler ranted against the Jews and celebrated the Aryan race. By Aryan, he meant white Europeans, and especially Nordic people.

The Nazis remained a fringe party in Germany until 1930, when they won more than 100 seats in the Reichstag. By this time, the Great Depression had started. Millions of people were out of work.

Germany's parliament, the Reichstag, burns in 1933. The Nazis under Adolf Hitler used this fire as an excuse to seize control of the German government.

The Nazis promised to promote economic recovery and restore German national pride. Their bitter rivals, the **Communist Party**, also promised economic recovery. Both parties wanted to seize control of the government, and neither had any respect for democracy. The difference was that the Nazis appealed to German traditions. The Communists wanted to destroy the traditional bases of German society.

At this time, the German system of government was one of the most advanced in the world. Germany's Constitution, drawn up after World War I, was designed to prevent a dictator from taking power. Representatives were elected to the Reichstag by a combination of geographic and proportional voting. Women had the right to vote.

The leader of the German government was the chancellor. Like Canada's prime minister, the chancellor was the leader of the party that held the most seats in the legislature. Unlike Canada's prime minister, however, the chancellor did not need to be an elected representative.

German voters also elected a president directly. The president had the power to dismiss the chancellor and appoint a new one if one party did not have clear control of the Reichstag.

Hitler seized control of Germany by manipulating these democratic institutions. He also played on people's fears and their unhappiness over Germany's economic situation. By the beginning of 1932, when the Great Depression was well under way, six million Germans were out of work. The Reichstag was in turmoil. No combination of the eight parties that held seats in the Reichstag could muster enough votes to pass laws.

As leader of the Nazi Party, Hitler had the backing of powerful people in business, the army, and the aristocracy. He also had the support of the son of the president, 84-year-old Paul von Hindenburg. Hitler used his influence to persuade Hindenburg to appoint him chancellor in 1933. Hitler's right-hand man, Hermann Göring, was appointed minister of the interior.

The minister of the interior was responsible for the largest police force in Germany. Within a month, Göring had replaced the upper ranks of the Prussian police service with Nazis, and given the Nazi storm troopers special policing powers.

Six days after he became chancellor, Hitler persuaded von Hindenburg to give him emergency powers. He cited the threat from the Communists. The government now had the power to ban all opposition and seize their offices. Dachau and nine other concentration camps were established in Germany at this time. At first, their purpose was to imprison Communists and other political enemies of the Nazis. These "enemies" had been arrested under the emergency decrees.

On February 27, 1933, fire engulfed the Reichstag. The fire was set on purpose. Hitler and his associates blamed the Communists.

Adolf Hitler, left, gives the Nazi salute to a crowd of supporters as Hermann Göring looks on.

A Dutch Communist was seized at the scene and charged with the crime. Though this man later confessed, many historians are suspicious of this confession. They have suggested that the Nazis set the fire and pinned the blame on a Communist. Their motive was to discredit their political enemies.

The Reichstag fire gave Hitler just the excuse he needed to demand — and get — even more power. He said that he needed these powers to protect the people from the Communist threat. People's civil rights were suspended. Nazi police and storm troopers could even throw people in prison without a trial.

As chancellor, Hitler also won the right to make laws without the approval of the Reichstag or the president. He used this power to outlaw all political parties except the Nazis. Finally, he abolished the presidency and took the title Führer, which means leader.

After he grabbed the power to make laws and got rid of all opposition, Hitler was free to pursue the Nazi program. With dizzying speed, the Nazis began to take away the civil rights of Jews.

Web Connection

http://www.school.mcgrawhill.ca/resources

To find out more about how Hitler manipulated the German democratic system to seize control of the government, go to History Resources. Then go to *Civics: Participating in a Democratic Society* to see where to go next.

The Nazis introduced more than 400 anti-Jewish laws and decrees. Civil servants of non-Aryan descent, for example, were ordered to "retire." Non-Aryans were decreed to include anyone descended from even one non-Aryan grandparent. Jewish laws governing the slaughter of animals for food were attacked, and Jews were barred from enrolling in institutions of higher learning, and participating in radio, film, and theatre. They were also barred from owning agricultural land.

After these laws were passed, there was a lull in the racist storm. It lasted for two years. Then, in a speech to a party rally in Nuremberg on September 15, 1935, Hitler announced the Reich Citizenship Law, the first of several decrees that deprived

This 1933 Nazi campaign poster reads: "Do you wish to be free from Jewish domination? Then vote the Nationalist Block!" What would happen if a political party tried to use a poster like this in Canada today?

Jews of their human rights. These laws, which became known as the Nuremberg laws, barred Jews from

- marrying Germans
- flying the German flag or the colours of Germany
- becoming citizens, voting, and holding public office

In the years that followed, these laws were made even stricter. By 1939, for example, every Jew over 10 years of age had to wear a yellow Star of David in public. Despite this, many Jews who chose to remain in Germany clung to the belief that the Nazi nightmare would end.

At this time, the Nazis' goal was to drive Jews out of Germany. On November 7, 1938, an orgy of anti-Jewish violence erupted across the country. Called *Kristallnacht*, or the Night of Broken Glass, the violence was aimed at persuading Jews to leave Germany. The Nazis also began to seize property owned by Jews.

When World War II began in September 1939, the Nazis used the concentration camps that had been set up to imprison Communists to harness Jewish manpower to help the country's war industries.

The **Holocaust**, or Sho'ah, began in 1941. This is when the notorious gas chambers and cremation ovens were introduced in some concentration camps. These camps became death camps instead of work camps. Hitler's so-called "Final Solution" escalated into a frenzy of murder, conducted with factory-like organization.

By the time the war ended in 1945, more than six millions Jews had died at the hands of the Nazis.

The Active Citizen

Think ... Discuss ... Act

Reverend Martin Niemöller was a Lutheran pastor who helped form a German resistance movement called the Confessional Church. In the 1930s, Niemöller spoke out against Nazi human rights abuses. As a result, the Nazis threw him into a concentration camp, where he spent seven years. After the war, Niemöller often spoke about people's responsibility to resist evil. This how he put it:

> *In Germany they came first for the Communists, and I didn't speak up because I wasn't a Communist. Then they came for the Jews, and I didn't speak up because I wasn't a Jew. Then they came for the trade unionists, and I didn't speak up because I wasn't a trade unionist. Then they came for the Catholics, and I didn't speak up because I was a Protestant. Then they came for me, and by that time no one was left to speak up.*

1. Explain the point Martin Niemöller was making with these words. Do you agree with him? Why?
2. Niemöller was not the only German who spoke out against the Nazis even though it became very dangerous to do so. Form a group and research to find out about other people and groups who tried to resist. What happened to them?

A Democracy Triumphs

Like Canada, South Africa was a British colony for many years. During this time, European settlers moved in and displaced African people in much the same way that they had displaced Aboriginal people in Canada.

When South Africa achieved independence from Great Britain in 1910, apartheid was already a way of life in the country. Apartheid means apartness in Afrikaans, the language spoken by many of South Africa's Dutch settlers.

Under apartheid, non-Europeans, who made up about 80 percent of the population, had few rights. The country's Constitution, for example, specified that only white men could become members of Parliament. In most areas of the country, only white men could vote.

Over the next 40 years, things got worse, not better, for Black Africans. The few rights they had were gradually taken away. Finally, in 1950, the government took even more extreme steps. The Population Registration Act classified all South Africans into three groups:

- Bantu — all Black Africans
- coloured — people of mixed race
- white

Later, a fourth category was added for Asians — people of Indian and Pakistani heritage who had started immigrating to South Africa in search of jobs.

Under apartheid, even everyday activities were segregated. In this 1969 photograph, spectators at a sports event in Bloemfontein, South Africa, sit in different areas of the stands.

The government then passed laws setting out areas of cities where people of each racial group were to live, operate businesses, and own land. It became illegal for members of one race to do any of these things in areas set aside for another race.

Blacks who had lived in mostly white cities were forced to move to poor townships far away. This meant that they often had to travel for hours to get to and from work. Those who had lived in the fertile countryside were moved to "homelands" in mostly infertile desert.

To enter an area set aside for whites, non-whites had to carry special passes. Other laws banned most social contact among people of different races, set up separate public facilities and education systems, and specified the jobs members of each race could hold.

People who objected to the laws were brutally beaten, jailed, or killed by police or other agents of the government. Still, protest movements continued to operate. One of these was the African National Congress, or ANC. The ANC began to use the tools of peaceful protest — civil disobedience, boycotts, and strikes.

Then, on March 21, 1960, things got even worse. To protest the pass laws, unarmed Black people had gathered outside police stations without their passes. In Sharpeville, near Johannesburg, police opened fire on the crowd. At least 67 people were killed and more that 180 were wounded. Many were shot in the back as they fled. The event became known as the Sharpeville Massacre.

As the world reacted in horror, a three-decade reign of terror began in South Africa. The ANC and other groups were outlawed. Many of their leaders, such as Nelson Mandela, were jailed. Mandela and many others became **political prisoners**, people who are imprisoned because of their political beliefs and actions.

The outlawed ANC and some other groups decided that peaceful protest was not working. As they turned to violence to try to achieve their goals, the struggle became more and more brutal.

In the meantime, other countries had started trying to pressure South Africa into changing its racist policies. South Africa was excluded from the British Commonwealth, an organization of independent countries that had once been British colonies. South African teams were barred from taking part in the Olympic Games and other international competitions. Corporations, banks, and entire countries refused to do business with South African businesses or the country's government.

As a result, South Africa became an outcast among nations. It was transformed from a wealthy country into a relatively poor one.

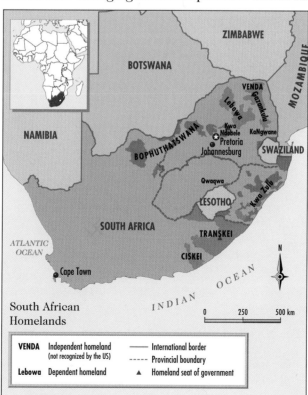

This map shows the location of the Black homelands in South Africa. More than 80 percent of South Africa's land ended up in the hands of the white minority.

South African Homelands

VENDA Independent homeland (not recognized by the US)
Lebowa Dependent homeland
— International border
----- Provincial boundary
▲ Homeland seat of government

0 250 500 km

Canada played an important role in bringing world opinion to bear on South Africa's leaders. In 1961, Prime Minister John Diefenbaker helped exclude South Africa from the British Commonwealth, an association of the United Kingdom and former British colonies. In 1974, Canada began to help liberation groups in South Africa indirectly. The Canadian government gave money to international aid organizations such as Oxfam, the Red Cross, and the World Council of Churches. These organizations were working in South Africa.

Canada also withdrew its trade representatives from South Africa and stopped funding trips to South Africa by Canadian athletes. When these measures did not work, Canada and other members of the British Commonwealth banned most trade with South Africa. Included in the ban were bank loans, air travel, and tourism. No longer were Canadian companies allowed to import South African agricultural products, or uranium, coal, iron, and steel. Canada also closed most of its consulates in South Africa.

Gradually, the government of South Africa came to realize that change was necessary. The governing party elected a new leader, F. W. de Clerk. De Clerk lifted the ban on the ANC and released Mandela from prison on February 11, 1990.

When terrible fighting broke out between rival Black groups, Mandela and de Clerk sat down to negotiate the establishment of democracy in South Africa. For their work, the two were awarded the 1993 Nobel Peace Prize. In South Africa's first truly democratic election in 1994, Mandela was elected president. At the age of 76, after spending more than one third of his life as a political prisoner, he became the first Black person to lead the nation of more than 43 million people.

When he sworn in as president, Mandela vowed: "Never, never and never again shall it be that this beautiful land will again experience the oppression of one by another and suffer the indignity of being the skunk of the world."

Despite its progress, South Africa's future remains uncertain.

Nelson Mandela dances at a concert celebrating his election as president of South Africa in 1994. When the country's Parliament adopted a new Constitution in 1999, Mandela stepped down. His work was finished.

Crime and poverty are everywhere. Violence flares nearly every day. Many white and Black people continue to view one another with fear and suspicion.

Still, South Africa stands as a beacon of hope for the rest of the world. It is one of the few countries that has overcome a violent regime without a bloody revolution. After decades of violence, its peaceful transition to democracy astonished the world. It gave heart to people who are suffering under oppressive regimes.

A woman and child stand in of their shack near Johannesburg in 1999. One of the challenges facing South Africa is to reverse the crushing effects of poverty on the Black majority. The government has been helping the poor build better housing.

THE QUEST FOR PEACE AND SECURITY

At the end of World War II, much of Europe and Asia lay in ruins. Even as the soldiers were washing the mud of battle off their boots, a new conflict erupted among the nations that had been allies during the war.

This conflict pitted the United States, Great Britain, and France against the Union of Soviet Socialist Republics, better known as the Soviet Union or USSR. The deadly rivalry between the Western democracies and the Communist Soviet Union and its allies became known as the **Cold War**. It was called the "cold" war because the two sides did not actually fight. Instead, they competed to build and stockpile bigger and better weapons of mass destruction. They also jockeyed for influence over smaller countries.

To force an end to World War II, the United States had dropped nuclear bombs on the Japanese cities of Hiroshima and Nagasaki in 1945. In the Cold War that followed World War II, both sides built up their arsenal of nuclear weapons. Each hoped that fear of the destructive power of its weapons would keep the other side from attacking. Though the Cold War is now over, the existence of nuclear weapons continues to threaten all humankind.

Nearly 100 million people died in World War I and II. After World War II, peace was threatened by the Cold War. Was the answer to these ruinous conflicts a form of world government? Peace-loving people everywhere hoped that the answer was yes. They pinned their hopes on an international oganization that was just forming.

CANADA AND THE UNITED NATIONS

After World War I, the Allies had formed an organization called the League of Nations. Though the goal of this organization was to promote co-operation among nations, it had been a dismal failure. It had not stopped the conflicts that led to World War II. Its small membership and limited powers meant that the League was all talk and no action.

Still, the leaders of many countries believed that an international organization of nations was needed. At the height of World War II in 1942, 26 Allied powers signed an agreement that would become the basis for such an organization. Then, in 1945, representatives of 50 countries met in San Francisco, California, to take this work a step farther. They formed a new organization called the United Nations.

The charter they created came into force on October 24, 1945, soon after the end of World War II. The charter begins with these words.

We the peoples of the United Nations (are) determined

- *to save succeeding generations from the scourge of war, which twice in our lifetime has brought untold sorrow to mankind, and*
- *to reaffirm faith in fundamental human rights, in the dignity and worth of the human person, in the equal rights of men and women and of nations large and small, and*
- *to establish conditions under which justice and respect for the obligations arising from treaties and other sources of international law can be maintained, and*
- *to promote social progress and better standards of life in larger freedom ...*

This photograph of Lester B. Pearson was taken in 1965, when he had become prime minister of Canada.

Though these goals were noble, it looked at first as if the United Nations — also known as the UN — might run into the same problems as the League of Nations. Ten years after it was formed, only 60 countries had joined. The Cold War was at its height.

Still, countries like Canada, one of the original members, worked hard to make the new organization a success. One of the people who worked hardest was Lester B. Pearson. After a career as a diplomat, Pearson became Canada's minister of external affairs in 1948. He was appointed to lead the Canadian delegation to the UN. Elected president of the General Assembly in 1952, he worked to promote the ideals of the UN and make sure that it did not suffer the same fate as the League of Nations.

Today, the UN represents nearly all the nations of the world — 188 at last count. This in itself is a success story.

The government of every member nation appoints a delegation to the UN. Every year, the delegations meet in a forum called the General Assembly. The General Assembly is headed by a president who is elected from among the members of the assembly.

In the General Assembly, each delegation has one vote. For most decisions, the principle of majority rule applies. The most important decisions, however, require 60 percent approval.

In the end, however, the General Assembly's power is limited to giving advice. The real power at the UN lies with the 15-member Security Council. The Security Council is always in session, ready to deal with any crisis at a moment's notice.

The creation of the Security Council made the UN different from the League of Nations, which did not have such a body. The Security Council has broad powers, which include the ability to send troops to keep peace in an area. First, however, it must try to negotiate a peaceful solution.

Five of the Security Council's 15 members are permanent. They are China, France, the Russian Federation, the United Kingdom, and the United States. Every year, the General Assembly elects five nations to sit as temporary members of the Security Council for a two-year term. This gives the Security Council 10 temporary members. The presidency of the Security Council rotates through the membership on a monthly basis.

Canada has been elected to sit on the Security Council six times. Its most recent term was in 1999–2000.

The General Assembly meets at the UN's New York City headquarters from September to December every year. Delegates debate important international issues, review UN actions, and plan future actions.

The 15 members of the Security Council sit at the big horseshoe-shaped table. Their advisers are behind them. Staff sit at the long table in the middle. The Security Council is the closest thing to world government that exists today.

Security Council decisions require 60 percent approval to pass. Nine members, including all the permanent members, must support decisions. This arrangement gives each of the permanent members the power to **veto** — defeat — a resolution, no matter how many others support it.

The way the Security Council makes decisions has been widely criticized. During the Cold War, for example, permanent members often used their veto power to defeat resolutions put forward by their rivals. The end of the Cold War triggered a change of attitude among the so-called superpowers. One indicator of the change is the fact that 15 new peace initiatives came before the Security Council in the three years after 1990. In the years before that, it had dealt with a total of only 17 issues.

In the field of security and peacekeeping, the UN has helped negotiate peaceful settlements in 172 conflicts. These include the Iran-Iraq war, the Soviet occupation of Afghanistan, and the civil war in El Salvador. It also helped ensure that free and fair elections were held in more than 45 countries, including Cambodia, Namibia, El Salvador, Eritrea, Mozambique, Nicaragua, and South Africa.

The secretary general, the person who is most closely identified with the UN, is appointed to a five-year term, which can be renewed. The appointment is made by the General Assembly on the recommendation of the Security Council. Seven secretaries general have held the office since 1945.

Though the secretary general has no power outside the UN, several have exerted great influence over international affairs, earning the UN greater prestige than the League of Nations ever commanded.

The secretary general is in charge of the day-to-day work of the UN — overseeing peacekeeping operations, mediating international disputes, surveying economic and social trends and problems, studying human

A Day in the Life

LLOYD AXWORTHY
SPEAKING OUT ON HUMAN RIGHTS

When Canada took over the presidency of the United Nations Security Council for the month of April 2000, Lloyd Axworthy stepped into the international spotlight. A veteran politician, Axworthy was first elected to the House of Commons in 1979 to represent the Manitoba riding of Winnipeg South-Centre.

Appointed Canada's minister of foreign affairs in 1996, Axworthy quickly made a name for himself in the international community. In October 1996, for example, he challenged the nations of the world to sign a treaty banning land mines, which maim or kill thousands of civilians every year. After delegates from 122 countries adopted an international treaty limiting the use of land mines, Axworthy was awarded the North-South Prize for his efforts.

In 1998, Axworthy began lobbying members of the United Nations General Assembly to elect Canada to a two-year term on the Security Council. His lobbying paid off, and Canada started its term in January 1999.

In February 1999, Canada took its first turn as president of the Council. Canada's second turn came in April 2000. The presidency gave Canada an important opportunity to control the Security Council's agenda for a month.

Axworthy planned to make good use of this opportunity. Along with members of Canada's UN delegation, he wanted the Security Council to focus on human rights issues.

As a result, the Security Council's calendar for April 2000 was packed with discussions of human rights. On the morning of April 7, for example, Security Council delegates heard a report on Afghanistan. There, a religious army called the Taliban Islamic Movement had taken over the government in 1994.

Taliban leaders had started a reign of terror that included murdering their foes. The Taliban laws were especially hard on women. Women could not go out in public unless they were covered from head to toe and accompanied by a close male relative.

In a speech to the Security Council on the morning of April 7, Axworthy did not mince words. He called the Taliban "a criminal gang." That afternoon, he summed up the Security Council discussion in a statement that condemned the regime. Of the Taliban's treatment of women, he said:

The Security Council condemns the continuing grave violations of the human rights of women and girls ... It remains deeply concerned about continued restrictions on their access to health care, to education, and to employment outside the home, and about restrictions on their freedom of movement and freedom from intimidation, harassment, and violence. The Council ... calls upon all parties ... to take measures to end all violations of the human rights of women and girls.

By the end of April 2000, Axworthy had achieved many of his goals for the month. Still, he knew that the struggle to end human rights abuses was far from over.

April 2000 was a busy month for Lloyd Axworthy, Canada's minister of foreign affairs. In this photograph taken on April 13, he is listening to a speech at the Commission on Human Rights in Geneva, Switzerland. Later, Axworthy made his own speech to the commission.

rights and development cases, organizing international conferences, and monitoring compliance with UN initiatives. The secretary general does this with the support 8600 staff, known as the secretariat.

In addition to the UN's New York City headquarters, the secretariat also runs UN offices in Geneva, Switzerland, which was the home of the League of Nations. This office is now a centre for diplomatic conferences and discussions of disarmament and human rights.

Another office in Vienna, Austria, is the UN headquarters for international drug-abuse control, crime prevention, criminal justice, space, and international trade law. A third office in Nairobi, Kenya, houses the headquarters for environment and human settlements.

One of the causes of war is the inequality between richer and poorer nations. The founders of the UN wanted to close the gap between the two by providing support for economic and social development. This idea, which was unheard of in the days of the League of Nations, has become one of the UN's most important goals.

The Economic and Social Council, known as ECOSOC, is the UN's main forum for dealing with international economic, social, cultural, educational, health, and related matters. It is also the central UN agency for promoting human rights and fundamental freedoms. ECOSOC has 54 members, elected for overlapping three-year terms by the General Assembly. It oversees a number of UN agencies that co-ordinate development in poorer countries. These include

- the United Nations Children's Fund, also known as UNICEF
- the Office of the United Nations High Commissioner for Refugees, also known as the UNHCR
- the World Food Program
- the United Nations Conference on Trade and Development
- the United Nations Development Program
- the United Nations Environment Program
- the United Nations International Drug Control Program

The UN also works closely with a variety of independent organizations, such as the United Nations Educational, Scientific and Cultural Organization (UNESCO), the World Health Organization (WHO), and the International Monetary Fund (IMF). UNESCO's purpose is to promote peace and security through education, science, culture, and communication. The WHO promotes good health by immunizing people against disease, educating them about health, and providing essential drugs. The IMF helps countries achieve financial stability.

The United Nations and the Rule of Law

The rule of law is important in the struggle to keep peace in the world. A growing body of international law is a tool that helps in this struggle. International laws now apply to issues such as how wars are conducted, the use of oceans and seas that cross international boundaries, upholding treaties, and respect for human rights.

Case Study

THE WATCHMEN OF HAIDA GWAII

In 1774, between 10 000 and 30 000 people lived in the Haida villages that dotted the Pacific coast of Northern British Columbia. One of these villages was SGaang Gwaii, the main village of the Kunghit Haida. Located on an island that is also called SGaang Gwaii, it was home to more than 300 people who lived in 30 longhouses.

The Haida carved totem poles to record their stories and the lineage of the people. Atop the poles, they often carved three human figures wearing high hats. These were the watchmen. The job of the watchmen was to warn of danger and other unusual happenings.

The coming of the Europeans in 1774 changed everything. European diseases nearly wiped out the Haida. By 1884, for example, 90 percent of the people of SGaang Gwaii had died. The village — and its totem poles — was all but abandoned. By 1900, only 600 Haida remained in two villages.

For decades after that, the Haida totem poles were left to the elements. Some were stolen. Others were damaged or destroyed by vandals. To try to save some totem poles, government officials moved them to museums.

By 1981, Haida such as Captain Gold had become concerned about the disappearance of their heritage. They started the Haida Watchmen Program, which was named after the carved figures that perched atop many of the totem poles.

Every summer, one or two watchmen travelled to each of the former villages. Their mission was to keep watch over the site and share their knowledge of Haida culture and customs with visitors.

In 1985, the Haida declared Gwaii Haanas, the South Moresby Island area of the Queen Charlotte Islands, a Haida heritage site. Since then, the area has become a National Park Reserve. It is now administered jointly by the Haida Nation and the Canadian government.

The former village of SGaang Gwaii, which contains the ruins of 10 longhouses and 32 memorial or mortuary poles, has been declared a World Heritage Site by UNESCO. It is one of 12 UNESCO World Heritage Sites in Canada.

Every summer, the Watchmen continue to travel to Gwaii Haanas to keep watch over the ancient villages and totem poles. Why? Perhaps the answer lies in the Haida Constitution. It says: "The living generation accepts the responsibility to insure that our heritage is passed on to following generations."

The Haida watchmen stand guard over memorial poles like these. The weathered poles at SGaang Gwaii are part of the most magnificent display of standing totem poles in the world.

The Active Citizen

1. Captain Gold, one of the Watchmen of Gwaii Haanas, is an example of a citizen who saw a need and acted to fill that need. Find an example of someone in your community who acted to preserve a historic or sensitive environmental site or to record information about an important person or event in the history of your community. If possible, invite this person to speak to your class.

2. Like SGaang Gwaii, some of the 11 other UNESCO World Heritage Sites found in Canada were drawn to global attention through the efforts of citizens who lived in the area. Find out what these citizens did and present your findings to the class.

In 1947, the UN General Assembly created the International Law Commission to develop laws to govern these matters. The commission has referred many issues to the General Assembly for approval. In 1974, for example, the Assembly adopted a definition of aggression. The definition said that aggression includes "military attacks, sending armed mercenaries against another state, and allowing one's territory to be used for perpetrating an act of aggression against another state."

The UN also set up the International Court of Justice to rule on disputes between member nations. Based in The Hague, Netherlands, the court is made up of 15 judges from 15 countries. The judges are chosen by the General Assembly and the Security Council.

Canada and the North Atlantic Treaty Organization

In addition to his work at the United Nations, Lester B. Pearson's influence on the world stage was also evident in the establishment of the North Atlantic Treaty Organization in April 1949. This alliance, which is usually called NATO, was established as a defensive military alliance to counter the threat posed by the Soviet Union.

Canada was one of 12 founding members of NATO, which provided security to all its members. If one member was attacked, the others agreed to help defend it.

Article 2 of the North Atlantic Treaty is often called the Canadian article. It was included because Pearson argued that NATO's role should not be limited to defence. He said that the alliance should also promote economic and social development. Article 2 says:

> *The Parties will contribute toward the further development of peaceful and friendly international relations by strengthening their free institutions, by bringing about a better understanding of the principles upon which these institutions are founded, and by promoting conditions of stability and well-being. They will seek to eliminate conflict in their international economic policies and will encourage economic collaboration between any or all of them.*

Boris Yeltsin, who was president of Russia at the time, speaks to NATO members at their headquarters in Paris during a summit in May 1997. Yeltsin signed a document giving Russia a consulting role in NATO affairs. Why would an agreement like this have been unthinkable even 10 years earlier?

Canada remains a committed member of NATO as the alliance carries out a new role as a stabilizing force in Europe. NATO's new purpose includes promoting peace and security as well as preventing and managing conflict in Europe. The organization also encourages nations to respect common values. These values include democracy, human rights, respect for minorities, and improved economic conditions. Some of the former allies of the Soviet Union, such as the Czech Republic, Hungary, and Poland have now joined NATO, which has grown to include 19 members.

CANADA AND THE COMMONWEALTH

Mozambique, a nation in Southeast Africa, is the only member of the Commonwealth — besides the United Kingdom — that was never a British colony. It was a Portuguese colony. Still, Commonwealth members voted to admit Mozambique in 1995 because its affairs are closely linked to those of its neighbours. All its neighbours are Commonwealth members.

Canada is one of 54 countries that belong to the Commonwealth. All except the United Kingdom and one other country are former British colonies. Formerly known as the British Commonwealth, the Commonwealth is the second-largest international organization after the UN.

The Commonwealth was formed in 1931 by the United Kingdom, Canada, Australia, New Zealand, South Africa, and the Irish Free State. It was to be an association of equals. Though Ireland has since withdrawn, membership in the Commonwealth grew as other British colonies achieved independence. In addition to Canada, Commonwealth members now include countries such India, the world's second most populous country, Malaysia, Cyprus, and Sri Lanka.

Commonwealth members endorse democracy and human rights, the rule of law, and improved economic and social development. Wealthier countries give economic aid to poorer member states in Africa, Asia, and Latin America and the Caribbean.

The Commonwealth has used its clout to force member states out of its ranks. South Africa, for example, was expelled in 1961 at the height of the apartheid régime. The country was readmitted to the Commonwealth after Nelson Mandela and the African National Congress won the country's first truly democratic election in 1994.

Nigeria was forced out in 1995 after its military rulers executed Ken Saro-Wiwa and other political activists. Four years later, it was readmitted when civilian democratic rule was restored. In 1999, Pakistan was suspended after military officers overthrew the democratically elected government.

CANADA AND THE FRANCOPHONIE

The Francophonie is an association of 49 countries that were once colonies of France or where French is an important language. As a former French colony in which French is an official language, Canada qualifies for membership on both counts. The provinces of New Brunswick and Québec, with their large French-speaking populations, hold their own seats in the Francophonie.

Like the Commonwealth, the Francophonie is a voluntary organization. Its purpose is to encourage co-operation and communication among countries with a French heritage and culture.

In September 1999, the eighth Francophonie Summit was held in Moncton, New Brunswick. New Brunswick Premier Bernard Lord (left), Prime Minister Jean Chrétien, Francophonie Secretary General Boutros Boutros Ghali, and French President Jacques Chirac walk to the final news conference of the Summit.

http://www.school.mcgrawhill.ca/resources
To find out more about the UN, NATO, the Commonwealth, and the Francophonie, go to History Resources. Then go to *Civics: Participating in a Democratic Society* to see where to go next.

CANADA AND OTHER INTERNATIONAL ORGANIZATIONS

The government of Canada also belongs to several international economic organizations that promote world trade and economic co-operation. These groups include:

- **Asia Pacific Economic Cooperation**. Known as APEC, this 21-member organization promotes global trade and economic co-operation. APEC members account for nearly 50 percent of the world's trade. APEC also encourages investment in its less-developed member states to help raise living standards and make them more competitive in the global economy.
- **Organization for Economic Co-operation and Development**. Known as OECD, this association of 29 countries encourages economic growth among industrialized countries. In 1998, the OECD began to promote a Multilateral Agreement on Investment, or MAI. This agreement would have loosened rules governing

investment in member countries. Many citizens' groups opposed this. They warned that signing the MAI would reduce the power of democratically elected governments to make their own decisions. In the end, the widespread protests scuttled the MAI.

- **World Trade Organization**. This association of 132 countries is known as the WTO. It was established in 1995 to regulate international commerce. The WTO is the only international organization with the power to establish and enforce rules of trade.

http://www.school.mcgrawhill.ca/resources

To find out more about APEC, the OECD, and the WTO, go to History Resources. Then go to *Civics: Participating in a Democratic Society* to see where to go next.

BUILDING RESPECT FOR HUMAN RIGHTS

In November 1945, a few months after the end of World War II, the International Military Tribunal gathered in the German city of Nuremberg to try 24 Nazi leaders for war crimes, crimes against peace, and crimes against humanity. This was not the first time that people had been tried for war crimes. It was, however, the first time that people had been tried for crimes against humanity.

These emaciated Jewish men were photographed the day after their camp at Ebensee was liberated at the end of World War II.

The idea that there was such a thing as a crime against humanity was new. It grew out of people's horror over the systematic murder of millions of Jews in Nazi death camps.

Controversy swirled around the Nuremberg trials from the beginning. British Prime Minister Winston Churchill was against holding the trials. He argued that Nazi leaders should be executed without trial. Others argued that the victors in the war should not try to disguise revenge as justice.

The Nazi leaders claimed that the trials were unfair. They said that they should not be prosecuted under laws that had been created especially to bring them to trial. Besides, they added, they were innocent because they had only been following orders.

Those who supported the trials argued that the civilized world had to do something to draw the line. Robert Jackson, the American lead prosecutor for the tribunal, said, "The wrongs which we seek to condemn and punish have been so calculated, so malignant, and so devastating that civilization cannot tolerate their being ignored because it cannot survive their being repeated."

After 11 months of testimony, 12 Nazis were condemned to hang. Hermann Göring, Hitler's right-hand man, was one of them. He committed suicide hours before he was to be executed. Another three were sentenced to life in prison. Four more received long sentences. Three — Hjalmar Schacht, Franz von Papen, and Hans Fritzsche — were acquitted. Two of the 24 accused never came to trial. One committed suicide while in prison, and the other was judged to be too sick to go through a trial.

Under heavy guard, the defendants at Nuremberg listen to testimony at their trial. In the front row, from left to right, are Hermann Göring, Rudolf Hess, Joachim von Ribbentrop, Wilhelm Keitel, Ernst Kaltenbrunner, Alfred Rosenberg, Hans Frank, Wilhelm Frick, Julius Streicher, Walther Funk, Hjalmar Schacht. In the back row from left to right are Karl Dönitz, Erich Raeder, Baldur von Schirach, Fritz Sauckel, Alfred Jodl, Franz von Papen, Arthur Seyss-Inquart, Albert Speer, Konstantin van Neurath, Hans Fritzsche.

PROTECTING HUMAN RIGHTS

FYI

The job of writing the Universal Declaration of Human Rights fell to John P. Humphrey, a young law professor from Montréal. An expert in international law, Humphrey was part of the Canadian delegation to the UN under Lester B. Pearson.

The founding of the United Nations and the Nuremberg trials ushered in an intense search for ways to guarantee and protect human rights. The United Nations became the vehicle for achieving this.

Countries that signed the United Nations Charter affirmed their goal of "promoting and encouraging respect for human rights and for fundamental freedoms for all without distinction as to race, sex, language, or religion." But would this noble-sounding goal protect human rights? Would it make a ruthless dictator like the Soviet Union's Josef Stalin, for example, stop ordering the murder of his political "enemies"? The answer to these questions was no.

The Charter also said that the UN could not "intervene in matters which are essentially within the domestic jurisdiction of any state" unless the Security Council decided that there was a "threat to the peace, breach of the peace, or act of aggression." This provision effectively barred the UN from interfering in the internal affairs of any country.

Clearly, more protection was needed.

As a result, the UN's Economic and Social Council created the Commission on Human Rights. Eleanor Roosevelt, widow of U.S. President Franklin D. Roosevelt, was appointed chair. The commission started working on creating an international bill of rights. The first step was to write the Universal Declaration of Human Rights. On December 10, 1948, the UN General Assembly adopted this declaration as a goal to strive toward.

Eleanor Roosevelt, first chair of the UN Commission on Human Rights, displays a copy of the Universal Declaration of Human Rights in 1949.

The Active Citizen

Think ... Discuss ... Act

Human beings learn from other human beings. This pattern of learning is evident in the wording of the Universal Declaration of Human Rights. Ideas in this document bear a striking similarity to ideas put forward by John Locke and rephrased by Thomas Jefferson in the American Declaration of Independence.

1. Compare the ideas set out by Locke (page 17) and Jefferson (page 18) with the ideas included in the Universal Declaration of Human Rights on page 107.
2. What rights did John Humphrey add to Locke's and Jefferson's ideas?
3. The actions of human beings often contradict their words. Cite examples in Canada and elsewhere that show that people do not always fulfil the expectations of the Universal Declaration of Human Rights.

The Universal Declaration of Human Rights is not law. The UN cannot force governments to obey its terms. Still, it sets a standard that countries are expected to follow.

What is more, the UN can — and does — investigate reports of human rights abuses. When it finds abuses, it can take action. In 1977, for example, the Security Council took steps against South Africa's apartheid regime. It imposed a mandatory arms embargo against South Africa. This meant that no country was allowed to ship weapons to South Africa.

Once the Universal Declaration of Human Rights was adopted, two other documents were created. One was the International Covenant on Economic, Social and Cultural Rights; the other was the International Covenant on Civil and Political Rights. The purpose of both was to set out codes of behaviour for governments that signed the declaration.

The General Assembly adopted both covenants in 1966, and both took effect in 1976. Under the International Covenant on Civil and Political Rights, the UN set up a Human Rights Committee to rule on complaints.

All members of the United Nations signed the declaration, but some refused to sign the covenants. They did not want to be forced to adhere to their terms. Canada, however, endorsed both covenants in 1976, with the agreement of all the provinces.

Together, the three documents are known as the International Bill of Rights. The UN monitors the agreements to make sure that countries are not violating their terms.

The UN has also taken many other steps to protect human rights. The Commission on Human Rights, for example, defines how the UN can protect civil liberties, redefine the status of women, assure freedom of information, protect minorities, and prevent discrimination.

Citizens in Action

This famous photograph was snapped by photographer Nick Ut in 1972 during the Vietnam War. Screaming children who have been badly burned by napalm flee the village of Trang Bang. Kim Phuc is the child in the centre of the picture.

On June 8, 1972, an airplane flew over the village of Trang Bang, South Vietnam. The plane was dropping napalm bombs. Vietnam, a country of rainforests in Southeast Asia, had been torn apart by war. South Vietnam and its American allies were fighting Communist North Vietnam and the dreaded Viet Cong guerilla army.

Napalm is a gasoline-based jelly that sticks to whatever it hits and makes it burn. The bombs were used to destroy forests and flush the Viet Cong out of their hiding places. The South Vietnamese believed that Trang Bang was a Viet Cong stronghold. They were wrong.

The napalm bombs killed many of the villagers and injured many others. Phan Thai Kim Phuc, a nine-year-old girl, was burned over 75 percent of her body. Her brothers and cousins died of their injuries. Kim Phuc and her neighbours ran down the road, screaming in pain. An American news photographer snapped a picture of this terrible scene.

The photographer, Nick Ut, and a nearby British television reporter helped get the young girl to a hospital. For the next 14 months, the hospital was her home. It took 17 operations to graft skin onto the burned parts of her body.

Meanwhile, the picture was published in newspapers around the world. It became a symbol of the harm that the Vietnam War was causing to innocent people. After seeing the picture, many people in the United States turned against their country's involvement in the war. Soon afterward, the United States withdrew its troops, and the Communist forces of North Vietnam took control of the entire country.

Later, Phuc immigrated to Canada. She now lives near Toronto with her husband and two children. She still feels the pain of her 30-year-old injuries. Amazingly, she bears no grudge against those who harmed her. She speaks to groups about the need to forgive the deeds of the past and work toward peace.

This work inspired a United Nations body to make her a Goodwill Ambassador for a Culture of Peace. Phuc's job is to "spread a message on the need for reconciliation, mutual understanding, dialogue and negotiation to replace confrontation and violence as a means of settling conflicts." She also lends her name to a foundation that helps children who have been injured in war.

This photograph shows Kim Phuc today. Phuc often speaks to groups about the need to forgive past injuries and work toward peace.

Other UN agencies have produced dozens of documents designed to make human rights protections stronger. These documents have helped enlarge the invisible blanket of protection that improves everyone's quality of life.

One of these documents is the Convention on the Rights of the Child, which was created in 1989. This convention is designed to

- protect female children
- prevent and eliminate the sale of children and the sexual exploitation and abuse of children
- protect children affected by armed conflict, children who are refugees, and children who work or live in the streets
- eliminate child labour
- promote and protect the rights of children involved with the justice system
- promote the rights of children with disabilities
- promote children's right to health and education

The Convention on the Rights of the Child has been ratified by more than 140 nations, including Canada.

Think ... Discuss ... Act

Canadian media philosopher Marshall McLuhan coined the term "global village" nearly half a century ago when he observed how improvements in communications were bringing the people of the world closer and closer together. He also said that that the media — newspapers, television, and radio — had a powerful influence on people. Since McLuhan's time, the pace of change in information technology has speeded up even more. Today, people anywhere in the world can communicate almost instantly via the Internet.

1. Scan a daily newspaper for five days. Clip articles showing that the so-called communications revolution has improved relations among peoples. Clip other articles showing that national, religious, ethnic, and income barriers continue to separate people.
2. Organize your evidence in two columns headed "Closer Together" and "Farther Apart." Be prepared to use your evidence to discuss whether relations among the peoples of the world are getting better or worse.
3. Some media critics believe that the news media focus on bad news. They believe that this distorts people's idea of the state of relations among the world's peoples. After your week of research, do you agree or disagree with these critics? Why?

Universal Declaration of Human Rights

The preamble states that the declaration is "a common standard of achievement for all peoples and all nations, to the end that every individual and every organ of society ... shall strive by teaching and education to promote respect for these rights and freedoms ..."
The following is a summary of the 30 articles included in the declaration.

1. All human beings are born free and equal.
2. Everyone is entitled to the same rights without distinction of any kind, such as race, colour, sex, language, religion, political or other opinion, national or social origin, property, birth, or other status.
3. Everyone has the right to life, liberty, and security of person.
4. No one shall be held in slavery or servitude.
5. No one shall be subjected to torture or to cruel, inhuman, or degrading treatment or punishment.
6. Everyone has the right to be recognized as a person before the law.
7. All are equal before the law and have the right to the protection of the law.
8. Everyone has the right to justice.
9. No one shall be subjected to arbitrary arrest, detention, or exile.
10. Everyone has the right to a fair trial.
11. Everyone has the right to be presumed innocent until proven guilty.
12. Everyone has the right to privacy and to be protected against attacks on his or her honour and reputation.
13. Everyone has the right to freedom of movement.
14. Everyone has the right to seek in other countries shelter from persecution.
15. Everyone has the right to a nationality.
16. Everyone has the right to marry and found a family.
17. Everyone has the right to own property and no one's property can be arbitrarily seized.
18. Everyone has the right to freedom of thought, conscience, and religion.
19. Everyone has the right to freedom of opinion and expression.
20. Everyone has the right to freedom of peaceful assembly and association.
21. Everyone has the right to take part in government.
22. Everyone has the right to social security and to share in the benefits of society's progress.
23. Everyone has the right to work, to equal pay for equal work, to a fair wage, and to form or join a trade union.
24. Everyone has the right to rest and leisure.
25. Everyone has the right to an adequate standard of living. Mothers and children are entitled to special care and help.
26. Everyone has the right to education, and parents have the right to choose the kind of education their children will have.
27. Everyone has the right to participate freely in the cultural life of a community.
28. Everyone is entitled to a social and international order in which the rights set out in the declaration can be fully realized.
29. Everyone has duties to the community. People's rights can be limited only by laws that recognize and respect the rights of others and that meet the just requirements of morality, public order, and the general welfare in a democratic society.
30. No one has the right to destroy any of the rights and freedoms set out in the declaration.

CHAPTER REVIEW

SUMMING IT UP

More than 325 years ago, the English poet John Donne wrote these words: "No man is an island, entire of itself." In Donne's time, the idea of becoming involved in humanity was revolutionary. Today, a more inclusive view prevails. In this age of instant mass communication, people understand that no nation stands alone — and no citizen stands alone. What happens in other parts of the world affects everyone.

1. Create a time line that emphasizes the main turning points in the evolution of people's thinking about human rights.

2. Why did World War II spark nations to band together to transform the ineffective League of Nations into the United Nations? Has the United Nations fulfilled the purpose set out in its Charter (see page 107). Why do you think so?

3. Add terms from this chapter to your list of New Words with Special Meaning.

GETTING THE FACTS

1. How are the Commonwealth and the Francophonie different from the United Nations?

2. Explain the differences among political, civil, equality, economic, social, and cultural rights.

3. Choose an international agency whose work interests you. The organization may be part of the United Nations, such as the United Nations Children's Fund (UNICEF) or the International Labour Organization (ILO), or it may be an independent organization that works closely with the United Nations, such the United Nations Educational, Scientific and Cultural Organization (UNESCO).

   Many of these organizations have Web sites. Visit the organization's Web site to find actions that demonstrate global citizenship.

   Report your findings to the class.

USING THE FACTS

1. Many international organizations are discussed in this chapter. In most cases, it is governments that are members of these organizations, not citizens. Do you think that citizens can influence the decisions made by these organizations? Why? How can citizens influence events that happen on the world stage?

2. Most of the organizations mentioned in this chapter have Web sites. Visit the Web site of the United Nations, NATO, the Commonwealth, or the Francophonie (see page 100). Whose point of view does the information on the Web site represent? Find two examples of statements made on the Web site that might be challenged. Note the statement and record an alternative point of view. Present your information on a chart like this.

Web site	Point of view	Statement	Alternative point of view

3. Canadian artist Emily Carr spent much of her career painting the totem poles and villages of British Columbia Aboriginal people including the Haida. Carr's paintings have been reproduced in many books. Was her decision to paint the Haida totem poles an act of preservation? Why?

4. There is a story about a man who wanted great wealth. He sold his farm and travelled the world searching for diamonds. Years later, he discovered that diamonds had been found on the farm he sold.

   The message of this story is that diamonds are often right beneath our feet.

   a) What could the word "diamonds" stand for in this story?

   b) What does your community do to recognize these diamonds?

   c) Invite a member of your community historical society or a community group such as the Rotary Club, Kiwanis Club, Lions Club, or the YMCA to speak to your class about people who are "diamonds" in your community.

5. Start a collection of information about citizens in your community who have made a difference in lives of others. Use the information collected to create a series of brief biographies of people in your community. Title the series "Making a Difference."

"I gazed upon the whirlpool of public life and saw the incessant movement of shifting currents [and] … felt dizzy."

Plato, an ancient Greek philosopher, in *Epistle Seven*

What did Plato mean when he described public life as a whirlpool?

Picture yourself as a citizen at the centre of the whirlpool Plato described. What ideas are swirling around you as you complete this unit? Copy the graphic organizer shown here onto a sheet of paper. Record an important idea from this unit in each blank circle. Not all informed citizens make the same choices, so be prepared to defend the ideas you select.

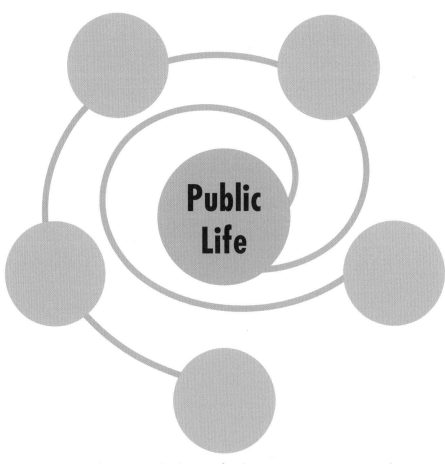

Public Life

Compare your choices with those of others in your group or class. Create a list of ideas that you and other students believe it is important for informed citizens to understand. After this discussion, review the ideas you chose originally. Have you changed your mind about including any of them? Record the changes on your organizer and save it.

FOCUS YOUR LEARNING

1. The human mind seems to like unravelling mysteries, trying to fit pieces into a jigsaw puzzle, tracking down information on the Internet, and sorting information into categories. Use your natural curiosity to advantage when preparing for a class assessment. Try following these four steps:

   a) Look at a topic (e.g., House of Commons).
   b) Convert the topic into a question (e.g., What is the House of Commons?).
   c) Make notes as you try to answer this question. Your notes might include points like the following:

   - place where laws are passed
   - place where elected members of Parliament sit

   d) Check your answer. Refer to the index of this book to locate the information you need to do this.

   Apply this technique to the following ideas found in Unit 1:

   totalitarianism, direct democracy, oligarchy, divine right of kings, responsible government, *Château Clique*, Family Compact, constitutional monarchy, federalism, political party, arbitration proportional representation, collective bargaining, the Francophonie, representation by population

APPLY YOUR LEARNING

1. As a class, create a 10-question survey based on the information in this unit. Include questions that you think informed, active citizens should be able to answer. Set up your survey like this:

Question	Respondent 1	Respondent 2	Respondent 3
1) Who is Canada's head of state?			

   Make copies of the survey, leaving space for each student in the class to administer the test to three people.

   Tabulate the results of the surveys. What do the results tell you about how informed the people surveyed are about Canada? Were you surprised by the results? Why?

2. Over a two-week period, collect newspaper articles highlighting the activities of the United Nations. Create a mini-scrapbook. Choose two of the articles and write a summary explaining what they are about. Then write a personal assessment of the articles. In your opinion, do they show the UN in a favourable or unfavourable light? Cite evidence from the articles to support your opinion. Conclude your assessment by commenting on the effectiveness of the United Nations.

REFLECT ON YOUR LEARNING

1. The ancient Romans believed that the proudest boast a person could make was "*Civis romanus sum*" — "I am a Roman citizen." In 1997, writer Richard Gwynn published a book titled *Rediscovering Our Citizenship*. In it, Gwynn suggested that today's equivalent boast should be "*Civis canadensis sum*" — "I am a Canadian citizen." Why would Gwynn be proud to say that he is a Canadian citizen? Do you agree with him? Why?

UNIT 2

THE PURPOSEFUL CITIZEN

Purposeful citizenship requires reflection and action. One Canadian who developed a strong sense of civic purpose was Terry Fox. Terry lost a leg to cancer when he was 18 years old. To raise money for cancer research, Terry set out from St. John's, Newfoundland, to run across the country. He called his run the Marathon of Hope.

When he discovered that the cancer had spread, Terry was forced to abandon his run after 143 days and 5373 kilometres. Though Terry died in June 1981, Canadians continue his quest to help find a cure for cancer by participating in the Terry Fox Run every September.

As a Canadian, Terry gave much to his country and the world — hope, courage, and pride in accomplishment. He was informed, found a purpose, and took action. This unit will help you explore the possibilities and meet the challenges of becoming an informed, purposeful, and active citizen of Canada and the international community.

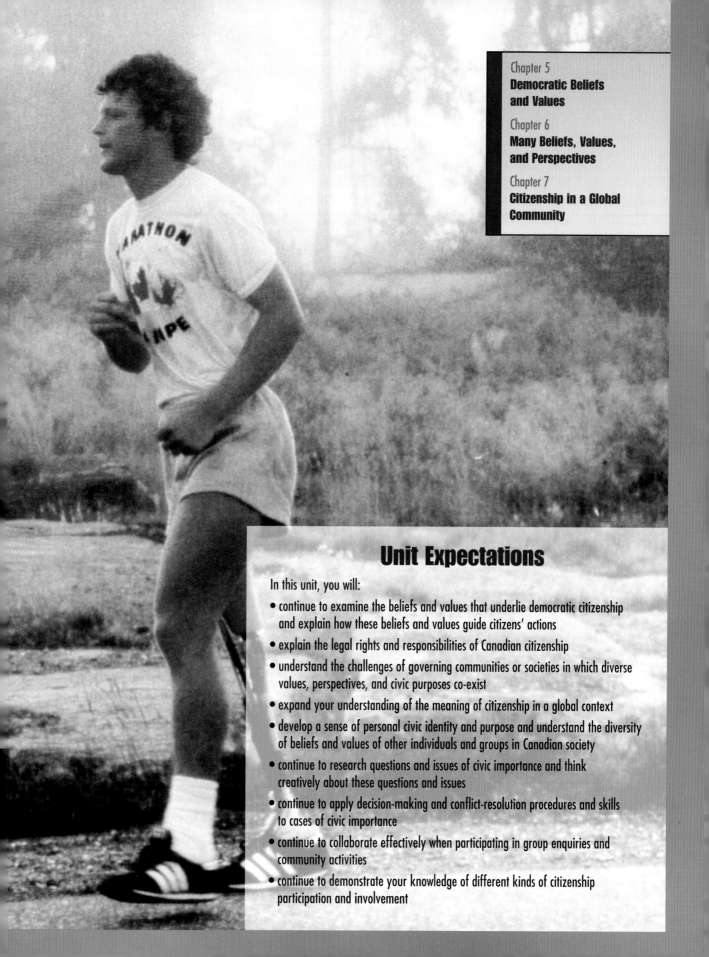

Unit Expectations

In this unit, you will:

- continue to examine the beliefs and values that underlie democratic citizenship and explain how these beliefs and values guide citizens' actions

- explain the legal rights and responsibilities of Canadian citizenship

- understand the challenges of governing communities or societies in which diverse values, perspectives, and civic purposes co-exist

- expand your understanding of the meaning of citizenship in a global context

- develop a sense of personal civic identity and purpose and understand the diversity of beliefs and values of other individuals and groups in Canadian society

- continue to research questions and issues of civic importance and think creatively about these questions and issues

- continue to apply decision-making and conflict-resolution procedures and skills to cases of civic importance

- continue to collaborate effectively when participating in group enquiries and community activities

- continue to demonstrate your knowledge of different kinds of citizenship participation and involvement

Chapter 5

DEMOCRATIC BELIEFS AND VALUES

"Democracy may be simply defined as the people in action."

Farm leader Henry Wise Wood in the *Grain Growers' Guide*, 1919

The firefighters battling this brush fire in Almonte, Ontario, are volunteers. Volunteer firefighters often hold other full-time jobs in their communities. When the fire alarm sounds, though, they drop everything and rush to help. They also devote hours of leisure time to maintaining equipment and upgrading their training. What conclusions might be drawn about the beliefs and values of these volunteer firefighters?

Everyone has beliefs and values. Beliefs influence people's values — and values influence people's beliefs.

A belief is a claim that a person accepts as true. Beliefs do not need to be proven and they may not be accepted by everyone. A value is an estimation of importance. Beliefs and values help people make decisions and decide how to act.

Think about what you value in a friend. Is it common interests, honesty, a sense of humour, or something else? How do your beliefs affect what you value in a friend? How does what you value in a friend affect your beliefs about friendship?

All people do not share the same beliefs and values. If you asked the students in your class about their beliefs and values, they would give you many different answers. People's beliefs and values are influenced by culture, religion, family, friends, education, and personal experience.

Chapter
Expectations

In this chapter, you will learn about:

- the beliefs and values of democratic citizenship
- the beliefs and values of Canadian citizens
- how people put their democratic beliefs and values into action
- how people create a sense of civic purpose based on their beliefs and values

Key
Terms

censorship	medicare	slander
civil disobedience	pluralism	social safety net
libel	secular	

BELIEFS, VALUES, AND GOVERNMENT

The political beliefs and values shared by the people who live in a society determine the system of government that organizes the society. As you think about your own beliefs and values, keep these questions in mind:

- How should society be organized to give people the opportunity to live the best lives possible?
- Is government necessary?
- If it is, who should govern and how?
- What role should government play in society?

These questions are not easy to answer. In fact, each raises many other questions. Previous chapters outlined how people of other times and places tried to answer these questions. They are questions that people are still struggling to answer today.

Think ... Discuss ... Act

Author William Golding's novel, *Lord of the Flies*, is about a group of young people whose plane crash-lands on a desert island. The crash kills all the adults on the flight. Imagine that you are one of these young people. You have always lived according to rules made by others. Suddenly, no parents, police, or school officials are around to enforce the rules. To survive, you and your friends must find food and shelter. You must also come up with ways of getting along with one another.

1. Would having a leader increase or decrease your chances of survival? How might the group choose a leader?
2. What rules would help everyone survive? Would the values that guide democratic decision making, such as the rule of law, common good, majority rule, and minority rights, as well as the values expressed in the Charter of Rights and Freedoms, help you create these rules?
3. How would you deal with conflict between those who want to uphold the rules and those who think the rules should be changed or eliminated?
4. How did your own beliefs and values affect your responses to the first three questions? How do your own beliefs and values affect the way you behave every day?

BELIEFS AND VALUES OF CANADIAN CITIZENS

In Canada, citizens come from a variety of backgrounds. As a result, it is often difficult to reach consensus about what is best for the country. Still, as Canada has evolved, people have come to believe in the importance of respecting human dignity. It might be said that respect for human dignity underlies all the democratic values that are cherished by Canadians and expressed in the Charter of Rights and Freedoms.

These university students are marching on Parliament Hill to urge the federal government to increase education funding so that universities can reduce tuition fees. The students believe that high tuition fees are putting a university education out of reach of many young Canadians. What democratic rights are the students exercising?

Think about what is necessary to live a dignified life. A list of basic physical needs might include such things as adequate shelter, satisfactory health care, and a safe environment. Meeting people's physical needs does not necessarily guarantee that they will be able to live with dignity, however. People must also be treated with respect by others in society. How can a society ensure that all its citizens are able to live with dignity? Whose job is it to ensure this? Is it up to individual citizens or to the government and society as a whole?

Most Canadians take pride in living in a caring society that looks after its citizens and helps people live with dignity. As a result, an important goal of governments is to ensure that people have opportunities to make the most of their lives. People often disagree, though, on exactly how this should be done.

Rock star Alanis Morissette leaves an Ottawa homeless shelter after paying a visit to support the volunteers who keep the shelter going. The volunteers include Morissette's aunt, who has helped out at the shelter for many years.

This disagreement among Canadians reflects the debate that takes place in many democratic countries. How much should governments do for people? How much should people do for themselves? In the United States, for example, governments are expected to lay the groundwork so that people can make the most of the opportunities available. Many Americans believe that taking advantage of these opportunities is up to individual members of society. Rising from rags to riches through hard work is often said to be the American Dream.

In Canada, governments have taken a different approach. Most Canadian citizens expect their government to do more than simply lay the groundwork for success. They expect the government to play an active role in making sure that everyone has an opportunity to live a dignified life.

A homeless man begs passersby for spare change near the Parliament Buildings in Ottawa. Are this man's needs being met? Is it the responsibility of society to make sure that his needs — and those of others like him — are met?

CANADA'S SOCIAL SAFETY NET

In Canada, a **social safety net** helps minimize poverty and maximize opportunity. The social safety net includes services, such as health care, that help all Canadians, as well as programs, such as welfare assistance, designed especially to help those in need. These services are funded by the taxes collected by federal, provincial, and municipal governments. The net is a safety device, like the nets used by trapeze artists or bungee jumpers. It is designed to catch people before they fall into poverty.

IF RENTS GO MUCH HIGHER

In the early 1900s, so many people were moving to Canadian cities that housing prices and rents increased rapidly. As a result, some people were even forced to live in tents. The artist who created this cartoon imagined what might happen if this trend continued.

Canada has not always had a social safety net. As the 19th century drew to a close, the country was changing from an agricultural to an industrial society. People were moving to towns and cities from rural areas. They were taking jobs in industry rather than on farms. When this happened, the income gap between the rich and poor started to widen.

During World War I, the federal government began to tax people's incomes. Though the tax on income was supposed to be a temporary measure to help fund the war effort, Canadians have paid taxes on their income ever since. These and other taxes now go into a pool of money that pays for services that contribute to the well-being of all Canadians, such as maintaining the armed forces and courts, as well as health care and other social services.

In the early decades of the 20th century, however, the role of governments in maintaining services was more limited. People often talked about the need for national social welfare programs that would be available to all citizens. The British North America Act stood in the way of this, however. The act had assigned responsibility for social services to the provinces. Some provincial governments had passed on the responsibility to municipalities or charitable groups. As a result, a patchwork of social programs existed across Canada.

The First National Social Program

The situation came to a head during the Great Depression of the 1930s. In 1929, only 2 percent of Canadians were unemployed. By 1933, 32 percent of wage earners had no jobs. Without a job, people had no income. And with no income, many people plunged into grinding poverty.

When World War II started in 1939, prosperity began to return to the country. Young men and women joined the armed forces and were sent overseas. Materials were needed for the war effort, and workers were needed to produce them. With so many people overseas and so many supplies to be produced, there were more than enough jobs to go around. Still, the memory of the hard times of the 1930s remained vivid. Many people feared what might happen if the country sank back into economic depression when the war ended.

To ease this fear, Prime Minister William Lyon Mackenzie King's Liberal government passed the Unemployment Insurance Act in 1940. Canada's first large-scale national social insurance program was in place.

When the members of this Montréal family could no longer afford to pay the rent during the Great Depression, they were evicted — thrown out of their home. Note their belongings piled in the street. This was a common sight during the 1930s when evicted families had nowhere else to go.

The program required employees in certain businesses and industries across the country to pay a small percentage of their salaries into an insurance fund. Then, if they lost their jobs, they could collect money from the fund. This meant that losing a job no longer condemned people to poverty.

Strengthening the Social Safety Net

In 1944, Prime Minister William Lyon Mackenzie King's government took the idea of national social welfare programs even farther. Promising Canadians "a new social order," King created the Department of National Health and Welfare and introduced the family allowance or "baby bonus." This program paid a monthly sum to all mothers of young children. Canada had taken the first steps toward developing a comprehensive social welfare system.

Not all Canadians agreed that King's government was on the right track, however. Many people opposed the idea of national social welfare programs. They argued that people would come to rely on government handouts and would lose the will to look after themselves.

Despite opposition, other social programs were also introduced. Many of them are still in place today. In 1945, for example, Saskatchewan launched Canada's first hospital insurance plan. Over the next two decades, other provinces followed suit. No longer were people who could not afford to pay for stays in the hospital simply dumped into charity wards.

Then, in 1962, Saskatchewan again blazed a new trail when the province became the first North American jurisdiction to introduce a tax-supported universal health-care program, often called **medicare**. Four years later, the federal government passed the Medical Care Act.

This paved the way for a national health-insurance program, which guaranteed medical care to all citizens, regardless of their ability to pay. Through their elected representatives, Canadians had put their beliefs and values into action.

In the 1990s, many taxpayers began to call for tax freezes and tax cuts. Responding to the pressure, many politicians began to shift their focus from meeting people's social needs to meeting their economic needs. Governments began to reduce the funds given to social programs. This sparked intense debate among citizens across the country — and it is a debate that continues.

Tommy Douglas, shown here in 1983, was the driving force behind Canada's universal health-insurance program. The former Baptist minister had witnessed the struggle and suffering of poor people during the Great Depression. As premier of Saskatchewan from 1944 to 1961, he had campaigned tirelessly for medicare. In 1961, he entered federal politics as the first leader of the newly formed New Democratic Party.

Can Canadian taxpayers afford to continue subsidizing people who are disadvantaged? Can Canadians afford not to? These questions are at the heart of the debate over social welfare programs. Those who say that governments must reduce spending on social programs complain about the high taxes needed to support these programs. Those who say that governments should not reduce social spending argue that cutting costs in one area simply leads to higher costs in another, such as providing shelters for homeless people.

To reduce the cost of medical care, the province of Alberta has started requiring people to pay for some services that were previously free. According to the cartoonist, where will this lead?

The Active Citizen

Think … Discuss … Act

In Canada today, some people earn barely enough to survive, while others make millions of dollars a year. In the 1950s, American sociologist Eric Fromm wrote about what he called a "sane society." He suggested getting rid of the gap between rich and poor by paying all workers the same wage, no matter what their jobs. If everyone earned the same wage, Fromm believed, people would be free to choose work they like and want to do. He was certain that this would improve society.

1. If you lived in a society like that envisioned by Fromm, what job would you choose? Why?
2. Would the society envisioned by Fromm eliminate the need for a social safety net? Why?
3. Some of Fromm's critics said that his vision of society was an impossible dream. What do you think? Could Fromm's idea work? Why?

RESPECTING DIVERSITY

In 1997, a public opinion research company asked people in 14 countries, including Canada, to rate their nation's tolerance of cultural diversity. The survey results are shown on the graph at the bottom of this page. Seventy-five percent of the Canadians surveyed agreed either strongly or moderately with a statement saying that people of different ethnic and language groups get along well in Canada. This response placed Canada at the top of the list of countries whose citizens participated in this part of the survey.

In a diverse society like Canada's, it is important to treat everyone respectfully. Everyone has rights, and respect for the rights of others is an essential element of human dignity. Canadian citizens, for example, respect others' right to privacy and their freedom to express their opinions.

Though everyone has rights, however, the rights of one person cannot interfere with the rights of another. For example, business owners have the right to hire whomever they want. If they eliminate some job candidates because of their race, religion, or sex, however, they are interfering with the right of these people to live lives free of discrimination. When the rights of one group in society clash with the rights of another, people can ask the courts to decide the issue or they can take their case to a provincial human rights commission.

In a diverse society, people must be tolerant. Respecting human dignity means more than tolerating other people's differences, however. It means keeping an open mind and attempting to understand their beliefs and values. It means accepting and learning from their differences. At school, what personal rights would you like to be respected by others?

A 1997 Angus Reid poll asked people in 14 countries to respond to this statement: "People of different ethnic and language groups get along fairly well in my country." Canada came out at the top of the list. Survey your class to find out whether the result would be similar.

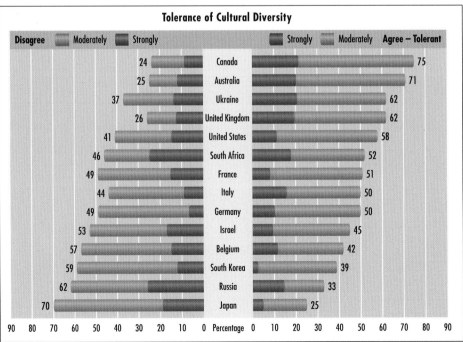

Tolerance of Cultural Diversity

	Disagree			Country		Agree – Tolerant	
		Moderately / Strongly		Canada	Strongly / Moderately		75
	24			Canada			75
	25			Australia			71
	37			Ukraine			62
	26			United Kingdom			62
	41			United States			58
	46			South Africa			52
	49			France			51
	44			Italy			50
	49			Germany			50
	53			Israel			45
	57			Belgium			42
	59			South Korea			39
	62			Russia			33
	70			Japan			25

Percentage scale: 90 80 70 60 50 40 30 20 10 0 — Percentage — 0 10 20 30 40 50 60 70 80 90

Canada and the World: An International Perspective on Canada and Canadians. Angus Reid Group Inc.

Democratic Values in Action

Since the Charter of Rights and Freedoms was entrenched in the Canadian Constitution in 1982, people have debated the meaning of the rights and freedoms guaranteed in the Charter. This sometimes involves weighing the rights of individual citizens against the common good or the public interest.

What happens when the rights of one citizen seem to trample on the rights of another? What happens when upholding the rights of individual citizens seems to be contrary to the common good? Individual citizens, governments, human rights agencies, and the courts are grappling with these questions.

Freedom of Worship

Canada is a **secular** nation. This means that the government and religion are supposed to remain separate. Religious leaders do not make laws or decide what is right or wrong in the courts. Politicians — the people who make the laws — have no say in deciding people's religious practices.

Today, Canada is a country in which people of many religions co-exist. Freedom of thought, conscience, and religion are guaranteed by the Charter of Rights and Freedoms, which means that people are free to practise the religion of their choice. The rights of agnostics, who question the existence of a supreme being, and atheists, who believe that there is no supreme being, are also protected by the Charter.

Things were not always this way, however. The first European settlers in Canada were Christian. Most of those who came from France were Roman Catholic, and most of those who came from Britain were Protestant. Even though Roman Catholics and Protestants are Christian groups, the two communities were deeply divided. Religious differences combined with language and cultural differences to increase the tension between people of British and French ancestry.

In 1991, Constable Baltej Singh Dillon became the first Sikh wearing a turban and beard to graduate from the RCMP training centre in Regina, Saskatchewan. Sikhs who joined the RCMP struggled for many years to win the right to wear turbans and beards, which are symbols of their religion.

Over the centuries, many people have struggled to win freedom of religion in Canada. At first, this struggle involved only Christian groups, as people tried to win the freedom to follow their own beliefs. Then, as people of other religious backgrounds began to arrive in Canada, the struggle broadened.

The struggle continues today. In Saskatoon, Saskatchewan, for example, a group of non-Christian parents went to court to challenge the practice of reciting the Lord's Prayer in the city's public schools. Members of the group argued that reciting this Christian prayer infringed their constitutional right to freedom of religion and conscience.

In July 1999, the courts agreed with the parents. A judge ordered the Saskatchewan government to change a 1901 law that required children to recite the Lord's Prayer in the province's public schools.

Schools across Canada have dealt with the issue of prayer in the classroom in different ways. Some provide a variety of religious readings throughout the week and combine these with non-religious, inspirational readings. Others observe a moment of silence to give staff and students the opportunity to pray privately. Still others have completely eliminated prayer from the school day. What is the situation in your school?

Rule of Law

Among other things, the Charter of Rights and Freedoms protects the legal rights of Canadians. According to the rule of law, the law applies to everyone equally. No one is supposed to be above the law or exempt from the law. This promises that the law will be impartial and will apply to all people and institutions, including the police, politicians, and governments.

Though laws are passed by a majority of members of Parliament, they are interpreted by judges who preside over the law courts. The judges are appointed by the government in power, but their duty is to apply the law impartially and independently. No one is allowed to influence, interfere with, or change court rulings. If politicians disagree with a court ruling, they cannot change the judge's decision. Instead, they must change the law.

One responsibility of citizens is to obey the law. What happens, though, when people believe that a law is unjust? What is a person's responsibility in this situation?

Many people believe that all laws must be obeyed, whether they are just or not. If they believe that a law is unjust, some people might decide to work to change it by legal means — writing letters, speaking to their political representatives, joining peaceful demonstrations, and so on.

Other people may decide to take their campaign to persuade the government to change an unjust law a step farther. They may decide to engage in acts of **civil disobedience**. Civil disobedience is non-violent public action that is illegal.

Deciding to engage in civil disobedience is an important step. People who make the decision to do this believe that it is an important citizenship responsibility. They accept that their actions might have serious consequences, which can include arrest, fines, and even imprisonment.

One famous example of organized civil disobedience occurred in the Clayoquot Sound area of British Columbia. Freshwater lakes and streams, mountains, and a coastal rainforest are features of this wilderness area.

Some cedar trees in the coastal rainforest are more than a thousand years old, and others are centuries old. The area is home to people,

One way the rule of law protects people is by ensuring that certain steps are followed when the law is enforced. These steps are called "due process of the law," a term that is often shortened to "due process." Everyone is entitled to due process. For example, police officers are not allowed to search people's homes without their consent or without a search warrant obtained through the courts.

THE PURPOSEFUL CITIZEN

McGraw-Hill Ryerson Ltd.

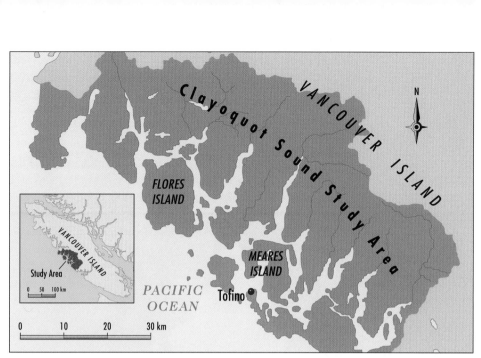

Clayoquot Sound is a body of water off the Pacific Coast of Vancouver Island.

black bears, cougars, wolves, bald eagles, orca and grey whales, sharks, salmon, tourists — and logging companies. It is very beautiful and rich in resources. It is not surprising that people clashed over how to use these resources.

Logging companies have been cutting timber in the Clayoquot area since the early 20th century. In 1984, a logging company decided to start clear cutting — cutting down all the trees — on Meares Island, a large island in the Clayoquot Sound area.

Aboriginal people and environmentalists wanted to stop this. They believe that clear cutting causes irreparable damage to the environment and Aboriginal culture.

The logging company, supported by many loggers and others who depend on the forest industry for their living, argued that logging creates employment and contributes heavily to the economy of British Columbia.

The islands in the foreground of this photograph of the Clayoquot Sound area are still covered in old-growth coastal rainforest. Part of the island in the background has been clear cut by loggers.

The dispute came to a head in the summer of 1993 when a group called the Friends of Clayoquot Sound decided to organize a protest based on principles set out by Mohandas Gandhi. On July 1, 1993, the Friends of Clayoquot Sound set up a Peace Camp on Vancouver Island. Over the next four months, more than 12 000 people visited the camp. These people came from all walks of life. They were professors, doctors, students, senior citizens, and parents and children.

More than 800 protesters were arrested for blocking a road that led to the logging camps. There was no violence, but the protesters interfered with the ability of the loggers to do their job. This act of civil disobedience gained widespread media attention in Canada and around the world.

Mohandas Gandhi led a successful campaign to win independence for India by engaging in non-violent protest. People who follow Gandhi's teachings engage in no verbal or physical violence, carry no weapons, and use no drugs or alcohol. They try to display a respectful attitude and conduct themselves with dignity.

In October 1993, the premier of British Columbia decided to appoint a panel of scientists to look into the issue and make recommendations. In 1994, Aboriginal representatives were added to the panel to ensure that the voices of Canada's First Nations were heard.

The panel recommended that future decisions about logging in the area place environmental concerns first. The protesters were pleased with the recommendations but continue to monitor logging in the Clayoquot area.

The Active Citizen

Think … Discuss … Act

"Unjust laws exist: shall we be content to obey them, or … shall we transgress [break] them at once?"

Henry David Thoreau in *On the Duty of Civil Disobedience*

Henry David Thoreau was an American philosopher and writer who believed that citizens have not only the right, but also a duty, to refuse to support laws that they believe are unjust. For example, Thoreau, who lived from 1817 to 1862, spent time in jail for refusing to pay a tax that he considered unfair.

Thoreau's ideas about civil disobedience have inspired people who hold minority opinions to show their disagreement with laws passed by governments elected by a majority of citizens.

1. Is a law unjust because a person like Thoreau believes it is unjust?
2. How should the police act when faced with people engaged in acts of civil disobedience? Why?
3. Do you agree with Thoreau? Is civil disobedience ever justified? Why?
4. Choose an example of an act of civil disobedience in today's society and find out about the outcome. Do you believe that this act of civil disobedience was justified? Why?

Svend Robinson is an outspoken New Democratic Party member of Parliament. He has represented the riding of Burnaby Douglas in the greater Vancouver area of British Columbia since 1979.

Educated as a lawyer, Robinson believes fiercely in democracy — and democratic values. As a result, he is often in the thick of debate on controversial issues.

As the first openly homosexual MP, Robinson has worked very hard to win equal rights for same-sex couples, homosexuals, and lesbians. He believes in equal rights for all Canadians, regardless of their sexual orientation.

Robinson often makes headlines by standing firmly behind his beliefs. As an advocate of environmental protection, Robinson has participated in peaceful acts of civil disobedience.

In 1993, for example, he took part in the anti-logging protest in Clayoquot Sound. With other protesters, Robinson blocked a road to prevent loggers from entering an old-growth forest. For his part in the protest, he spent two weeks in jail.

The same year, Robinson also made news by supporting a movement to help people die with dignity. He believes that Canadian laws must be changed to give people who are terminally ill the right to end their lives in a dignified way.

The issue came to a head over the case of Sue Rodriguez, a woman who was suffering a slow, painful death from Lou Gehrig's disease. Though Rodriguez had asked the courts to give her the right to end her own life, her request was turned down. Still, she decided to go ahead — and Robinson was present at her illegal doctor-assisted suicide.

Whether people agree or disagree with Robinson's actions, he is an example of someone who stands firmly behind his beliefs and values. In the process, he forces Canadians to examine difficult moral issues.

In the House of Commons, MP Svend Robinson reads a petition signed by 1000 people. The petition requested that mention of God be deleted from the Constitution because it interferes with freedom of religion and conscience. Robinson's action sparked an outcry from people who told him to leave the Constitution alone.

Freedom of Expression

The Charter of Rights and Freedoms guarantees freedom of thought, belief, opinion, and expression. These freedoms are considered essential in a democracy. If people are to participate in the democratic process, they must be free to express their political beliefs without fear.

Pluralism, or the acceptance of varied beliefs and values, is necessary for democracy to function. A government that bars people from expressing opposing views might be an effective decision-making body, but it would not be democratic.

It is also essential that the media, such as newspapers, television, and radio, be free to report events without interference from the government. Some countries that claim to be democratic censor the press or shut down media organizations when they become too critical.

People in Canada do not have complete freedom to write or say whatever they want, however. The Charter specifically states that laws may be passed to impose "reasonable limits" on citizens' rights and freedoms.

To prevent people from being harmed when others make untrue statements about them, for example, the law forbids **libel** — damaging someone's reputation by writing something that is not true. It also forbids **slander** — damaging someone's reputation by saying something that is not true. What is more, it is illegal to tell a lie in court and to make false statements in advertising. In addition, Canada has adopted anti-hate laws. These laws make it illegal to promote hatred of an identifiable group.

The case of James Keegstra, an Alberta high-school teacher, shows how Canada's anti-hate laws work. Keegstra told the students in his classes that the Holocaust — the systematic murder of Jews, Roma, homosexuals, and other so-called undesirable people by the Nazis during World War II — did not happen. He also made negative comments about Jews. As a result, he was charged with the "wilful promotion of hatred" against an identifiable group.

In court, Keegstra argued that his right to express his thoughts, opinions, and beliefs was protected by the Charter of Rights and Freedoms. The court decided otherwise. In convicting Keegstra of the charges against him, the court upheld the idea that freedom of speech can be limited, as long as the limitation is reasonable and justified in a free and democratic society.

WHAT OUR FRIENDLY DEMOCRATIC SYSTEM HAS BECOME -

HATE

The cartoonist who created this image showing the power of hatred was American. Does his message apply in Canada too? Why is this image so effective?

THE PURPOSEFUL CITIZEN

http://www.school.mcgrawhill.ca/resources

To find out more about free speech and hate crimes, go to History Resources. Then go to *Civics: Participating in a Democratic Society* to see where to go next.

The widespread use of the Internet has raised new questions about freedom of expression. Though the Internet is not regulated, it is considered "a telecommunications undertaking" under Canadian law. As a result, it is subject to the same restrictions as any other form of publication.

Controlling the Internet is difficult, however, because Web sites originate all over the world. In some cases, Canadians have moved offensive sites to the United States to avoid being prosecuted in Canada.

Representatives of many countries, including Canada, have discussed the possibility of creating a global agreement about Internet content. Reaching agreement is difficult, however. Sometimes, content that is considered offensive in one country is not considered offensive in another. Opponents of **censorship** also argue that the Internet should not be regulated. As a result, a global agreement is a long way off.

In the meantime, software companies have developed programs that can block or filter content. This idea, too, raises many questions. What content should be blocked? Who would decide what to block? Many people oppose this kind of intrusion. What do you think?

A PERSONAL SENSE OF CIVIC PURPOSE

Along with the rights set out in the Charter of Rights and Freedoms come certain responsibilities. Voting in elections is one of the most basic of these. Before casting their ballots, informed voters consider the issues and think seriously about which candidate will do the best job of representing their interests.

Voters line up to cast their ballots in the 1997 federal election. According to Elections Canada, only 67 percent of eligible voters exercised their right to vote in this election. Does this mean that only 67 percent of Canadians are good citizens? Why?

In 1999, Vancouver's Park Board received a petition from dog owners. The petition asked the board to increase the number of off-leash dog runs in city parks.

At the time, nearly 30 Vancouver parks already had designated off-leash areas during early morning and evening hours. Some city residents thought that more than enough had already been done to accommodate dogs and dog owners.

Other people argued that free-running dogs had no place in parks. They believed that people, especially children, should be able to use the parks without fear of being attacked by dogs or of being infected by their waste.

As debate raged over this issue, people fell into three main groups:

- those who asked for more designated off-leash zones in city parks
- those who telephoned city councillors or spoke out at meetings against increasing the number of off-leash zones
- those who did not care enough about the issue to become involved

Whenever a community deals with an issue that some people feel strongly about, people can often be divided into two groups: active citizens and passive citizens. Before a decision is made, the active citizens on both sides of the issue often try to persuade the passive citizens to become active. They try to encourage people to write letters, make phone calls, or come out to public meetings. The more supporters the two sides can muster, the better their chances of influencing the elected officials who will make the decision.

On every issue, some citizens choose to remain passive. These people may, however, become active on other issues, such as the need for new sidewalks or increasing education taxes. This is typical human behaviour. People may be active citizens on some issues, and passive citizens on others.

Two dogs — one on leash and one off — enjoy an outing on a sunny day in Vancouver's Stanley Park. Which side of the debate do you think the in-line skater was on?

The Active Citizen

1. If you were against setting up off-leash zones in your community's parks, what arguments might you use to convince passive citizens to become active — on your side of the issue?

2. What would you say to someone who believes that the whole dogs-in-parks issue is dividing people and should never have been raised in the first place?

3. List some issues that people are debating in your school or community. Place an "A" beside the issues on which you are an active citizen. How are you active? How do these issues reflect your beliefs and values?

The responsibilities of citizens do not end when the votes are counted, however. Democratic governments may be responsible to the people, but it is up to the people to make sure that the politicians who form governments take this responsibility seriously and use their power wisely.

Citizenship in a democratic society involves more than simply voting in elections. It is also up to Canadians to fulfil other citizenship responsibilities. These include:

- understanding and obeying Canadian laws
- allowing other Canadians to enjoy their rights and freedoms
- helping to preserve Canada's diverse cultural heritage

Citizenship responsibilities can be fulfilled in many ways. One of these is to work with other people to create a safe, enjoyable environment for families, friends, and neighbours. People often band together in service clubs, religious groups, and other organizations. People in many communities across Canada, for example, have formed neighbourhood watches to make their neighbourhoods safer for everyone. Neighbours keep their eyes open for problems, and volunteer block parents put signs in their windows to tell children that they can get help by ringing the doorbell. Good neighbours and good citizens look out for one another.

People also contribute to the common good in other ways. For example, they pay taxes to help fund services such as health care and garbage pick-up. After a snowfall, urban homeowners shovel the sidewalks in front of their houses to enable people to walk safely in the streets. What are some other things people do to contribute to the common good?

These young people are contributing to the common good by helping out at a food bank.

Democratic Beliefs and Values

CRAIG KIELBURGER
FREE THE CHILDREN

Craig Kielburger of Thornhill, Ontario, is a young Canadian who set out to make a difference.

When Craig was 12 years old, he read a newspaper article that changed his life. The article told the story of Iqbal Masih, a Pakistani boy who had been sold into slavery at the age of four. Shackled to a carpet loom and forced to work for the next eight years, Iqbal managed to escape when he was 12. As he was about to tell his story, though, he was murdered.

Iqbal's story inspired Craig and some of his Grade 7 classmates to found an organization called Free the Children. They spoke at neighbouring schools, educating other young people about the horrors of child labour. Craig was very successful in drawing attention to his cause and raising money for programs to help child labourers.

One of Craig's mentors, Alam Rahman, was so impressed by this young man's dedication that he invited Craig to accompany him on a trip to Asia to visit child labourers. Reluctantly, Craig's parents gave their son permission to go and helped him organize the trip.

The trip won Craig international recognition and drew attention to the issue of child labour. He met many child labourers and heard their stories first-hand.

On the trip, Craig also had an opportunity to talk to Prime Minister Jean Chrétien, who was in Asia on a trade mission.

Since this trip, Craig has travelled to many countries with other young members of Free the Children. In their attempts to end child labour and the exploitation of children, they have carried their message to government officials and aid organizations.

Craig believes that children deserve to live dignified lives and have the right to an education. He also believes that Canadians can help stop child labour by boycotting products produced by child labour.

Free the Children is now an international organization with chapters in 20 countries. For his efforts, Craig has been named a Global Leader of Tomorrow and awarded the Governor General's Award for Meritorious Service.

On his 1996 trip to Asia, Craig Kielburger talked to Munna, a 10-year-old food vendor in New Delhi, India. Craig also talked to government officials in the countries he visited.

Because the voting age in Canada is 18, most teenagers are not old enough to vote. Does this mean that teenagers cannot be contributing citizens? Few would answer yes to this question. Would you?

Students contribute to their school, neighbourhood, and community in many ways. Many students become active members of the school community by taking part in extracurricular activities such as clubs or sports teams. Others become involved in the student council. Participating in school government enables students to help run the school and organize activities, including community outreach programs.

These high-school students in Welland, Ontario, organized a spaghetti-eating contest to raise money for their student council's scholarship fund.

What citizenship opportunities are available to students in your school? What issues would you like to see addressed by your school's student council?

For democracies to function, people must be able to freely exercise their rights and fulfil their responsibilities. Are you able to put your personal citizenship values into action? If roadblocks prevent this, are you willing to accept things the way they are or can you do something to improve the situation?

Web Connection

http://www.school.mcgrawhill.ca/resources
To find out more about organizations that need volunteers, go to History Resources. Then go to *Civics: Participating in a Democratic Society* to see where to go next.

The Active Citizen

Think ... Discuss ... Act

The United Nations has repeatedly ranked Canada as the number one country in the world in which to live. In ranking the countries of the world, the United Nations considers many criteria.

1. What do you think makes Canada a great place to live?
2. What things would make Canada an even better place to live? What can you and other students do to make these things happen?

CHAPTER REVIEW

SUMMING IT UP

Canadians have developed a unique perspective on the meaning of democratic citizenship. Canada is a society that believes strongly in the rule of law. It is also a caring society that stresses the importance of human dignity, respecting the rights of others, and working toward the common good. To continue enjoying the rights and freedoms of democratic citizenship, though, Canadians must participate in the democratic process and fulfil their citizenship responsibilities.

1. Choose one of the following scenarios from in this chapter and explain what it says about democratic beliefs and values.

   - Civil disobedience and Clayoquot Sound
   - Anti-hate laws and James Keegstra
   - Off-leash dogs in Vancouver parks
   - Reciting the Lord's Prayer in public schools
   - Child labour and Free the Children
   - Regulating Internet content

2. Is deciding how city parks will be used as important as deciding how wilderness areas will be used? Is regulating the content of material published on the Internet as important as limiting hate messages? Why? Explain your position on each of these issues.

3. Add terms from this chapter to your list of New Words with Special Meaning.

GETTING THE FACTS

Suppose you are preparing a class assignment on this chapter for your class.

1. Here is one question that you would like to ask:
   Explain or define the following five words or phrases: civil disobedience, rule of law ...

   List three other words or phrases that you would add to this list. What answers would you expect?

2. Here is another question you want to ask:
   Why did a group of people form the Friends of Clayoquot Sound?

   What are two important points you would expect students to include in their answers?

3. Make up two other questions for the assignment and outline the answers you would expect.

1. a) With your eyes closed, ask yourself what you remember most about this chapter. What images come to mind? Are issues related to basic beliefs and values easier to recall than "smaller" pieces of information or vice versa?

   b) Share what you remember with classmates. On the chalkboard or a large sheet of chart paper, create a graphic organizer to outline the group's recollections.

   What conclusions can you draw about the kinds of information most people were able to recall easily?

2. People do not always share the same beliefs and values. Sometimes good citizens have different beliefs and values.

   Skim the chapter to find examples of value conflicts. What benefits might be gained from bringing together — in a neutral setting — groups of citizens who seem to have conflicting values?

3. What might you say to comfort people who are feeling left out or ignored because an issue they really believe in was defeated in a democratic vote? With a partner or group, prepare a scenario showing this and present it to the class.

4. How involved are you and your classmates in your school? Conduct a survey to find out. Rate each person's involvement on a scale of 1 to 4. Use the following survey statements.

   1) I am actively involved. I participate in at least two extracurricular activities.

   2) I am somewhat involved. I participate in at least one extracurricular activity.

   3) I am not very involved. I am interested in my school but participate in no extracurricular activities.

   4) I am not involved at all. My only involvement is to attend classes.

   Tabulate the results and show them on a bar graph. Into which category do most students fall? Why do you suppose this is so? Why have some students become active citizens of your school? Why do some students choose to remain passive?

Chapter 6
MANY BELIEFS, VALUES, AND PERSPECTIVES

"Canada has no cultural unity, no linguistic unity, no religious unity, no economic unity, no geographic unity. All it has is unity."

American economist and pacifist Kenneth Boulding

In 1996, thousands of flag-waving Montrealers gathered to mark the first anniversary of a unity rally that had attracted tens of thousands of Canadians to the city just before the 1995 referendum on Québec sovereignty. Quebeckers who want to remain part of Canada won the referendum by a narrow margin. Would the people gathered for this anniversary rally have agreed with Kenneth Boulding's thoughts on Canadian unity? Would people who favour an independent Québec have agreed with him? Why?

In a country that encourages diversity, it is impossible for everyone to share the same beliefs, values, and perspectives. Diversity, which gives Canada its strength, also presents challenges. Some of the differences in the beliefs, values, and perspectives of Canadians are rooted in history that stretches back over centuries. Other differences exist because variations in beliefs, values, and perspectives always occur in society.

Think about how your own beliefs, values, and perspectives differ from those of your friends, classmates, or family members. Is it important to get along with people who do not share your views? Why?

Chapter
Expectations

In this chapter, you will learn about:

- the beliefs and values that unite Canadians
- Canadian citizenship
- how diverse beliefs and values have influenced, and are influencing, Canadian perspectives on issues such as Aboriginal self-government, the role of Québec in Canada, and constitutional reform

Key
Terms

allophone	francophone	regionalism
anglophone	melting pot	separatist
conscription	multiculturalism	sovereignty association
cultural mosaic	naturalization	

THE CANADIAN MOSAIC

During the 20th century, immigration changed the face of Canada. Today, at the dawn of the 21st century, the country has become a nation of diverse peoples, many of whom came to Canada seeking a better life.

The diversity of this country's society means that many Canadians do not share a common first language, religion, or cultural heritage. People who live in different regions of the country also have different visions of the nation.

What, then, is a Canadian? Ask 10 people this question and they will probably come up with 10 different answers. Some people might define themselves by what they are not. They might say, "We are not Americans!" Others might even say, "Canadians do not have an identity." What would you say?

Canada has not always welcomed immigrants. In 1885, Chinese immigrants like those shown in this photograph were forced to pay a head tax of $50 before entering the country. In 1895, they were barred from voting and, in 1903, the head tax was raised to $500, a huge sum at the time. In 1923, immigration from China became illegal and, in 1931, a law barred people of Asian heritage from becoming citizens. These harsh restrictions began to ease only during World War II.

Canadian Citizenship

Some people might define a Canadian as someone who holds Canadian citizenship. In Canada, citizenship is a birthright. This means that anyone born in Canada is automatically a citizen. Many people who were not born in this country have chosen to become Canadian citizens. To do this, they must go through a process called **naturalization**. This involves applying to become a citizen.

People from other countries can apply to become Canadian citizens if they

- are at least 18 years old
- have lived in Canada for at least three of the previous four years
- can speak, read, write, and understand English or French
- can pass a test on the rights and responsibilities of Canadians, Canada's history and geography, and Canada's political system

An Asian mother and daughter who became naturalized Canadians at a citizenship ceremony in Lethbridge, Alberta, smile as they examine their citizenship papers.

People who fulfill these requirements become Canadian citizens with the same rights and responsibilities as those born in Canada.

Children and teenagers younger than 18 cannot apply for citizenship on their own. Their parents must apply for them — and parents can do this only if they are already citizens themselves or are about to become citizens.

There was no stopping Vancouver resident Elizabeth Nash, who is visually challenged, once she decided that the city's annual dragon boat festival presented a unique opportunity for people with impaired vision. Dragon boats are long, colourfully decorated racing canoes.

Two of Nash's children were dragon boat racers. As she listened to their stories, she asked herself: Do people need good eyesight to paddle a dragon boat? She believed that the answer was no. Timing, teamwork, and technique seemed more important.

Nash got to work. Along with other members of the Canadian National Institute for the Blind, she began forming a unique dragon boat team called Eye of the Dragon. By 1994, she had recruited enough people to enter that year's festival. Like other dragon boat crews, Eye of the Dragon was made up of 20 paddlers, a steersperson, and a drummer. Unlike other crews, however, it included several members who were either completely blind or had low vision.

Nash, the team manager, was fondly called the Dragonlady by crew members. To help finance the team, she set up a memorial fund in the name of her son Stephen, who had gone missing and been presumed drowned a number of years earlier. Inspired by what she was trying to do, Concord Pacific Group, a residential and waterfront development corporation, donated the use of its boat to Eye of the Dragon to help the crew train.

When they competed in their first festival, team members were thrilled to know that visually challenged paddlers were competing not in a special event for others like themselves but against sighted racers.

"Out on the water, we're equal," said Richard Marion, one of the team's visually challenged paddlers.

In 1995, at the festival's closing ceremonies, Eye of the Dragon received the David Lam Award, which is named after one of British Columbia's former lieutenant governors. The award recognized the "team which best exemplifies community service, dedication, and the multicultural spirit of the festival."

The next year, Eye of the Dragon placed in the top half of the novice division. Known for their positive attitude, crew members were pleased not only by their performance, but also because their participation raised public awareness of the abilities of the visually challenged.

Much of the credit for this goes to the feisty "Dragonlady" who turned her physical limitation into an opportunity to help others and make her community a better place to live.

Dragon boats and their crews prepare to race in Vancouver's annual dragon boat festival. Dragon boats originated in China more than 2000 years ago. Dragon boat racing is now a popular sport in many Canadian cities — and around the world.

Multiculturalism

To ensure that all Canadians enjoy the rights of citizenship and take pride in their heritage, the government of Prime Minister Pierre Trudeau adopted an official policy of **multiculturalism** in 1971. The government decided that Canada would become a **cultural mosaic** where peoples' ethnic and cultural roots would be celebrated. This policy made Canada different from the United States. In the American **melting pot**, immigrants are expected to assimilate as quickly as possible.

In 1988, the federal government went a step farther and became the first country in the world to pass a multiculturalism act. The Canadian Multiculturalism Act officially recognized "the equality of all Canadians in the economic, social, cultural and political life of Canada ... "

From the beginning, the government's adoption of official multiculturalism sparked debate — and this debate continues. Some Canadians believe that official multiculturalism is an essential part of the Canadian identity; others believe that it weakens the country.

Is it important for Canadians to define themselves according to their cultural roots? There is little agreement on the answer to this question. On the 1995 Canadian census, for example, one in five people specified "Canadian" as their ethnic origin. Three and half million others checked "Canadian" in combination with another ethnic origin.

Web Connection

www.school.mcgrawhill.ca/resources

To find out more about Canada's multicultural history, go to History Resources. Then go to *Civics: Participating in a Democratic Society* to see where to go next.

Regionalism

In addition to being a country of diverse peoples, Canada is a nation of diverse regions. **Regionalism** — loyalty to the interests of a particular region — contributes to the difficulty of defining Canadians. Regional histories differ, as do the cultures of various parts of the country.

The lifestyle of a Newfoundland fisher is different from the lifestyle of a Prairie grain farmer or a Vancouver businessperson. The economic priorities and needs of people in various regions also differ. For example, the priorities and needs of a New Brunswick logger are very different from those of an Alberta cattle rancher.

The picture on the left shows the Newfoundland fishing village of Conception Bay. The picture on the right shows Saskatchewan's Qu'Appelle Valley. How might the identity, culture, and political concerns of someone living in Conception Bay differ from those of someone living in the Qu'Appelle Valley?

THE PURPOSEFUL CITIZEN

McGraw-Hill Ryerson Ltd.

With the exception of Aboriginal people, all Canadians are either immigrants or descended from immigrants. This can sometimes cause problems. When people from diverse backgrounds live in the same community, conflicts may erupt because they do not understand and respect one another's beliefs, values, and perspectives. People can be even less tolerant when they are afraid of something.

When World War I started in 1914, many Canadians wondered whether to trust the Ukrainian immigrants who had arrived from various parts of the sprawling Austro-Hungarian Empire of Europe. After all, the Austro-Hungarian Empire was now at war with Canada. Where would the loyalties of Ukrainian immigrants lie?

After some debate, the federal government decided that the Ukrainian immigrants could not be trusted and classified them as enemy aliens. As a result, 80 000 people, most of them of Ukrainian background, were required to report regularly to local police.

Things were even worse for Ukrainian immigrants who had not yet become citizens. More than 5000 of them — mostly men, though some women and children were also included — were ordered to pack their belongings. They were then loaded onto sleighs, trucks, cars, and trains and shipped to tent camps in wilderness areas across the country. There, they were forced to do jobs such as clearing brush along railway lines, building a golf course, and clearing land for returning soldiers and their families.

The politicians who passed the law took away the rights of Ukrainian immigrants, saying that these people did not share the values of Canadians of other ethnic origins.

These Ukrainian immigrants are working near their internment camp at Castle Mountain, Alberta, in 1915. Even when World War I ended in 1918, the interned immigrants were not freed. Some were forced to remain in the camps until 1920.

The Active Citizen

1. Canadians who supported interning Ukrainian immigrants often did so out of fear. What do you think they might have been afraid of? Do you think that their fears were justified? Why?

2. Does war make some citizens less equal than others? Why?

3. Research and report on what happened to other groups of Canadians who were classified as enemy aliens during World War I or II.

4. Prepare arguments for or against interning so-called enemy aliens in times of war. Debate the issue in class.

Dealing with regional diversity is a difficult challenge for the Canadian government. It is hard to create policies that satisfy the needs of people with such a wide variety of perspectives.

MANY PERSPECTIVES ON THE FIRST FOUNDING PEOPLES

When Europeans arrived in the New World, about 300 000 Aboriginal people lived in what is now Canada. These Aboriginal people belonged to different nations, with different languages, customs, and forms of government. When Aboriginal Nations made treaties with one another, the agreements were viewed as sacred.

Big Snake, a Blackfoot chief, tells the story of his exploits to subordinate chiefs. This picture was painted by artist Paul Kane in the 1850s, just as the lives of the Aboriginal people of the Prairies were beginning to change forever.

National Gallery of Canada, Ottawa/Musée des Beaux-arts du Canada, Ottawa

What is more, the Aboriginal people's attitude toward land was different from that of the European settlers. Aboriginal people believed that they shared the land where they lived, hunted, trapped, and fished.

Europeans valued individual ownership of land and did not understand the Aboriginal idea of sharing. As a result,

FYI

The Royal Proclamation of 1763 declared that land occupied by Aboriginal Peoples would remain theirs unless they agreed to turn it over to the British monarch. Though some Aboriginal Nations signed treaties giving up their land, others, such as the Nisga'a of Northern British Columbia, did not. As a result, some of today's Aboriginal land claims are based on this proclamation.

Europeans and Aboriginal people brought different perspectives to the treaty-making process. To the Europeans, a treaty was like a real estate deal. It was simply an agreement to change the ownership of a parcel of land.

Aboriginal people, on the other hand, believed that a treaty involved much more than this. They believed that the spirit of the treaty was as important as what was recorded on paper. For them, the spirit of a treaty defined the way the people of the nations involved would treat each other.

In 1867, the British North America Act placed Aboriginal Peoples under the control of the Canadian government — without consulting them. Nine years later, in 1876, the federal government passed the Indian Act, which set out rules for Aboriginal people. Once again, no one consulted the people of Canada's First Nations.

Under the Indian Act, Aboriginal people living on reserves were not considered Canadian citizens. They were not allowed to vote or leave their reserve without a special pass. An Indian agent, who worked for the federal government, controlled everything that happened on the reserve. Later, the government also outlawed traditional Aboriginal ceremonies such as the potlatch, sun dance, and the buffalo jump.

In the 20th century, life on many reserves got worse and worse. Aboriginal people could no longer follow their traditional ways, but they were not welcomed into the Canadian community. On many reserves, few jobs existed. People struggled with high unemployment and poverty, which contributed to social problems in their communities.

Government officials watch an Aboriginal drum dancer perform. During this 1998 ceremony, the federal government apologized for the abuse suffered by many Aboriginal children at residential schools. For decades, Aboriginal children were sent far away to these schools. There, they were forbidden to speak their own language, learned nothing about their own culture, and were sometimes abused.

To survive, many Aboriginal people applied for welfare. This system of individual survival was different from the communal way of life they had followed for centuries. Those who left the reserves to seek a better life risked losing their Aboriginal status.

The Indian Act satisfied no one. Aboriginal people were not assimilated into Canadian society, nor was their traditional way of life or culture preserved. The Act made Aboriginal communities dependent on the federal government. Many people believe that it set up the conditions that led to the poverty that now exists on many reserves.

Aboriginal people who stayed on reserves had little control over their own lives. Though they won the right to vote in federal elections in 1960, they had to wait another 22 years for their rights to be recognized officially. Finally, these were confirmed in the Constitution Act of 1982. It states: "The existing aboriginal and treaty rights of the aboriginal peoples of Canada are hereby recognized and affirmed."

To many Aboriginal people, this statement marked an important turning point in their struggle to regain control of their lives and future. They believe that it recognizes not only their right to govern themselves, but also their claims to all land that was not surrendered through treaties.

Not everyone agrees with this interpretation of the statement, however. Some Canadians still expect Aboriginal people to assimilate and adopt European-based Canadian values.

Some people fear that self-government will lead to special treatment for Aboriginal people. Others say that settling land claims and helping Aboriginal Nations make the transition to self-government costs too much. Still, public opinion polls show that a majority of Canadians support righting the wrongs suffered by Aboriginal people.

To do this, two routes have been followed. The first route has involved the courts. In 1990, for example, the Supreme Court of Canada confirmed the Aboriginal view of treaties. The court's decision said that treaties and laws relating to Aboriginal people "should be liberally construed and uncertainties resolved in favour of the Indians."

The second route has involved negotiations. Since 1973, more than 220 claims have been settled. Many more are still being negotiated.

Confirming Mi'kmaq Treaty Rights

Sometimes, the issue of Aboriginal treaty rights ends up in court. The case of Donald Marshall Jr. shows how this can happen. Marshall, a

When Mi'kmaq fishers like this man began trapping lobster outside the official season, non-Aboriginal fishers protested and the conflict turned violent. More than 40 of this man's traps were destroyed in one incident.

Mi'kmaw from New Brunswick, was arrested for fishing out of season. At his trial in 1999, the court ruled that he had not broken the law because the Mi'kmaq have a treaty right to live by fishing, hunting, and gathering food throughout the year.

The court decision focused on treaties negotiated between the British and Mi'kmaq in 1760–1761. Until 1759, the Mi'kmaq had been allies of the French. After the fall of Québec, the British wanted to make sure that the Mi'kmaq would either support Britain or remain neutral in future wars against the French.

The treaties established trading relationships between the Mi'kmaq and the province of Nova Scotia. Until they were raised in the Marshall case, these treaties had never been studied by historians.

As a result of the court ruling, Mi'kmaq fishers began to trap lobster before the official season began. This provoked violent conflicts between Aboriginal and non-Aboriginal fishers, who can fish only during the official season. The federal government tried to resolve the dispute by negotiating with the two groups, but neither side was satisfied.

Though the court ruling confirmed Mi'kmaq treaty rights, it left many other questions unanswered. Does the ruling apply to all Aboriginal people? Is logging considered gathering?

The dispute that erupted in 1999 between Aboriginal and non-Aboriginal fishers was sometimes dubbed the "lobster wars." The artist who created this cartoon portrayed the dispute from a lobster's point of view.

Nunavut: Canada's Newest Territory

Nunavut means "our land" in Inuktitut, the Inuit language. This name was chosen because Nunavut, Canada's newest territory, established a homeland for the Inuit who make up about 85 percent of the territory's population of 27 219. Because the Inuit are in the majority, they control the decisions made by the territory's elected government. The Legislative Assembly is made up of 19 elected representatives, none of whom belong to a political party. The premier is elected by members of the assembly.

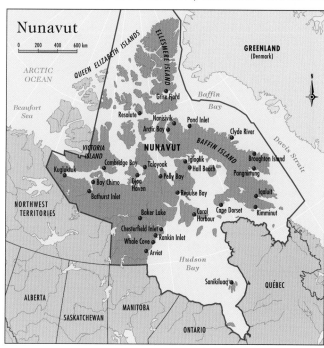

After more than 20 years of negotiating with the federal government, the new territory of Nunavut came into being on April 1, 1999. The territory, which is entirely north of the tree line, was created from the eastern section of the Northwest Territories. It covers about 20 percent of Canada, includes two thirds of Canada's coastline, and traverses three time zones.

Many Beliefs, Values, and Perspectives

The goal of the territorial government is to integrate traditional Inuit values into a Canadian system of government. Though Inuit and non-Inuit residents have equal rights, an affirmative action program promotes Inuit participation in the territory's civil service.

Some people have criticized the creation of the new territory. They say that it segregates the Inuit from the rest of Canada. Those who support the idea of Nunavut believe that it will enable the Inuit to participate more fully in Canadian life.

The government of Nunavut faces many economic and social challenges. Unemployment is high, education levels are low, and substance abuse is a problem in many communities. The territory's suicide rate is six times higher than the national average, and the cost of providing services to isolated communities is high.

Still, the Inuit are confident that controlling their own government will help them tackle these challenges. For example, their justice system will incorporate traditional practices such as healing circles and community-based policing.

As part of the settlement with the federal government, Nunavut will receive financial help. At first, the federal government will foot the bill for more than 90 percent of the territory's expenses. This will help Nunavut develop an economy based on mining, commercial fishing and hunting, and tourism.

The flag of Nunavut is rich in symbols. The blue and gold stand for the riches of the land, sea, and sky. The red symbolizes Canada. The inuksuk at the centre is a traditional stone monument that guides people and marks sacred places. The Niqirtsuituq is the North Star. It is also a guide. In addition, it symbolizes the leadership of elders in the community.

www.school.mcgrawhill.ca/resources
To find out more about Nunavut, go to History Resources. Then go to *Civics: Participating in a Democratic Society* to see where to go next.

One day in the early 1960s, RCMP officers arrived at the remote northern hunting camp of Paul Okalik's family. Pulling out their guns, the police officers shot the family's sled dogs.

This scene was repeated many times at other Inuit camps. It was part of a federal government plan to force the Inuit to give up their nomadic way of life and move to settled communities. Without dogs to haul their sleds, the Inuit could not survive on the land. The Okaliks moved to Pangnirtung on Baffin Island, where Paul was born in 1964.

In Pangnirtung, the family had access to food, health care, and education. Like other Inuit families, though, they no longer had a way of making a living. A once-proud family of hunters entered a cycle of poverty and despair.

Paul, the youngest of the family's seven children, was shipped to residential school in Iqaluit, 300 kilometres away. In Iqaluit, the unhappy teenager dropped out of school and turned to alcohol. After an older brother committed suicide, he started drinking even more and spent three months in prison for breaking into a post office to steal a bottle of liquor.

Once out of jail, Okalik picked up work here and there. Finally, he talked his way into a job researching Aboriginal land claims. The job changed his life. As he learned more about his people, he discovered a sense of purpose. He started to take pride in his Inuit heritage. Within a few years, he had entered a recovery program for alcoholics, travelled to Ottawa to enrol in university, and launched a new career as a lawyer.

The job also sparked Okalik's interest in politics. After he won a seat in Nunavut's new Legislative Assembly, the members elected him the territory's first premier.

As premier, Okalik has a clear vision of the territory's future. He believes that the education system must respect and reflect Inuit culture. The skills that disappeared when people were forced off the land must be taught to a new generation, and those who want to travel south to attend university must receive support. In addition, he wants to diversify Nunavut's economy so that the territory can become self-sufficient.

Okalik's personal journey has created a model for many young Inuit, who share his hopes for the future in the new territory.

When members of the Nunavut's Legislative Assembly chose Paul Okalik as the new territory's first premier in February 1999, he became the youngest premier in Canadian history.

Self-Government for the Nisga'a

In 1999, Parliament approved a landmark treaty with the Nisga'a of Northern British Columbia. The agreement, which took more than 100 years to negotiate, is expected to become a model for similar treaties with other Aboriginal Nations.

Like most of the First Nations of British Columbia, the Nisga'a had never signed treaties giving up their land or resources. Yet non-Aboriginal people and businesses were moving into their territory in the Nass River Valley, and there seemed to be little they could do to stop this. They had been trying since 1887, when Nisga'a chiefs first travelled to Victoria to try to negotiate a treaty that would recognize their claim to their land and their right to govern themselves.

Finally, in 1976, the Nisga'a tribal council started treaty negotiations with the federal government. The British Columbia government joined the process in 1990. In 1996, a draft treaty was approved by Nisga'a voters, but it would take another three years for a final treaty to be approved by everyone.

When the treaty was finally signed by the federal government on May 4, 1999, it gave the 6000 Nisga'a a form of self-government over the 1992 square kilometres of land they now own collectively. In this territory, they have the power to grant their own citizenship, tax their own citizens, and decide how to use the land. They also manage and operate their own government, including family, social and health services, police, the courts, and schools. Perhaps most important, they control forestry, mining, and fishing rights, which are keys to economic self-sufficiency.

The Nisga'a treaty was not without critics. Many people in British Columbia opposed it. They urged Parliament to reject it because they

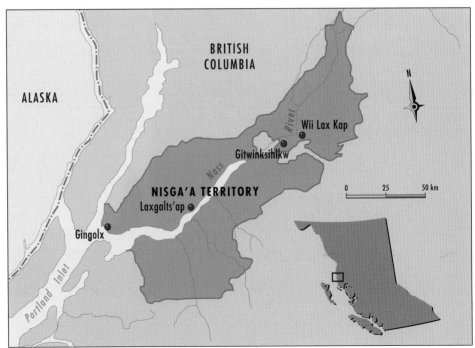

The treaty negotiated with the British Columbia and federal governments gives the Nisga'a power to decide their own destiny in this area of Northern British Columbia.

THE PURPOSEFUL CITIZEN

McGraw-Hill Ryerson Ltd.

said that it gave the Nisga'a special status within Canada. They said that this set a dangerous and potentially expensive precedent.

In 1999, Joseph Gosnell, president of the Nisga'a tribal council, entered the Senate chamber in Ottawa to hear the governor general deliver the Speech from the Throne. For the Nisga'a, it was an important moment. The speech opened the session of Parliament that would approve a treaty giving their nation a form of self-government.

Some Aboriginal groups also criticized the treaty, saying that the Nisga'a gave away too much. The Nisga'a, for example, agreed to give up the tax-exempt status enjoyed by all Aboriginal people covered by treaties.

Self-government does not give the Nisga'a complete independence, however. The Charter of Rights and Freedoms continues to apply in the territory, as do federal and provincial laws. Still, the Nisga'a agreement rights old wrongs and sets an important precedent for future treaty negotiations.

The Active Citizen

Think ... Discuss ... Act

"Our fathers held out to [European settlers] the hand of friendship. The strangers then asked for a small piece of land on which they might pitch their tents; the request was cheerfully granted. By and by they begged for more, and more was given to them. In this way, they have continued to ask, or have obtained by force or fraud, the fairest portion of our territory."

Chief Peter Jones, chief of the Credit River band of the Mississauga, made this statement in the 1840s. At the time, the members of his band were outnumbered more than 100 to one by European settlers. Today, the sprawling city of Mississauga, just west of Toronto, occupies the territory that was once home to Jones and his people. In 1847, the 226 Mississauga who remained in the area agreed to "surrender" the last fragment of their land to the British. The Mississauga were resettled on a reserve just south of Brantford, Ontario.

1. How would you explain the idea of private property to an Aboriginal person who believes that land is to be shared?
2. About 1360 Mississauga now live on the New Credit Reserve near Brantford, Ontario. The population of the city of Mississauga is approaching one million. Does the fact that the Mississauga signed a treaty surrendering their land make what happened to them fair? Why?
3. Invite an Aboriginal person to explain his or her view of land-claims issues to your class.

The conflict between Québec and the rest of the country is one of the most divisive issues facing Canada today. At the heart of the issue is the desire of Québécois to preserve their language and culture.

The differences in perspective between French- and English-speakers have sometimes erupted into open conflict. During both World War I and World War II, for example, **conscription** — compulsory military service — was an issue that deepened the division. Many English-speakers favoured conscription; many French-speakers opposed it. They did not want French-speaking young people forced to fight — and possibly die — in a European war.

This cartoon pokes fun at Canadians who expected Québécois to endorse conscription when it was introduced during World War II.

In both wars, the voices of people who opposed conscription were drowned out by those who favoured it — and laws bringing in conscription were passed. For many Québécois, the defeat sounded a warning: on the national political stage, they were too few in number to make their voices heard.

Think ... Discuss ... Act

During World War I, opposition to conscription was not limited to French-speakers. Conservative Prime Minister Robert Borden's decision to introduce compulsory military service in 1917 nearly tore Canada apart. Liberal Opposition Leader Wilfrid Laurier felt compelled to oppose the conscription bill, even though he had done much to support the war effort. This meant that there was division along political party lines as well as along French-English lines. What is more, many farmers across the country opposed conscription because they needed their sons to help produce food at home.

1. What were some of the values that came into conflict over conscription in 1917?
2. Imagine it is 1917. Do you agree or disagree with Borden's decision to bring in conscription? Would your opinion be different if you were a farmer? If you were a Québécois? Why?

The Quiet Revolution

In the years after World War II, English-speakers in Québec, though fewer in number than French-speakers, held most of the economic power in the province. **Anglophones** — people whose first language is English — filled the senior ranks of business. They were often influential in government as well.

Economically, anglophones seemed to be better off too. Their average salaries were higher than those of **francophones** — people whose first language is French.

In response to this, a new movement started to grow among francophones who wanted the same social, economic, and political opportunities as anglophones. This movement was given a voice by Jean Lesage, a politician who appealed to the Québécois by saying that it was time for them to become "*maîtres chez nous*" — "masters in our own house."

Lesage was elected premier of Québec in 1960. For the next six years until his party's defeat in 1966, his government carried out what has become known as the Quiet Revolution. He reformed the government of the province and strengthened the French language. He also demanded more recognition of and power for Québec on the national stage.

Jean Lesage, who was leader of the Québec Liberal Party, on the campaign trail in the 1962 provincial election. His slogan — "*maîtres chez nous*" — became a rallying cry for Québécois who believed that taking control of their own affairs was the only way to preserve their language and culture.

For some people, though, this was not enough. More and more Québécois were coming to believe that declaring independence was their only chance to become truly *maîtres chez nous*. The **separatist** movement was born.

The Quiet Revolution Turns Violent

From the beginning, separatists were not unified. They had many different ideas about the best form of independence and the best way of achieving it.

One group of separatists wanted independence right away. The Front de Libération du Québec, also known as the FLQ, was founded in 1963 and immediately began a campaign of terror. Its members, though few in number, believed that violence was the only way to achieve what they wanted.

Members of the FLQ divided themselves into smaller groups called cells and launched a series of bombings in Québec. From 1963 to 1970, the FLQ was responsible for 200 bombings. On May 17, 1963, a day that became known as Black Friday, FLQ members placed 17 bombs in mailboxes in the mainly English-speaking Montréal suburb of Westmount.

A Canadian Army engineer who was trying to dismantle one of the bombs was killed when another exploded nearby. Other people were also killed during the FLQ's seven-year campaign of terror.

On October 5, 1970, members of one FLQ cell kidnapped James Cross, the British trade commissioner. Five days later, another cell kidnapped Pierre Laporte, the Québec labour minister. These events set off what became known as the October Crisis.

In response to the kidnappings, the Québec government called in the armed forces to help the police, and Prime Minister Pierre Trudeau proclaimed the War Measures Act. This act gives emergency powers to the federal Cabinet and limits the rights and freedoms of Canadians during times of "war, invasion or insurrection, real or apprehended."

Tanks rolled in the streets of Montréal and Québec City, and soldiers seemed to be everywhere. More than 450 people, most with no connection to the FLQ, were arrested and held in jail without bail.

Armed soldiers patrol the streets of Montréal during the October Crisis. This is the only time the War Measures Act has been proclaimed in peacetime. Opinion polls showed that most Canadians supported the federal government's action. Québec nationalists, however, were outraged, saying that it was an overreaction. What do you think?

On October 18, Laporte's murdered body was found in the trunk of a car. On December 4, Cross's kidnappers released him into the care of a Cuban diplomat. Cross's kidnappers and some of their family members were then flown to Cuba, where they were safe from prosecution in Canada. Four men who had been involved in Laporte's kidnapping were captured and convicted of various charges, including murder.

The violence of the October Crisis was over, but the voices of Québec separatists were about to grow louder.

The Independence Movement Grows

In 1968, Quebeckers who wanted independence formed a provincial political party dedicated to this goal. Led by René Lévesque, the Parti Québécois — or PQ — won the provincial election in November 1976. For the first time, people who supported Québec's independence had a government dedicated to separation.

When the Parti Québécois came to power, less than 20 percent of the people of Québec favoured separating completely from Canada. Hoping to attract more support, Lévesque came up with a plan called **sovereignty association**. This plan called for Québec to become a self-governing nation, while keeping its economic ties to Canada. Québec would control immigration, relations with other countries, and who could become citizens.

René Lévesque speaks to a crowd of jubilant supporters after the Parti Québécois election victory on November 15, 1976. The election of a party dedicated to independence propelled the debate over Québec's separation to intense new levels.

On May 20, 1980, the Parti Québécois held a referendum on Lévesque's plan. A referendum is a special vote to find out what voters think about one issue.

On referendum day, 60 percent of all voters, including 60 percent of francophones, cast ballots against sovereignty association. This was a bitter defeat for separatists. Their hopes for an independent Québec had been dashed — for the time being.

Though the Parti Québécois lost the referendum, the question of Québec's place in Canada was far from settled.

A Second Referendum

In 1994, the Parti Québécois again formed a government in Québec, this time with Jacques Parizeau as leader. For Parizeau and the PQ, the election victory was an opportunity to hold another referendum on Québec sovereignty. A date was set for the vote: October 30, 1995.

At first, Parizeau wanted to ask voters to approve independence, but polls showed that this idea was not popular. Instead, the PQ drafted a referendum question that asked whether Quebeckers, both English- and French-speaking, supported a sovereign Québec in "a new economic and political partnership" with Canada. No framework for this kind of partnership existed, and the debate leading up to the referendum showed that no one was sure exactly what it meant.

Still, as referendum day neared, it began to look more and more as if Quebeckers might approve the idea. When voting day arrived, more than 93 percent of eligible voters cast ballots. That night, Canadians in every part of the country sat in front of TV sets to watch the results roll in from polling stations across Québec.

At one point, it looked as if the YES side might win, but the final tally gave the NO forces a very narrow victory — 50.6 percent to 49.4 percent. For the time being, Québec would remain part of Canada.

An analysis of voting patterns revealed that 60 percent of francophone voters had voted YES to the question, but their votes had been outnumbered by ballots cast by anglophone and **allophone** voters. An allophone is an immigrant whose first language is neither English nor French.

Angered by this turn of events, Parizeau publicly blamed the loss on "money and ethnic votes." His comments drew harsh criticism, and Parizeau resigned three days after the vote. Lucien Bouchard, leader of the Bloc Québécois in the federal Parliament, replaced him as PQ leader and premier of Québec.

With Bouchard as leader, the PQ won another majority government in the 1998 provincial election. During the campaign, Bouchard assured Quebeckers that a vote for the PQ was not necessarily a vote for independence. He promised that another referendum would be held only under "winning conditions" — but never explained exactly what winning conditions were.

Since the PQ election victory, public opinion polls have shown that support for separation is not growing in Québec and may even be declining. They also show that a majority of Quebeckers do not want another referendum.

On October 27, 1995, just three days before the referendum, tens of thousands of people from all over Canada gathered for a huge rally in the streets of Montréal. They wanted to show their support for Canadian unity.

"Do you agree that Québec should become sovereign, after having made a formal offer to Canada for a new economic and political partnership, within the scope of the bill respecting the future of Québec and of the agreement signed on June 12, 1995?"

This was the question that appeared on the 1995 referendum. The "bill respecting the future of Québec" referred to a proposed new law that set out what Québec would do if the YES side won. The "agreement of June 12, 1995," referred to an agreement between Parizeau, Bloc Québécois leader Lucien Bouchard, and Mario Dumont, leader of the Parti action démocratique. The three had agreed on an offer of partnership with the rest of Canada.

1. What might have happened if the YES side had won the referendum?
2. Since the referendum, the Supreme Court of Canada has ruled that Québec has the right to hold a referendum on separation — if the question is clear and if the vote for separation wins by a "clear majority." Do you think the 1995 question was clear? How do you think it might have been made clearer? What do you think a clear majority should be? Why?
3. If Québec has the right to separate from Canada, should the people of various regions of Québec, such as the James Bay Cree, also have the right to decide their own future? Why?
4. What can individual Canadians do to ensure that Québec stays in Canada?

The Language Debate

For many Québécois, the struggle to protect their language is a symbol of their struggle to protect their culture. As a result, the battle over language rights in Québec has been long and bitter.

In the 1960s, the government of Premier Jean Lesage introduced policies to promote the use of French in Québec. Then, in 1969, Prime Minister Pierre Trudeau's federal Liberal government passed the Official Languages Act to make Canada officially bilingual. This act made English and French the official languages of the country and Parliament. It also guaranteed that federal government services would be available in either English or French.

In 1974, the government of Québec Premier Robert Bourassa passed a law making French the only official language of the province. When the Parti Québécois came to power in 1976, however, Premier René Lévesque decided that the laws did not offer enough protection for the French language.

In 1977, Lévesque's government passed Bill 101, which is also known as the Charter of the French Language. This law confirmed French as the only official language of the province — but also went

Although Canada is officially bilingual, the only officially bilingual province is New Brunswick. The official language of Québec is French, and English is the official language of the other eight provinces. The language of the government of the new territory of Nunavut is Inuktitut, but government services are also available in English and French.

much farther. It decreed that only French could be used on business and road signs — and required all students to enrol in French-language schools unless one parent had attended an English school in Québec.

In this area of Montréal, which is home to many Chinese businesses, merchants are asking to be exempted from a law that requires the language on their signs to be predominantly French. They want to display their signs in Chinese.

The law immediately became a lightning rod for protest in Québec and elsewhere in Canada. People asked why it was necessary to restrict the rights of some Quebeckers in order to protect the French language. Groups and individuals launched court cases saying that the law violated the Charter of Rights and Freedoms. As a result of court challenges, some parts of the law have been changed. The battle, however, is far from over.

MANY PERSPECTIVES ON CONSTITUTIONAL REFORM

When Prime Minister Pierre Trudeau patriated the Constitution in 1982 without the consent of Québec, he set in motion a debate that still divides the country. Though two important attempts were made to settle the debate, both failed. The constitutional impasse between Québec and the rest of Canada has not been resolved.

The Meech Lake Accord

Progressive Conservative Prime Minister Brian Mulroney, an anglophone Quebecker, tried to find a way to bring Québec into the Constitution in the mid-1980s. For months, Mulroney negotiated with the provincial premiers, trying to reach an agreement that would satisfy all 10, including Québec. Finally, in April 1987, Mulroney and the provincial premiers reached an agreement known as the Meech Lake Accord.

The agreement included five key points.

- Québec would be recognized as a distinct society, though the agreement did not specify what "distinct society" meant.
- Future constitutional amendments would require the approval of Parliament and the legislatures of all 10 provinces.
- The Supreme Court would be entrenched in the Constitution, ensuring that politicians could not change or abolish it by simply passing a new law.
- The prime minister would select senators from lists submitted by the provinces. Every province would have the right to veto changes to the Senate.
- Provinces would have the right to opt out of federally sponsored social programs. Provinces that did not participate would receive federal money to set up their own programs.

To be adopted, the Meech Lake Accord needed to win the approval of Parliament and all 10 provincial legislatures within three years. Though the accord pleased Québec, it ran into opposition elsewhere in Canada.

Many Canadians disagreed with giving Québec distinct-society status. Others complained that the agreement weakened the federal government by handing too much power to the provinces. Aboriginal people voiced a complaint that was echoed by many other Canadians: they had been left out of the negotiations.

As he voted against debating the Meech Lake Accord in Manitoba's Legislative Assembly, Elijah Harper drew spiritual strength from an eagle feather that he held in his hands. Harper's action made him a hero among Aboriginal people — and served notice that they intended to make their voices heard in future constitutional talks.

Still, the federal Parliament endorsed the agreement. In fact, in a rare show of parliamentary solidarity, the accord won the support of opposition Liberals and New Democratic Party members. Québec was the first province to endorse the agreement. One by one, the rest followed suit — with the exception of Manitoba.

As the deadline neared, Manitoba's Legislative Assembly called a special session to debate the agreement. The legislature's rules of procedure required all members to agree to a motion to hold the special debate.

People were shocked when Elijah Harper, an Oji-Cree member of the legislature, rose and voted against the motion. He said that he could not support the accord because Aboriginal people had been left out of the process. Harper's action scuttled the accord. Because the debate did not go ahead, the accord did not have the required approval of all the provinces.

In the meantime, Newfoundland's Legislative Assembly had reopened debate on the accord, which the province's legislature had already approved. A different government was now in power. At the last minute, this new government withdrew its approval of the accord.

Without the approval of either Manitoba or Newfoundland, the Meech Lake Accord was dead. Québec was still not included in what Mulroney had called "the Canadian family."

The Charlottetown Accord

In 1992, Prime Minister Brian Mulroney tried again to bring Québec into the Constitution. This time, he believed that he had learned from his earlier mistakes.

Mulroney decided to involve more people much earlier in the process. First, public discussions were held. Then, Mulroney called Aboriginal

In this cartoonist's opinion, what was the difference between the Confederation conferences of 1864 and the constitutional talks of 1992?

THE PURPOSEFUL CITIZEN

McGraw-Hill Ryerson Ltd.

leaders and the provincial premiers to a conference in Charlottetown, Prince Edward Island. On August 28, 1992, the delegates reached an agreement. This time, the federal government decided to hold a national referendum on the agreement.

The Charlottetown Accord built on the ideas of the Meech Lake Accord. Once again the agreement identified Québec as a distinct society. The Charter of Rights and Freedoms was to be amended to protect Aboriginal languages, culture, treaties, and right to self-government. Protections for universal health care, social services and benefits, and workers' rights such as collective bargaining were to be built into the Constitution. Senate reform was to include five-year terms for elected senators.

In Parliament, Progressive Conservative, Liberal, and NDP members of Parliament voted to endorse the agreement. This set the stage for the national referendum, which was to be held on October 26, 1992.

As the referendum date neared, debate raged across the country. Few people supported everything in the accord. This placed them in a dilemma. Should they vote YES, even though they disagreed with parts of the agreement? Or should they vote NO, even though they supported most of the accord?

Onlookers wave the flags of Québec and France as a statue of Charles de Gaulle is unveiled in Québec City in 1997. As president of France, de Gaulle had visited Québec 30 years earlier. In a famous speech to a cheering crowd in Montréal, he had galvanized the separatist movement, and outraged many other Canadians, by declaring: "*Vive le Québec libre*" — "Long live a free Québec."

In the end, 54.4 percent of voters said NO. Another constitutional agreement was defeated. Québec remained outside what Mulroney had called the "Canadian family."

After the turmoil created by the debate over the Meech Lake and Charlottetown Accords, many Canadians wanted to stop focusing on constitutional reform. With the country in the middle of the recession of the 1990s, people urged their governments to turn their attention to improving the economy. The constitutional debate was placed on the back burner — but it has continued to simmer.

CHAPTER REVIEW

SUMMING IT UP

As a nation of diverse peoples and regions, Canada is a country in which it is impossible for everyone to share the same beliefs, values, and perspectives. At times, people's differing perspectives have sparked violent conflict. Still, Canada is a country with a long history of negotiation and compromise. It is also a country in which individual citizens try to understand and respect the perspectives of others.

1. This chapter described three important issues — Aboriginal self-government, the role of Québec in Canada, and constitutional reform — that continue to divide Canadians. Explain your stand on each of these issues.

2. Skim the chapter and add to your list of New Words with Special Meaning.

GETTING THE FACTS

1. Choose one of the issues — Aboriginal self-government, the role of Québec in Canada, or constitutional reform — described in this chapter. Identify the debate and create a graphic organizer that summarizes the main arguments.

2. The Mi'kmaq, Inuit, and Nisga'a are not the only Aboriginal Peoples struggling to right old wrongs. Choose an Aboriginal group that is negotiating a land claim. Find out the basis for the claim and report your findings to the class.

3. The Citizenship Act prevents certain people from becoming Canadian citizens. Find out what this law says. Are these restrictions fair? Why?

4. The issues described in this chapter are not the only ones that divide Canadians. Form groups and choose one of the following issues. Research the arguments at the heart of the debate and present them to the class.

   • The Privacy Act and protecting personal information

   • The proposed Youth Criminal Justice Act and tougher penalties for crimes committed by young people

   • The Canada Elections Act and extending voting rights to prison inmates

   • The Firearms Act and controlling guns

USING THE FACTS

1. Assume that you will be taking part in a debate on this topic: Canadians today should not be required to pay for the wrongs committed by governments of the past.

   a) Would you choose to be on the team that argues for or against this statement? List the points you would make to support your side of the argument.

   b) Compare your list with that of someone who took an opposing position.

   c) After you heard the arguments for the other side, did your position change? Or did you think of more arguments to support your point of view? Revise you list to reflect the changes in your ideas.

   d) After hearing and thinking about the arguments on both sides of the issue, what recommendations would you make? To whom could you make your recommendations?

2. Choose one of the issues mentioned in this chapter, such as Aboriginal self-government, the role of Québec in Canada, or constitutional reform. Write a letter to a newspaper editor explaining how you would resolve the issue.

3. Relationships among Canadians have usually been peaceful. Still, violence has sometimes erupted. With a group, prepare a presentation that refutes the idea that the Canadian civic experience has been peaceful by identifying some of the conflicts you have studied so far.

4. Many people believe that citizenship means much more than the strictly legal definition set out in this chapter. Discuss this idea in a group.

   a) Record the group's ideas and compare them with the ideas of other groups in the class. How are the ideas similar? How are they different?

   b) On a larger sheet of chart paper, create a graphic organizer that shows the similarities and differences. Display the graphic organizer so that it can be used for discussion purposes.

5. Review the news clippings you have been collecting since the end of Chapter 2. Choose the clippings that you believe are the most important and organize them into a "thoughtful scrapbook."

   Tape or glue the clippings into a scrapbook in chronological or thematic order. With each clipping, include a paragraph that explains its meaning and why you think it is important to the debate.

Chapter 7
CITIZENSHIP IN A GLOBAL COMMUNITY

"Human rights and true peace — which is more than the absence of war — are closely linked. As long as human rights are violated, there can be no foundation for peace."

Dalai Lama, spiritual leader of Tibet and winner of the 1989 Nobel Peace Prize, in a speech to the Inter-American Court of Human Rights, 1989

The Dalai Lama applauds a speech to the French National Assembly during a celebration of the 50th anniversary of the signing of the Universal Declaration of Human Rights in 1998. The Dalai Lama believes that people can achieve true happiness only by developing love and compassion for all beings. Do you agree with this belief? Why?

Setting *the Stage*

The people of Canada have acted together to create a country in which people enjoy certain rights in return for taking on certain responsibilities. But should Canadians, as well as Canadian governments and institutions, also be concerned about what happens outside Canada? Do Canadians, as well as Canadian governments and institutions, have a responsibility to ensure that people living in other parts of the world are able to live in dignity? If so, how far does this responsibility go?

As the 21st century begins, these questions are being debated not only in Canada but also in other countries. Rapid changes in transportation and communications technology, as well as the removal of many of the barriers that restricted trade and immigration, have intensified the debate. These changes have also sparked the development of new ideas about the meaning of citizenship. As more and more people come to view themselves as citizens of a global community, they are expanding their definition of the rights and responsibilities of citizenship.

Chapter *Expectations*

In this chapter, you will learn about:

- Canada's immigration and refugee policies
- Canada's involvement in international organizations
- how the world community deals with human rights violations
- the role of non-governmental organizations in world affairs
- international trade and its effect on the world
- how citizens participate in the global community

Key *Terms*

biodiversity
biotechnology
deport
Geneva Convention

intellectual property
maquiladora
non-governmental
   organization (NGO)

prisoner of conscience
reconciliation
refugee
tariff

IMMIGRATION AND REFUGEES

Immigration has always been important to Canada. Every year, more Canadians die than are born. Without immigration, the country's population would shrink rather than grow. How would this affect the economy?

From Confederation until after World War II, Canada's immigration policies were designed to attract British and European immigrants — and limit the number of non-Europeans. In the late 1800s and early 1900s, for example, Chinese immigrants were forced to pay a head tax before entering the country. European immigrants were not required to pay this tax. Later, immigrants from China were barred completely.

During World War II, when Canada was at war with Japan, tens of thousands of people of Japanese heritage who lived within about 160 kilometres of the Pacific Coast were rounded up. Branded enemy aliens, they were interned in camps until the end of the war. Their property was confiscated and sold, often at bargain-basement prices.

At the time, Canada was not much more welcoming to refugees fleeing Nazi persecution in Europe. During the 1930s and 1940s, only 5000 Jewish refugees were allowed into the country. The United States accepted 200 000. In one case, a ship carrying 930 Jewish refugees tried unsuccessfully to land in Cuba, the United States, Argentina, Panama, and Uruguay. When it was turned away by Canada too, the SS *St. Louis* sailed back to Europe. Several European countries eventually agreed to take some of the refugees. When Germany invaded these countries, many of the refugees ended up in concentration camps.

After World War II, the Canadian economy continued the boom that had started with the war. Employers needed workers, and the only way to meet the demand was to attract more immigrants. Gradually, the government relaxed its restrictive immigration policies.

Today, three principles guide decisions about who can immigrate to Canada:

- promoting Canada's economic development
- reuniting families
- protecting refugees

Immigrants from Galicia, a region that includes parts of Poland and Ukraine, arrive in Canada early in the 20th century. Clifford Sifton, minister of the interior, said that the immigrant he wanted to attract was "a stalwart peasant in a sheepskin coat, born on the soil, whose forefathers have been farmers for 10 generations ..." What jobs did Sifton have in mind for settlers?

A points system is used to decide whether independent immigrants — those who are not entering Canada as refugees or to join family members — qualify to immigrate. The system measures an immigrant's potential for contributing to the Canadian economy.

Points are awarded based on an applicant's qualifications in many categories. These include age, education and training, occupation, prearranged employment, work experience, and ability to speak English or French. Bonus points are offered to entrepreneurs and investors, as well as to those who already have relatives in Canada.

Applicants must score at least 60 out of 100 points in order to be invited to an interview. At the interview, additional points are awarded based on an applicant's potential for adjusting to Canadian life. The final step is a medical examination.

Once immigrants arrive in Canada, they have the same legal responsibilities as Canadian citizens. Until they become citizens, however, they do not enjoy all the rights of citizens. They cannot vote or hold some public offices. Immigrants can also be **deported** — sent back to their home country — if they are convicted of a serious crime or have lied about their background.

Immigration in the 20th century changed Canada profoundly. At the beginning of the century, most people were of British heritage. Since then, the population has become a mosaic of people from many different cultures.

Statistics Canada estimates that visible minorities will make up 16 percent of Canada's population by 2005. In big cities such as Montréal, Toronto, and Vancouver, this percentage is likely to be much higher.

After World War II, some Japanese immigrants chose to return to their home country. Their experiences in Canada had not been pleasant, as this cartoon points out.

Refugees

People from other countries do not always choose to immigrate to Canada. Sometimes, they do so only because they have been forced to leave their homes to escape war or political persecution. People fleeing for their lives can seek refuge in Canada as **refugees**. Refugees are not required to meet the qualifications required of other immigrants.

In 1951, the Geneva Convention Relating to the Status of Refugees defined refugees as "those who have fled their countries because of a well-founded fear of persecution for reasons of their race, religion, nationality, political opinion, or membership in a particular social group, and who cannot or do not want to return." This description applies to about one of every 280 people in the world. Refugees count on other countries to provide a safe haven for them and their families.

About 25 000 people claiming refugee status enter Canada every year. Those who claim this status must be granted a hearing to decide whether they are genuine refugees. They are provided with legal counsel to help them through the hearing process. The wait for a hearing can be long. Because there is a backlog of about 20 000 refugee claims, it takes about 11 months before claims are heard.

About 45 percent of refugee claims are eventually accepted. Once their claim is accepted, refugees have 180 days to apply to become permanent residents of Canada. During this time, they are eligible for publicly funded health care and may request permission to look for a job. Their children may attend school.

Most Canadians sympathize with refugees fleeing war or political persecution. Many Canadians, however, have little sympathy for people who try to enter Canada illegally. Sometimes called economic refugees, these illegal migrants are usually seeking better economic opportunities.

In recent years, smuggling humans has become big business. International crime rings charge high fees to sneak people into countries such as Canada and the United States. In 1998, for example, smugglers earned about $180 million sneaking human cargo into Canada.

In the summer of 1999, the plight of illegal migrants touched off a controversy. At different times, four ships carrying Chinese migrants were caught on their way to secret landing spots on the coast of British Columbia. Canadian officials found that the smugglers had charged the migrants an average of $57 000. Most migrants had made a down payment of $15 000. They then signed contracts promising to pay the rest of the money after they landed in North America.

The issue of illegal migrants inspired many editorial cartoonists during the summer of 1999. This cartoonist focused on what might have happened if the Coast Guard had discovered the characters on the long-running TV show *Gilligan's Island*. What is this cartoonist's message?

Illegal migrants who make it into North America are often exploited. The smugglers sell their contracts to employers, who pay the migrants low wages until their debt is paid off. This can take many years. In the meantime, the migrants cannot complain. If they seek help from the police or government officials, they risk being deported because they entered the country illegally.

Many of the illegal migrants on the four ships captured in 1999 tried to stay in Canada by claiming refugee status, but most were turned down. People who are simply seeking better economic opportunities are not considered refugees. What is more, known terrorists and war criminals, and people who have been convicted of serious crimes cannot be accepted as refugees.

In fact, most people claiming refugee status in Canada enter by land at the Canadian-American border. Another 5000 a year arrive by air. And every year, the government also chooses about 7300 refugees overseas.

Still, some people say that Canada has become a target for smuggling rings because illegal migrants can falsely claim refugee status. This delays their deportation until they are granted a hearing. When their hearing date finally arrives, some illegal migrants do not show up. Knowing their application will be turned down, they have slipped out of reach of the government officials who want to deport them.

Others Canadians believe that Canada has no choice but to respect international human rights agreements by allowing all refugees the opportunity to prove that their claims are real. If this means that a few people take advantage of the system, they believe that this is a small price to pay.

In April 2000, the minister of citizenship and immigration introduced new legislation in the House of Commons. Called the Immigration and Refugee Protection Act, the bill was designed to close Canada's back door to people who make false refugee claims or who try to sneak into the country.

The proposed law aims to do this by streamlining the refugee system. Its goal is to reduce the time it takes to go through the process of claiming refugee status. The law would also impose stiff penalties — fines of up to $1 million and life in prison — on people convicted of smuggling humans into Canada.

The minister also promised to change the rules to attract more immigrants to Canada through the front door. Rules governing family-class immigrants will be loosened, for example, so that people can sponsor more family members.

Most Canadians believe that Canada should

Some of the illegal migrants who arrived in the summer of 1999 are escorted off the ship that brought them to the coast of British Columbia.

help true refugees. There is less agreement, however, on how to define a true refugee. Some people say that the definition of refugees should include people fleeing desperate economic situations. Other people say that it should not.

http://www.school.mcgrawhill.ca/resources

To find out more about refugees, go to History Resources. Then go to *Civics: Participating in a Democratic Society* to see where to go next.

Think ... Discuss ... Act

Two of the Chinese women migrants who arrived in Canada on boats in 1999 argued that they should be granted refugee status because families in China are limited to one child. The women said that they wanted more than one child.

1. Do you think that this claim qualified the women to be true refugees? Why?
2. No country has a completely open-door immigration policy. Why not?
3. With a group, prepare an immigration policy that does not discriminate and is also realistic. Compare your group's policy with those of other groups. Pick the best of each and prepare a class policy.

RESOLVING INTERNATIONAL CONFLICTS

Since World War II, Canada has emerged as a middle power among the nations of the world. It is not a military superpower like the United States, nor does it have the power to influence the decisions of other countries.

Still, Canada has carved out a respected role in the world community and has been active in international organizations such as the United Nations and the North Atlantic Treaty Organization. Individual Canadians, too, have often played important roles on the international stage.

When nations are in conflict, countries and organizations in the international community use many tools to try to resolve disputes peacefully. Some of these tools are

- peacemaking — negotiating to prevent disputes from arising in the first place and to prevent existing disputes from erupting into armed conflict
- peacekeeping — placing troops between warring sides until a conflict can be resolved peacefully
- peace enforcement — sending troops to an area to stop one nation from attacking another

CANADA AND PEACEKEEPING

Involvement in international peacekeeping is a longstanding tradition in Canada. It is a cornerstone of Canadian foreign policy. Canada has taken part in most UN-sponsored missions. Since the early 1990s, Canadian forces have also participated actively in NATO-sponsored peacekeeping missions.

The United Nations Charter, the document that guides the operations of this international organization, requires peacekeeping missions to be approved by the Security Council.

Between 1957 and 1990, the Security Council authorized 18 peacekeeping missions. In the 1990s, however, the number of missions increased dramatically. Since 1991, the number of UN-sponsored peacekeeping missions has exceeded the total of the previous 43 years. The increase occurred because the Security Council became more willing to use peacekeeping as a tool for preventing and resolving conflicts. During the 1990s, Canadian peacekeepers took part in missions to countries such as the former Yugoslavia, Somalia, Rwanda, and Haiti.

As the number of peacekeeping missions has increased, the nature of peacekeeping has become more complicated. As well as the armed forces, missions may now include civilian police officers, advisers from Elections Canada, and health workers from organizations such as the Red Cross.

This is because restoring peace to war-torn regions is a long, difficult process. The process may include

- monitoring cease-fires and disarming warring factions
- providing medical attention to the sick and injured
- distributing relief supplies and helping refugees resettle in their homes
- preventing the spread of disease
- helping to organize a new government and hold elections

A Canadian peacekeeper wearing the blue helmet that identifies members of UN peacekeeping forces amuses a child in Bosnia. More than 30 000 Canadians have taken part in peacekeeping missions in various parts of the former Yugoslavia.

Not all Canadians support this country's active role in peacekeeping missions. Some people argue that the costs are too high. Although the United Nations provides some funding for Canadian troops on UN missions, the Canadian government pays most of the bill. People who oppose this expense say that the money would be better spent in Canada or in providing different kinds of help to war-torn areas.

More than 100 Canadians have been killed on peacekeeping missions. As a result, some critics say that peacekeeping is too dangerous.

An RCMP officer teaches a member of the Haitian police force how to question a suspect. Members of the RCMP were part of a peacekeeping force in Haiti. Their role was to help train Haitian police officers.

Criticism of peacekeeping is not restricted to Canada. The United Nations has been criticized for taking three to six months to organize peacekeeping missions. Critics say that this is too long.

As a result of the criticism, some member states, including Canada, have contributed troops to a 5000-member stand-by force. In an emergency, these troops can be sent quickly to trouble spots where they stay until they are replaced by regular UN peacekeepers.

Not all nations approve of the stand-by force. Some believe that it is the first step toward creating a standing army for the United Nations. They say that a standing army would give the UN — and the countries that dominate this organization — too much military power. What do you think?

More than 100 000 Canadians have served on international peacekeeping missions since 1949. This monument, which was unveiled in Ottawa in 1992, commemorates their contribution. The monument, which is called "Reconciliation," was the first of its kind in the world.

RECONCILIATION

Web Connection

http://www.school.mcgrawhill.ca/resources

To find out more about Canada's contributions to peacekeeping, go to History Resources. Then go to *Civics: Participating in a Democratic Society* to see where to go next.

Enforcing international human rights agreements is one of the most challenging issues facing the world today. The nations of the world must decide what steps, if any, should be taken to deal with people who violate these agreements.

During the 1990s, the United Nations grappled with a series of conflicts marked by extreme brutality. In countries such as Rwanda and the republics of the former country of Yugoslavia, people caught in the middle of these violent conflicts found that they had become the targets of genocide.

The Former Yugoslavia

Since 1991, bloody conflicts have raged in the republics of the former country of Yugoslavia. The conflicts involve rivalries among ethnic and religious groups that have been bitter enemies for centuries.

After World War I, Yugoslavia was created as a homeland for a variety of ethnic and religious groups who live in the Balkan Peninsula. From the beginning, the alliance was troubled.

After World War II, the Yugoslav federation was held together for 35 years by Josip Broz, a powerful communist dictator who was better known as Tito. When Tito died in 1980, Yugoslavia gradually began to break apart.

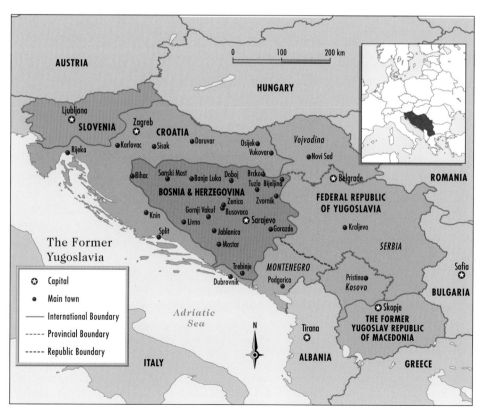

The Former Yugoslavia

Legend:
- ⊙ Capital
- ● Main town
- —— International Boundary
- ----- Provincial Boundary
- ----- Republic Boundary

Today, the Federal Republic of Yugoslavia includes only Serbia and the provinces of Vojvodina and Kosovo. Bosnia and Herzegovina, Croatia, Montenegro, and Macedonia broke away from the former Yugoslav federation in the early 1990s.

During the early 1990s, various republics that had been part of the federation declared independence and were recognized as independent states by the United Nations. In response, the government of Serbia — the largest and most powerful of the former Yugoslav republics — sent troops to these areas. Their mission was to protect the Serbs who lived in the breakaway republics. Most Serbs belong to the Eastern Orthodox church, a Christian faith.

Bosnia and Herzegovina was one of the republics that declared independence. There, Muslims made up 44 percent of the population. When the Serbian troops marched in, the Muslim population became the target of so-called ethnic cleansing, an organized campaign of terror and murder. At least 140 000 people were killed and another two million fled their homes.

Rwanda

Like the former Yugoslavia, the African country of Rwanda was also divided by bitter conflict between rival ethnic groups: the Hutu and the Tutsi. In 1994, the presidents of Rwanda and neighbouring Burundi met in Tanzania to talk about resolving the strife that was tearing apart both their countries. As the leaders flew home, their airplane was shot down. Everyone on board was killed.

The Hutu, who made up 90 percent of the population of Rwanda, blamed Tutsi terrorists for shooting down the plane. The word went out: kill all Tutsi. Soldiers, police officers, militia, and civilians participated in the systematic slaughter of about 800 000 Tutsi in a matter of months. More than two million other people fled the country.

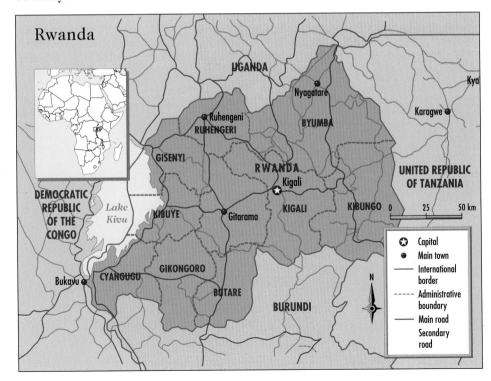

FYI

A Canadian peacekeeper tried in vain to sound the alarm about the coming genocide in Rwanda. Major-General Roméo Dallaire commanded a small United Nations mission in that country. Dallaire read the signs and realized that a terrible slaughter was looming. He appealed to UN officials to send more troops, but his warnings were dismissed. Once the killings started, his small force could do little to stop them.

Rwanda is a landlocked country in Central Africa. Burundi, Tanzania, Uganda, and the Democratic Republic of the Congo are its neighbours.

THE PURPOSEFUL CITIZEN

McGraw-Hill Ryerson Ltd.

International Criminal Tribunals

To deal with the genocide in Rwanda and the republics of the former Yugoslavia, the United Nations set up International Criminal Tribunals to investigate crimes against humanity and bring to justice those who had committed them. In the case of Rwanda, the UN was stepping into uncharted territory. Although it had sponsored similar hearings in Nuremberg after World War II, the Rwanda tribunal was different. It was set up to prosecute war criminals who had committed their crimes only within the borders of their own country.

Historically, the UN had become involved only in conflicts between nations. When civil conflict erupts within the borders of a sovereign nation, the UN says that this is a domestic affair. It must be resolved by the people of the country in their own way.

At the United Nations, some countries argued that the UN tribunal interfered in the domestic affairs of Rwanda. Other nations urged the UN to create a permanent tribunal to investigate human rights abuses, no matter where they occur, because they violate international human rights agreements. They say that the International Court of Justice deals only with disputes between governments. A permanent court is needed to deal with crimes against humanity, which are committed by individual people.

Some countries, such as the United States, supported setting up the Yugoslavia and Rwanda tribunals because each had a specific job. These countries stopped short of endorsing a permanent tribunal, however. They fear that a permanent tribunal with broad powers might try to interfere in *their* domestic affairs.

Today, some countries also question whether a permanent tribunal would treat all nations equally. They wonder whether alleged abuses by people in wealthy, powerful nations such as the United States would be treated the same as alleged abuses by people in poor and less powerful countries.

The UN tribunals have also been criticized for taking so long to lay charges in many of the cases — and for hesitating to lay charges in others. Some people have wondered, for example, why individual decision makers at NATO have not been called to account for their actions during the conflict between Serbia and the breakaway province of Kosovo.

Many of the people of Kosovo are ethnic Albanians who are mainly Muslim. When Kosovo tried to break away from Serbia, Serbian troops marched into the province and attacked ethnic Albanian communities.

When stories of atrocities in Kosovo started to appear in newspaper headlines, the international community feared a repeat of the so-called ethnic cleansing that had occurred earlier in Bosnia and Herzegovina. The UN Security Council debated a motion to intervene, but Russia and China vetoed the action. They said the conflict was a domestic matter within Serbia.

As a result of this decision, NATO decided to step in. NATO first asked the Serbian government to withdraw its troops from Kosovo.

A Day in the Life

LOUISE ARBOUR
BRINGING WAR CRIMINALS TO JUSTICE

When members of the United Nations Security Council named Canadian Louise Arbour chief prosecutor of the International Criminal Tribunals for Rwanda and the former Yugoslavia, they handed her one of the toughest jobs in the world. As chief prosecutor, Arbour's job was to bring to justice some of the most vicious war criminals of recent times.

The Security Council had set up the Yugoslavia tribunal in 1993 and the Rwanda tribunal in 1994. Based in The Hague, a city in the Netherlands, the mission of the tribunals was to find out what had happened during the brutal conflicts in both countries and bring to justice those who had committed crimes against humanity.

Arbour and the other prosecutors spent long hours searching out the evidence needed to bring charges against suspected war criminals. In both Rwanda and the former Yugoslavia, they visited mass burial sites and interviewed people who had witnessed atrocities. Arbour also negotiated with countries around the world to persuade them to share information that would help build the cases against the alleged criminals.

On August 18, 1999, the tribunal for the former Yugoslavia charged Slobodan Milosevic, president of Serbia, with committing war crimes. For Arbour and her colleagues, this was a big step. It marked the first time that a serving head of state had been called to account for allegedly committing war crimes — and served notice that Arbour did not consider anyone above the law.

To prove Milosevic's guilt, however, tribunal prosecutors must now present evidence that he personally ordered specific atrocities. So far, Milosevic has refused to co-operate with the tribunal. He has also eluded prosecutors' efforts to arrest him so that he can be taken to The Hague to stand trial.

If Milosevic is ever brought to trial, Arbour will not lead the prosecution. In September 1999, she decided that it was time to move on. She left the international tribunal to take up an appointment as a justice of the Supreme Court of Canada.

Arbour is proud of her role in helping bring to justice those who committed crimes against humanity. She brought credibility to the chief prosecutor's position by convincing Western governments to help the tribunal. In one case involving the Rwanda conflict, she recorded the first conviction for genocide since the international law against genocide was created in 1948.

On one of her trips to gather evidence of war crimes, Louise Arbour talks to an ethnic Albanian woman in Kosovo. Before being appointed chief prosecutor for the UN's International Criminal Tribunals, Arbour was a lawyer and judge in Ontario.

When Serbia refused, NATO forces began to bomb Serbian targets far from the Kosovo war zone. The bombings killed or injured many civilians and destroyed billions of dollars worth of civilian property.

When Serbian government officials were unable to persuade the international criminal tribunals to charge individual NATO decision makers with war crimes, they took their case to the International Court of Justice. They charged 10 countries, including Canada, Spain, the United Kingdom, and the United States with violating the UN Charter. The Charter bars UN members from using force against other member countries.

When NATO peacekeepers entered Kosovo, ethnic Albanians who had been hiding from Serbian troops started to emerge from hiding places in the country around their villages. Hundreds of thousands of other Kosovars had escaped to refugee camps.

The International Court ruled that it had no right to hear the case against the United States and Spain. It is still hearing arguments about whether it had the right to rule on the charges against the eight other countries, including Canada.

NATO officials argue that the bombings were justified because they saved countless lives. They say that this was the only way of forcing Serbia to pull its troops out of Kosovo so that NATO peacekeepers could move in and restore order.

Truth and Reconciliation Commissions

In some countries where human rights abuses have occurred, people have chosen a different way of dealing with these crimes. When apartheid was finally abolished and all South Africans gained full civil and human rights in 1993, for example, the South African government decided to set up the Truth and Reconciliation Commission. **Reconciliation** means settling a conflict by helping the two sides accept and co-operate with each other.

The commission's goal was to promote national unity by healing the terrible wounds that had been inflicted during the apartheid era. This was to be achieved not by punishing those who had committed the crimes, but by trying to reconcile those who had committed the abuses and those who had been victims of the abuses.

Under the leadership of Archbishop Desmond Tutu, the commission is hearing the stories of victims and making reparations — compensating victims for the harm suffered. The commission also has the power to grant amnesty to people who come forward and confess their crimes, provided they meet the following conditions:

- the crime happened between 1960 and 1993
- the crime was politically motivated in keeping with either government policy at the time or the policy of a liberation movement
- the person who committed the crime tells the complete truth about what happened

Tutu expressed the goals of the commission in a speech that opened its first session in 1995. He said, "Freedom and justice must become realities for all our people, and we have the privilege of helping to heal the hurts of the past, to transcend the alienations and hostilities of that past so that we can close the door on that past and concentrate on the present and our glorious future."

Countries such as Chile, Argentina, and Brazil have established similar commissions to deal with human rights abuses that occurred in the 1960s and 1970s when those countries were ruled by military dictators.

A truth and reconciliation commission is effective, however, only when everyone is willing to participate and truly wants reconciliation. If one side wants revenge, reconciliation may be impossible.

Archbishop Desmond Tutu, chair of South Africa's Truth and Reconciliation Commission, welcomes a witness to the commission's opening session. The woman planned to give evidence about the kidnapping and disappearance of her husband during the apartheid era.

Think … Discuss … Act

Some people say that the strains created by global instability have reduced the effectiveness of the United Nations. Others argue that the UN is poised to enter a new era when it will become even more important than ever.

1. Has the UN set a dangerous precedent by interfering in the internal affairs of some countries? Why?
2. Find out more about the conflicts that led to outbreaks of violence in Somalia, Rwanda, the former Yugoslavia, or another country. Describe the conflict and suggest ways of resolving it peacefully. Should the Canadian government play a role in this process? How?

A VOICE FOR CITIZENS OF THE WORLD

When government leaders gather to debate issues within organizations such as the United Nations and NATO, individual citizens have little opportunity to influence decisions. To make their voices heard, citizens of many countries have turned to **non-governmental organizations**, also known as NGOs.

NGOs are non-profit, non-partisan, independent organizations dedicated to making the world a better place. Many people in many countries volunteer their time and money to help NGOs achieve particular goals. Amnesty International, Greenpeace, the Red Cross, and Médecins sans frontières (Doctors without Borders) are examples of NGOs that play active roles in the global community.

Rock star Bruce Springsteen was one of many performers who volunteered to take part in a concert in Paris. The 1998 concert, sponsored by Amnesty International, celebrated the 50th anniversary of the Universal Declaration of Human Rights.

Amnesty International

In 1961, a British lawyer read about Portuguese students who had been thrown in jail for toasting freedom in a restaurant. At the time, Portugal was ruled by the dictator António de Oliveira Salazar.

The lawyer began a letter-writing campaign. If enough people wrote to Salazar, the lawyer believed that the dictator would be forced to free the students. This campaign evolved into Amnesty International, which now has members in 162 countries.

Members of Amnesty International work to ensure that the rights enshrined in the Universal Declaration of Human Rights are respected around the world. Their goals are to free **prisoners of conscience** — people who have been sentenced to prison because of their beliefs — and to end political killings and human rights abuses, such as the death penalty, torture, and other cruel punishments. To do this, its members monitor government actions in countries around the world.

Greenpeace

Greenpeace was founded in Vancouver in 1971. It started as the Don't Make a Wave Committee. The committee's goal was to prevent the United States from conducting nuclear tests on an island off the coast of Alaska. The island was home to many endangered species, such as sea otters, bald eagles, and peregrine falcons.

Though the committee failed to stop the nuclear tests, it kept working. It eventually evolved into an international organization dedicated to making the world green and peaceful. It called itself Greenpeace.

Greenpeace often organizes high-profile protests against actions that threaten the environment. Its other work, which attracts less publicity, is just as important, though. Its goals are to protect the environment; end pollution and nuclear threats; and promote peace, disarmament, and non-violence by researching solutions to problems and offering alternatives.

Red Cross

The familiar flag of the lifesaver — a red cross on a white background — first appeared in Canada on the battlefield near Batoche, Saskatchewan, in 1885. In the confrontation between Gabriel Dumont's Métis forces and the Canadian militia, 50 men died and dozens more were injured. The death toll would have been higher had it not been for George Sterling Ryerson. This volunteer doctor drove his wagon onto the battlefield to care for the wounded of both sides. Everyone knew that the red cross on the side of Ryerson's wagon meant that he was neutral and was not to be fired on.

The Red Cross, which is called the Red Crescent in Islamic countries, had been founded more than 20 years earlier by Jean-Henri Dunant, a young Swiss businessperson. In 1859, Dunant witnessed the Battle of Solferino, which occurred during the Italian war for independence. In the battle, about 29 000 people were killed or wounded. Dunant organized a group of volunteers to help the victims.

In 1864, Dunant persuaded the Swiss government to hold an international conference to found a volunteer society to help war victims. The conference drafted the first **Geneva Convention**, which set out rules for the treatment of soldiers and civilians during wartime. Within three years, the convention had been signed by all the major European powers.

In 1909, the Canadian government established the Canadian Red Cross Society. Canadian Red Cross volunteers saw action in both

FYI

Since 1864, other international conventions, or treaties, have also been signed. This collection of rules is called International Humanitarian Law or the "laws of war." These laws set out how soldiers, prisoners of war, and civilians caught up in war must be treated. The laws also govern how wars are fought and the weapons that can be used. The Red Cross and Red Crescent are responsible for promoting the rules, which most countries have agreed to.

World Wars. They operated ambulances, staffed hospitals, and cared for veterans and orphaned children.

Today, Red Cross and Red Crescent societies exist in more than 170 countries. Red Cross volunteers number about 250 million. The work of

the Red Cross and Red Crescent has expanded greatly. Providing disaster relief is one of their biggest tasks today. When Hurricane Mitch ripped through the West Indies in 1998, for example, Red Cross volunteers were there. They helped people get food, water, shelter, and clothing. Today, the Red Cross continues to provide medical services in some of the 40 wars that are now being fought around the world.

Recently, the Red Cross spearheaded the battle to save civilians from land mines. Land mines are small bombs that are hidden under the surface of the soil in war zones. When armies withdraw from these zones, they

After his experience at Batoche, Dr. George Sterling Ryerson campaigned for a Red Cross society in Canada. He set up a Canadian branch of the British Red Cross Society in 1896. This work led to the founding of the Canadian Red Cross Society in 1909.

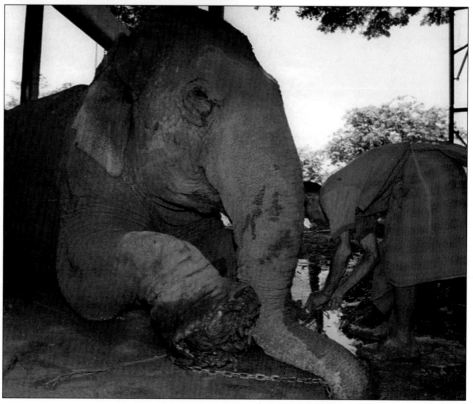

A 40-year-old cow elephant waits for treatment after her right front foot was injured when she stepped on a land mine in Thailand.

often leave live mines behind. About 26 000 people are injured every year when they step on unexploded land mines.

Because they help victims of war, Red Cross workers often see the damage done by land mines. In the 1990s, the organization worked with other NGOs to persuade more than 100 countries to sign the International Land Mines Treaty, a 1997 agreement banning the use of the mines. This agreement is sometimes called the Ottawa Treaty because it was signed in Canada's capital.

The Canadian government has played an active role in the campaign to ban land mines. In 1998, for example, Canada donated more than US$10 million to help remove mines that had been left behind after the conflict in Bosnia and Herzegovina.

Web Connection

http://www.school.mcgrawhill.ca/resources

To find out more about the Red Cross, Amnesty International, Greenpeace, or Médecins sans frontières (Doctors without Borders), go to History Resources. Then go to *Civics: Participating in a Democratic Society* to see where to go next.

Think ... Discuss ... Act

At the end of 1999, *Time* magazine declared Albert Einstein the most important person of the 20th century. Though Einstein is most famous for his theories that led to the development of nuclear energy, he was also very concerned about citizenship. He believed that people need a sense of community. At the same time, he recognized that a sense of community can lead to blind nationalism — and that blind nationalism can spark intolerance, prejudice, and even warfare. As a result, Einstein did not believe in national borders — or the standing armies that protect national borders.

1. Is it possible for a country to exist without an army? Explain why you do or do not think so.
2. Can someone who believes strongly in Canada and Canadian values also respect the values of people of other countries and cultures? Why?
3. Work with a group to make a list of the rights and responsibilities of global citizens. Compare your group's list with those of other groups. Create a declaration of global citizenship for your class.
4. Discuss the process of creating your class declaration. Does it reflect everyone's ideas? How much negotiation was involved? Did the process involve consensus or majority rule? What did you learn from the process?

JAMES ORBINSKI
MÉDECINS SANS FRONTIÈRES

When James Orbinski, a Canadian doctor, stepped to the lectern to accept the 1999 Nobel Peace Prize on behalf of Médecins sans frontières — also known as MSF — the audience was in for a big surprise. Instead of delivering the standard acceptance speech, Orbinski took the opportunity to denounce Russia for continuing its bombing campaign in Chechnya.

"The people of Chechnya ... today and for more than three months are enduring indiscriminate bombing by the Russian army," Orbinski told the audience. "For them, humanitarian assistance is virtually unknown."

These were tough words — but toughness is an MSF tradition. Members of the organization, which is better known in North America as Doctors without Borders, believe that humanitarian agencies have the right to interfere to save lives. They also believe in speaking out, loudly and publicly, when they see abuses.

MSF was founded in 1971 by two young French doctors who had worked with the Red Cross during the Biafran War in Nigeria. At the time, it was customary for aid agencies to enter countries only with government permission. After returning to Paris, the men decided to found a group of dedicated physicians who would be willing to provide medical help wherever it was needed — without waiting for government permission.

Their first mission was to help earthquake victims in Nicaragua in 1972. Four years later, MSF volunteers went to Lebanon, which marked their first experience in a war zone. MSF volunteers from more than 45 nations now work in more than 80 countries around the world.

Most physicians, nurses, and other staff donate between six months and two years of their time. Funded by private donations, MSF is dedicated to providing medical relief to those in need because of natural disasters, human-made disasters, war, or poverty.

The Nobel Peace Prize recognized MSF's contribution to world peace. In bestowing the award, the Nobel committee said, "... [MSF] calls attention to humanitarian catastrophes, and by pointing to the causes of such catastrophes, the organization helps to form bodies of public opinion opposed to violations and abuses of power."

James Orbinski speaks during the ceremony awarding the Nobel Peace Prize to Médecins sans frontières (Doctors without Borders). Orbinski co-founded MSF Canada in 1990 and became president of the group's international council in 1998.

As the last half of the 20th century unfolded, many businesses were no longer content to attract customers only from their own community, region, or country. Improvements in transportation and communication meant that they could sell — and buy — products in countries around the world. By 1997, the value of international trade was 14 times higher than it had been in 1950. Businesses everywhere were plunging into the global marketplace and lobbying governments to streamline the process of trading with other nations.

Free Trade

The Canadian government and many Canadian businesses have embraced the idea of a global marketplace where trade barriers will be reduced or even eliminated completely.

In 1989, the Canadian government signed its first comprehensive free trade agreement with the United States. This agreement started a process of eliminating **tariffs** between the two countries. Tariffs are taxes on goods and services imported from other countries.

The agreement also set up a panel to resolve trade disputes between the two countries. The Canadian government agreed to ease its laws limiting American investment in Canada and to stop restricting sales to the United States of Canadian energy resources, except in times of shortage.

This cartoon voiced the fears of many people when free trade was introduced: that the Canadian identity would be swallowed up by the United States. What was the cartoonist's message about these fears?

Five years later, the North American Free Trade Agreement, known as NAFTA, replaced the original agreement. NAFTA includes Canada, the United States, and Mexico. These three countries are members of the world's largest free trade zone.

The World Trade Organization

Until after World War II, most national governments imposed tariffs on products imported from other countries. By making imported goods more expensive, tariffs protected domestic industries against competition. This also protected jobs. Tariffs were also a source of money for governments.

FYI

Mexico had no environmental protection laws until 1988. It took another four years for the country to create an agency to enforce the laws that had been passed. This meant that companies did not worry about controlling pollution from their manufacturing operations.

During the Great Depression of the 1930s, many countries raised their tariffs on imports to try to stimulate their own economy, create jobs, and generate government revenue. These policies had the opposite effect, however. As international trade ground to a near halt, the prices of many goods increased. For people who were already struggling to make ends meet, higher prices made life even harder.

After World War II, countries did not want to repeat the mistakes made during the Depression. In 1947, representatives of 23 countries that accounted for 80 percent of world trade met in Geneva, Switzerland. There, they signed the General Agreement on Tariffs and Trade, also known as the GATT.

The GATT was both an agreement and an organization. Its purpose was to reduce tariffs among countries and streamline international trade. As an organization, the GATT was supposed to be temporary. It was to operate only until a United Nations organization could be set up to replace it. The UN organization never materialized, however. As a result, the GATT existed for nearly 50 years.

During this time, world trade grew even more important, and GATT members met frequently to work out trade issues. Finally, in 1995, the World Trade Organization, also known as the WTO, was created to replace the GATT. The GATT agreement was incorporated into WTO agreements on international trade.

The WTO plays a larger role in world trade than the GATT did. The GATT was concerned only with trade in manufactured products. WTO rules apply to trade in products, services, and **intellectual property**. Intellectual property is the name given to the products of creative efforts, such as patents and copyrights.

By the end of 1999, the WTO included 135 member nations. Its goals are to promote freer trade and settle trade disputes by setting out clear rules that member states must follow. One of these rules requires member nations to treat other member nations equally.

These cars were manufactured in Canada. To protect auto-manufacturing jobs in Canada, the Canadian government imposes tariffs on cars imported from Japan. Both Canada and Japan are members of the WTO. The Japanese government has said that the Canadian import tariff on cars violates WTO rules. If this is true, should the WTO be able to stop the Canadian government from taxing Japanese cars?

Supporters of freer trade believe that getting rid of trade barriers is the best way to increase wealth and improve living standards around the world. They also believe that having a body to mediate trade disputes eliminates costly trade wars between nations.

Many people oppose the WTO and its rules, however. To ensure fairness in trading, for example, the WTO can overrule the decisions of democratically elected governments. Some people believe that this makes the WTO too powerful. Other people worry that the WTO is too focused on business interests and ignores social, health, and environmental concerns.

Many Canadians and Americans, for example, complain that the new trading rules have drained well-paid manufacturing jobs out of their countries. They point to the many companies that have closed factories in Canada and the United States and moved to countries where wages are lower and rules about working conditions and the environment are less strict. These conditions mean that factories in other countries can produce cheaper goods.

In Mexico, for example, special manufacturing zones called *maquiladoras* have been set up along the border with the United States. Factories called *maquilas* locate in the *maquiladoras* to take advantage of cheap Mexican labour.

In the Mexican *maquilas*, workers complain about abusive working conditions, extremely low wages, and terrible living conditions. Many children are forced to work instead of going to school because their families need the money. This creates a cycle of poverty that is hard to break.

The issue of low wages and poor working conditions in developing countries raises difficult questions for citizens of developed countries. The current system benefits consumers in countries like Canada. Products made by low-paid workers in developing countries can be imported to Canada and sold cheaply. This keeps prices down for consumers — but at what cost?

A worker in a Mexican *maquila* puts together seat belt components that will be exported to the United States.

As citizens in a global economy, should Canadian consumers be concerned about environmental, social, and labour issues in developing countries? Should Canadian citizens press the government to raise these issues with the WTO? Some people believe that the answer to these questions is yes.

From November 30 to December 3, 1999, for example, WTO delegates met in Seattle, Washington. Environmentalists and social and labour activists gathered outside the meeting to express their dissatisfaction with WTO policies. The protest became the largest in the United States since the Vietnam War.

In the end, little was achieved at the Seattle talks. Developing countries lobbied successfully to keep delegates from discussing labour issues. These nations complain that pressure to improve conditions for workers in their countries is nothing but a ploy to protect jobs in wealthier nations.

What comment is the cartoonist making about the protest at the 1999 WTO meeting in Seattle, Washington?

Many Canadian farmers were unhappy that WTO delegates were unable to reach an agreement on agricultural subsidies. Canadian farmers have trouble competing with farmers in Europe and Japan, where agricultural products are heavily subsidized by governments.

When some people at the 1999 WTO meeting in Seattle, Washington, began to vandalize buildings and loot stores, police used tear gas and force to break up the crowds. Finally, the National Guard was called in to restore order and a curfew was imposed.

Canadian farmers believe that this amounts to unfair competition and want the WTO to do something about it.

The issue of freer trade raises many questions for Canadians. Does it create or destroy jobs? Does it threaten Canadian culture? Does it threaten Canadian political sovereignty and decisions made by democratically elected governments? Does it encourage or discourage foreign investment in Canada? Does it benefit the people of Canada or big business — or both? The debate over these questions has just begun.

THE GLOBAL ECONOMY, HUMAN RIGHTS, AND THE ENVIRONMENT

If governments can agree to take action on trade issues, many Canadians believe that they should also be able to agree to take action on human rights and environmental issues. Some non-governmental organizations have lobbied leaders of developed countries such as Canada to use trade as a lever to persuade other countries to improve their human rights and environmental protection records.

So far, developing countries have resisted this idea. In 1993, for example, China and other nations attending an Asian conference endorsed the Bangkok Declaration. The declaration included a statement saying that the countries that signed the agreement would discourage attempts by other countries to use human rights as a condition for extending development assistance.

For human rights activists, the Canadian government's reluctance to require their trading partners to improve their human rights records is frustrating. In Indonesia, for example, Canada continued to trade with and offer aid to the government of President Suharto. At the same time, Indonesian troops were engaged in a violent campaign to force the former Portuguese colony of East Timor to become a province of Indonesia.

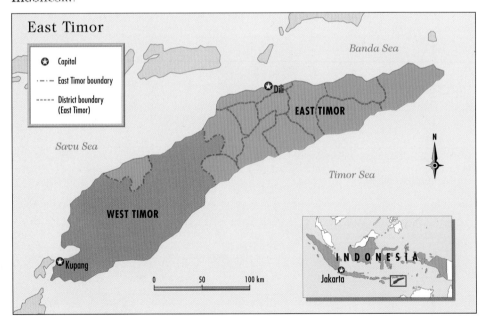

When the people of East Timor resisted Indonesian President Suharto's plans to make their country a province of Indonesia, Indonesian troops moved in and waged a brutal campaign to make the East Timorese change their minds.

THE PURPOSEFUL CITIZEN   McGraw-Hill Ryerson Ltd.

The issue of using **biotechnology** to alter the food people eat has sparked intense debate among scientists, farmers, corporations, consumers, and governments. Biotechnology is the science of using technology to change the natural biology of plants and animals.

In January 2000, delegates from 130 countries gathered at a conference in Montréal to talk about making rules for using biotechnology to alter foods.

A group of 150 Canadian scientists wrote an open letter supporting biotechnology. They argued that it helps create more nutritious food that can also protect people against disease and allergies. "We know, for example, that foods like tomatoes and broccoli contain phytochemicals that can help protect us against cancer and heart disease," wrote the scientists. "Through biotechnology, we can enhance the levels of these chemicals in foods and, perhaps, transfer them to other foods."

The scientists appealed to the public not to overreact to fears about the harmful potential of biotechnology.

At the same time, protesters gathered outside the meeting hall to urge delegates to impose strict rules on the use of biotechnology. "[Scientists] are putting plant genes into animals and animal genes into plants, and they are changing nature, and we don't really know what will happen to us in the future," one protester said.

A nutritional consultant said that she is "very concerned about the lack of knowledge the public has about the effects of genetically altered foods. We don't want to be used as guinea pigs in order to find out what the end result is. We may not know for 50 years or so."

Some governments have already tried to restrict imports of genetically modified foods, also known as genetically modified organisms or GMOs. They believe that GMOs pose a risk for people and the environment.

Countries such as Canada, the United States, Argentina, Australia, Uruguay, and Chile have protested the trade restrictions. They say that many farmers in their countries grow food from genetically altered seeds. These farmers will suffer if they cannot export their produce.

Right now, all the groups involved in the issue can agree on only one thing: the debate over the ethics and safety of biotechnology is just beginning.

A Greenpeace member is hoisted past the mouth of a giant corn cob outside an international conference on genetically modified foods in Montréal in January 2000. The man was helping to string up a banner protesting the use of biotechnology to alter food.

The Active Citizen

1. What role can everyday citizens play in the debate over biotechnology? Brainstorm to create a list of things that citizens can do.

2. Choose one of the actions on this list. With a partner or group, carry out the action and report the results to the class.

Even when reports started to surface that Timorese people were being starved and murdered, other governments took no action. It took NGOs years to persuade the international community to pay attention to what was happening in the remote area. All this time, trade with Indonesia was never interrupted.

People have also come to realize that protecting the environment is an international challenge that is closely linked to economics. Water and air pollution do not heed international boundaries. Other environmental issues that concern the world community are soil erosion and reduced soil fertility and **biodiversity**. Biodiversity refers to diverse plant and animal species. As plants and animals become extinct, biodiversity is reduced. As the number of species shrinks, scientists fear that a plague or other disaster could easily wipe out the species that remain.

Dealing with hazardous waste is also an environmental challenge that is linked to economics. Hazardous waste is the toxic or radioactive material created by manufacturing processes. It is hazardous to human and environmental health. Hazardous waste must be disposed of safely or recycled into other products.

Global warming is another environmental concern. Canada experienced record-breaking warm temperatures in the 1990s, sparking fears that pollution has speeded up global warming.

In 1992, an Earth Summit was held in Rio de Janeiro, Brazil. There, Canada and other countries signed an eco-pact. The pact recognized the link between poverty and the degradation of the environment, pledged to protect biodiversity, and set goals for reducing pollution.

As his Chinese government-appointed guard runs alongside, Prime Minister Jean Chrétien rides a bicycle in Shanghai. Though Chrétien has discussed human rights with leaders of developing countries, he has not linked the issue to trade or aid.

The countries at the summit also agreed to pass laws requiring industries to reduce greenhouse gas emissions. Greenhouse gases such as carbon dioxide cause global warming. They absorb heat radiated from the earth's surface and help keep this heat in the earth's atmosphere.

The agreement called for reducing greenhouse gas emissions to 1990 levels by the year 2000. In fact, most developed countries failed to reach this target because introducing equipment to reduce emissions is costly for industries.

In 1997, representatives of many countries gathered to talk about climate change at a UN-sponsored conference in Kyoto, Japan. Conference delegates endorsed the Kyoto Protocol. This is an agreement to limit carbon emissions from cars, power plants, and major users of fossil fuels such as coal.

Prime Minister Jean Chrétien addresses a 1997 meeting of the United Nations General Assembly. The meeting was called to monitor the progress of agreements made at the 1992 Earth Summit.

Not everyone agreed that the protocol was a good idea, however. The American Senate, for example, voted to reject it. Senators opposed to the agreement warned that its restrictions would lead to job losses and reduced economic growth.

The senators' position highlights the difficulty of striking a balance between protecting the environment and maintaining economic growth.

Think ... Discuss ... Act

Corporation X wants to build a large factory in your community, where many people are unemployed. The factory would create hundreds of jobs, including summer jobs for students. As a result, many residents welcome the factory. There is one problem, however. The manufacturing process used by the factory creates hazardous waste. This waste would raise the level of air, water, and soil pollution in your community. As a result, some people in the community are trying to stop the project. The community is split over whether to accept or reject the factory.

1. Describe how you would decide where you stand on this issue.
2. Are accepting or rejecting this factory the community's only options? Discuss other options that might be explored.
3. In taking a stand on this issue, is your only responsibility to the people of your community? Create a graphic organizer showing how your stand might affect the people of your province, region, country, and the world.

CHAPTER REVIEW

SUMMING IT UP

Many challenges face the international community. No individual citizen, non-governmental organization, or national government can successfully meet these challenges without the support and co-operation of others. People who want to help make the world a better place have found many ways of doing this. They have made choices about when and how they wish to contribute to the world community.

1. Choose several issues raised in this chapter and rank them according to their importance to you. Record your responses on a chart. Use the following headings as a guide:

Most Important Issues	Reasons I Think So	Action I Could Take

2. Compare your choices and ideas with those of the other students in the class. Using the same headings, rank the issues according to their importance to the class.

3. Add terms from this chapter to your list of New Words with Special Meaning.

GETTING THE FACTS

1. Distinguish between political and economic refugees. Should they be treated the same or differently? Why?

2. Write a few sentences identifying the importance of the following issues and organizations in the global community:

   biotechnology   Médecins sans frontières
   Amnesty International   peacekeepers
   global warming   Red Cross
   Greenpeace   Truth and Reconciliation Commission
   International Criminal Tribunal   United Nations Security Council
   maquiladoras   World Trade Organization

3. Many non-governmental organizations, such as Earth Summit Watch and Project Ploughshares, were not mentioned in this chapter. Brainstorm to make a list of other NGOs you have heard about. Choose one and report to the class on its role in the international community.

4. Many students in your class or school may already be active in organizations whose goal is to make your school, community, country, or the world a better place. Invite several of these students to your class to talk about how they contribute to the work of the organization they belong to. Prepare for the visit by creating a list of questions to ask.

USING THE FACTS

1. Though individual citizens can take action on issues that concern the global community, many people believe that combining their efforts with those of others is more effective. Refer to the chart of important issues created earlier. What can you or your class do to help resolve these issues?

2. Clip a newspaper article that deals with one of the issues raised in this chapter. Make a list of people whose comments on the issue are quoted in the article. Beside each name, record the name of the organization the person represents. If the person is speaking as an individual citizen, record this information. Then assess the bias of each person. Record the information on a chart like the following.

Name	Organization	Bias

Which person's comments do you take most seriously? Why? Do you think the writer of the article presented the debate impartially? Why?

3. Research and report to the class on how one of the following people — or another person you may know about — has helped make the world a better place:

Jean Vanier
David Suzuki
Mother Teresa
Cardinal Paul-Émile Léger

4. Amnesty International is a non-governmental organization that tracks and reports on human rights abuses. Go to the Amnesty Web site (see directions on p. 180) to find out about violations this organization has "red-flagged." Report to the class on one of these violations. What action could you take to help correct it?

Review the words of Plato quoted in the Unit Review on page 110 and refer to the graphic organizer you created at that time.

Picture yourself as the citizen at the centre of the whirlpool Plato described. What ideas are swirling around you as you complete this unit?

As you did at the end of Unit 1, create a graphic organizer like the one shown here. Begin by filling in the five ideas you recorded at the end of Unit 1. Then record an important idea from this unit in each of the five blank circles that are left. Once again, be prepared to defend your selections.

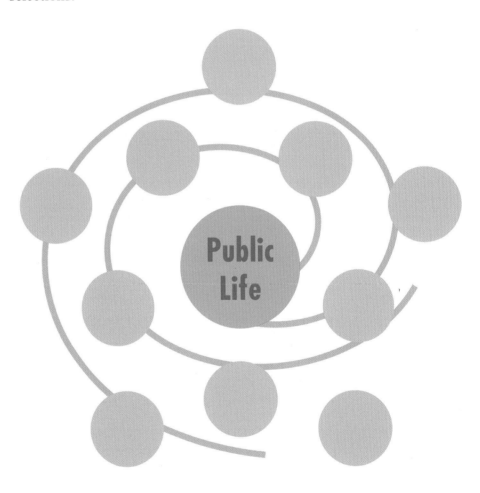

Prepare a brief class lesson based on one of the ideas recorded on your organizer. Create another organizer to record points you plan to include in your lesson. Once your lesson is planned, teach it to your classmates.

FOCUS YOUR LEARNING

1. Andy Warhol, an American pop artist and philosopher, once wrote: "In the future, everyone will be world-famous for 15 minutes." Though Warhol was probably joking when he made this statement, the idea that fame passes quickly has caught people's imaginations. The names of some people mentioned in this unit are likely to be forgotten quickly. Other names will be remembered because of the issues they raised or the actions they took. Classify the people listed below under the following headings:

   Terry Fox   Svend Robinson   Sue Rodriguez   James Keegstra   Craig Kielburger
   Paul Okalik   Pierre Trudeau   Elijah Harper   Louise Arbour

Name	Issue Raised	Will the name be remembered or forgotten?	Why?

2. a) How does Canada contribute to the international community through the following organizations?

   United Nations, North Atlantic Treaty Organization, non-governmental organizations, such as Greenpeace and Doctors without Borders, World Trade Organization

   b) Do you contribute to any of these organizations? How? If you do not contribute now, do you think you will in the future? Why?

3. Invite a peacekeeper to visit your class to explain his or her role. Prepare for the visit by finding out about the country where the peacekeeper served. Before the visit, create a list of things you would like to learn from the visit. After the visit, create a list of things you learned.

APPLY YOUR LEARNING

1. Citizenship is a lifelong experience where some people become increasingly conscious of the community, region, and nation in which they live. Others do not.

   Debate the truth of this statement. How would you rate your own civic awareness and sense of civic purpose?

3. With a partner, choose a local, provincial, national, or international issue that is currently in the news. For two weeks, collect information about the issue — newspaper articles, magazine articles, material from the Internet, or videotapes of television news or current affairs programs. With your partner, prepare a conversation that might take place between two people involved in the issue. To bring out the arguments on both sides, choose people whose views conflict. Present your conversation to the class.

REFLECT ON YOUR LEARNING

1. Terry Fox is a shining example of a Canadian whose sense of civic purpose inspired him to take action. Many other Canadians have done the same. If asked to pick one person as an example of a good citizen, whom would you choose? Your choice might be someone mentioned in this book, a national or international figure, or a parent, friend, or neighbour. Write a short editorial explaining your choice. Title the editorial "A Good Citizen."

GLOSSARY

Absolute monarch An all-powerful king or queen who makes laws that his or her subjects must obey.

Allophone An immigrant, usually to Québec, whose first language is neither English nor French.

Amending formula A procedure for changing the Constitution.

Amnesty A pardon, often for political crimes, that usually applies to everyone.

Anarchy A breakdown of law and order, in which the government is ineffective or non-existent.

Anglophone Someone who speaks English.

Apartheid A South African system of segregating people according to their race. Apartheid was abolished in 1993.

Arbitration The hearing of a dispute by a referee or arbitrator who has the power to decide on a settlement. Before the hearing, both sides usually agree on the identity of the arbitrator and to abide by the arbitrator's decision.

Authoritarianism A kind of government system that requires complete obedience to the will of the ruler. No individual freedom is allowed.

Balance of power The power held after an election by a political party with a small number of seats when the number of seats held by two or more other political parties is equal or nearly equal.

BCE Before the Common Era. This refers to the years before the birth of Christ and is often used instead of BC, which means Before Christ.

Biodiversity A variety of species of plants and animals.

Biotechnology The science of using technology to change the natural biology of plants and animals.

Boycott To punish a company or country by refusing to buy its goods or services.

CE The Common Era. This refers to years after the birth of Christ and is often used in place of AD, which is an abbreviation of the Latin phrase *Anno Domini* (in the year of the Lord).

Censorship The act of examining books, films, television programs, and other media to delete material or information that is considered offensive. In peacetime, governments sometimes introduce censorship to protect public morals or to stop the spread of political ideas they do not like. In wartime, it may be introduced to safeguard national security.

Citizen Someone who is by birth or naturalization a legal member of a nation and who, as a result, has the rights and responsibilities of citizenship.

City state An independent, self-governing city that is not part of a larger nation.

Civic conflict A dispute or disagreement between citizens.

Civil disobedience The refusal to obey laws in order to force a government to change the laws.

Civil law Laws that relate to disputes or disagreements between citizens, rather than to criminal acts, which are considered crimes against the state.

Civil war A war between the citizens of a country.

Coalition The joining together of people, political parties, or nations.

Cold War A rivalry between countries that stops short of full-scale war. From 1945 to 1990, the United States and the Soviet Unions, along with their allies, engaged in the Cold War.

Collective bargaining The act of negotiating a collective agreement between unionized workers and their employer. Collective

McGraw-Hill Ryerson Ltd.

agreements usually cover issues such as wages, benefits, and working conditions.

Communist Party A political party whose members believe that the state should control the economy and the means of production.

Conscription Compulsory military service.

Consensus General agreement, usually reached after an issue has been thoroughly discussed.

Constituency A geographical area in which the people elect a representative to a provincial or federal legislature. In Canada, a constituency is also called a riding and an electoral district.

Constitution A written or unwritten collection of laws, court decisions, and conventions that sets out how a government will operate.

Constitutional monarchy A system of government in which a monarch is the head of state. The monarch's powers are, however, limited by the country's constitution.

Co-operative federalism A power-sharing arrangement between the federal government and the provincial governments.

Coup The sudden overthrow of a government. It is a short form of the French phrase *coup d'état*.

Cultural mosaic A situation in which people of various origins are encouraged to remember and take pride in their cultural roots. A mosaic is a picture or design created by setting small pieces of coloured glass, stone, or tile onto a surface.

Democracy A government system in which the people rule.

Deport To banish or expel someone from a country, usually to his or her country of origin.

Direct democracy A government system in which the people make decisions directly.

Federal, federalism A government system in which provinces or states share certain powers with the national government.

Francophone A French-speaking person.

Geneva Convention Any of a series of international treaties signed at Geneva, Switzerland. The purpose of the conventions is to set out rules governing how soldiers and civilians must be treated in times of war.

Genocide The planned extermination of people from a cultural or racial group. The Holocaust was an attempted genocide of the Jewish people.

Hazardous waste Toxic or radioactive material created by manufacturing processes.

Head of government A political official, often elected, who leads a government. In Canada, the prime minister is the head of government.

Head of state An official, who may be elected or unelected, who performs ceremonial functions on behalf of the people of a country and who stands apart from political debates and conflicts. In Canada, the head of state is the British monarch, who is represented by the governor general.

Holocaust The Holocaust, which is usually spelled with a capital letter, refers to the systematic murder of millions of Jews by the Nazis during World War II. In Hebrew, it is called the Sho'ah.

Indirect democracy A government system in which people do not make decisions directly; instead, they elect representatives to make decisions on their behalf. This system is sometimes called representative democracy.

Intellectual property The product of creative efforts, such as patents and copyrights.

Junta A group of military officers who rule a country after taking over the government by force.

Legislature A body that has the power to make laws.

Libel The act of damaging someone's reputation by writing something that is not true.

Lobby Try to persuade.

Majority government A government formed by the political party whose representatives won more seats in a legislature than all the other political parties combined.

Maquiladora A special manufacturing zone on the Mexican side of the Mexico-United States border. *Maquiladoras* are set up to take advantage of lower wages in Mexico. Factories in the *maquiladoras* are called *maquilas*.

Means of production Factories, farms, and so on where goods are produced.

Medicare A tax-supported universal health-care program in which everyone has access to medical care regardless of income.

Melting pot A situation in which immigrants from other countries are encouraged to integrate into the dominant culture as quickly as possible. This term is often used to refer to the treatment of immigrants in the United States.

Minority government A government formed by a political party whose representatives did not win more seats in a legislature than all the other political parties combined. When this happens, the party with the most seats requires the support of another party to form a majority.

Monarchy A government system headed by a king or queen.

Multiculturalism A system in which people of various cultural backgrounds are encouraged to preserve their cultural identities while coexisting in one nation.

Naturalization The process of becoming a citizen of another country.

Non-governmental organization, NGO A non-profit, non-partisan, independent organization dedicated to making the world a better place.

Oligarchy A government system in which the many are ruled by the few.

Parliament An elected assembly that is responsible for making laws.

Parliamentary democracy A kind of representative or indirect democracy in which the head of government is often called a prime minister and must be an elected member of the national legislature

Pluralism A system in which people of various cultural backgrounds coexist in one nation.

Political party An organized group of people who share ideas about governing. Political parties compete with others for the support of voters during elections. The goal of a party is to win enough seats to gain control of the legislature and form the government.

Political prisoner Someone who has been imprisoned because of his or her political beliefs or political actions.

Popular vote The total number of ballots cast in an election.

Portfolio The department supervised by a Cabinet minister.

Pressure group An organization that tries to advance specific causes, issues, or interests.

Precedent A legal case or action that establishes a rule or pattern that will be used to guide subsequent cases or actions.

Prisoner of conscience Someone who has been sentenced to prison because of his or her beliefs.

Proportional representation A system of government in which the number of elected members of a particular party in a legislature is decided on the basis of the number of votes the party received in an election.

Racial segregation A system in which people of various races are segregated or kept apart.

Reconciliation The act of accepting someone or something after a conflict or separation.

Referendum A special vote to find out what voters want to do about an issue.

Refugee People who have fled their countries because of a well-founded fear of persecution for reasons of race, religion, nationality, political opinion, or membership in a particular social group, and who cannot or do not want to return.

Regionalism Loyalty to the interests of a particular region.

Republic A country in which a monarch is not the head of state. Republics may be democratic or non-democratic.

Representation by population An electoral system in which each of the elected members of a legislature represents about the same number of voters.

Representative democracy A government system in which people do not make decisions directly; instead, they elect representatives to make decisions on their behalf. This system is sometimes called indirect democracy.

Representative government A government system in which representatives of the people make decisions on their behalf.

Residual powers Leftover powers that were not assigned specifically to a particular level of government.

Responsible government A system of government in which the executive branch remains in office only as long as it has the support of a majority of the legislature.

Roma The name preferred by Gypsies. Many Roma detest the term "Gypsy."

Secular Referring to the material world rather than the spiritual world. A secular state is a country in which religion and government are separate.

Separatist Someone who wants Québec to separate from Canada and become an independent country.

Slander The act of damaging someone's reputation by saying something that is not true.

Social safety net An expression that refers to a range of tax-funded services, such as health care and pensions, that are available to everyone. Other programs, such as welfare assistance, are designed especially to help those in need.

Society A group of people gathered together in a community of some kind.

Sovereignty association A term used by Québec Premier René Lévesque to describe his proposal for Québec's new relationship with Canada. Québec was to become a self-governing nation in control of immigration, relations with other countries, and citizenship. At the same time, Québec would keep its economic ties with Canada.

Tariff A tax or duty levied by a government on imports or exports.

Totalitarian, totalitarianism An authoritarian system of government that requires total obedience to the ruler.

Treason Betrayal of the ruler or government.

Veto The right to reject a law.

Visa A special pass that allows someone to enter or leave a country.

CREDITS

Front Cover
left, Mark Richards/Photo Edit; **middle left**, Phil Snel/Canadian Press MACLEANS, **middle right** Bettman/CORBIS, **right** Adrian Wyld/Canadian Press CP.

Back Cover
left, Tom Prettyman/Photo Edit; **middle left**, David Lucas/Canadian Press CP, **middle right** Mary Kay Denny/Photo Edit, **right** Tony Freeman/Photo Edit.

Photo credits
viii Peter Bregg/Macleans/Canadian Press CP; viii Photo RMN/ /Versailles et Trianon 69252/ Musée de Versailles; ix National Archives of Canada C-15418; ix Courtesy of the Chambers Family; ix Metropolitan Toronto Reference Library, J. Ross Collection MTL 1826; ix Canadian Press CP; x Donald Stampfli/Associated Press AP; 1 Peter Bregg/Macleans/Canadian Press CP; 2 Photo RMN/ /Versailles et Trianon 69252/ Musée de Versailles; 4 David K. Crow/Photo Edit; 5 Bettmann/CORBIS; 6 U.S. National Archives and Department of Records Administration; 7 Photo RMN-Herve Lewandowski/Louvre; 8 top The Granger Collection, bottom Girdaudon/Art Resource, NY; 10 The Granger Collection; 11 Marie Mauzy /American School of Classical Studies, 54 Souidias Str. Athens, Greece 10676; 12 Erich Lessing/Art Resource; 14 Photodisc TR 005393; 15 Michael Stephans Pool/Associated Press AP; 16 British Museum Photographic Services/ 342526; 17 By Courtesy of the National Portrait Gallery, London REG NO: 3846; 18 U.S. National Archives and Department of Records Administration; 19 Cranbrook Institute of Science; 20 Giraudon/Art Resource, NY; 21 top By Courtesy of the National Portrait Gallery, London REG NO: 1237, bottom Leonard de Silva/CORBIS; 24 Ian McKain/Canadian Press CP; 26 Tom Hanson/Canadian Press CP; 27 James Stevenson/Canadian Press CP; 28 top National Archives of Canada C-16758, bottom National Archives of Canada C-1247; 31 Bettman/CORBIS; 33 National Archives of Canada C-47783; 35 Metropolitan Toronto Reference Library, J. Ross Collection MTL 1826; 36 National Archives of Canada C-121846; 37 National Archives of Canada C-018454; 38 top National Archives of Canada C- 26743, bottom National Archives of Canada

C-9220; 39 National Archives of Canada C-041067; 40 top National Archives of Canada C-733, bottom Courtesy Canadian Heritage Department Ac4c195; 41 National Archives of Canada C-15418; 43 U.S. National Archives and Department of Records Administration; 45 Courtesy of the Chambers Family; 48 Jonathon Hayward/Canadian Press CP; 50 Tom Hanson/Canadian Press CP; 51 top Comstock Photofile Ltd/KARSH, bottom left Comstock Photofile Ltd./KARSH, bottom right Sgt. Julien Dupuis, Rideau Hall; 52 top Adrian Wyld/ Canadian Press CP, middle Ontario Archives S2626, bottom left Ontario Archives S2630, bottom right National Archives of Canada/Robert Cooper PA-142647; 53 Ron Poling/Canadian Press CP; 54 Graham Harrop/Back Bench; 56 top Tom Hanson/Canadian Press CP; 58 Reuters/Archive Photos; 59 Courtesy Alvin Curling M.P.P.; 61 Photodisc AA001921; 64 "Get Fuzzy" reprinted with permission of United Features Syndicate, Inc.; 65 Aaron Harris/Canadian Press CP; 67 Canadian Press CP; 68 left Courtesy the Supreme Court of Canada/Yves Lefebre authorized by Desnoyers Mercure & Associates, right Tom Hanson/Canadian Press CP; 69 Cam/Ottawa Citizen; 70 National Archives of Canada C-11508; 71 Canadian Press CP; 72 Ron Poling/ Canadian Press CP; 78 Beth A. Keiser/Associated Press AP; 80 Fred Chartrand/Canadian Press CP; 81 J. Scott Applewhite/Associated Press AP; 82 John Moore/Associated Press AP; 83 Daniel Morel/Associated Press AP/World Wide Photos Inc.; 84 U.S. National Archives and Department of Records Administration 0541; 85 Bettman/COR-BIS/Magma; 86 Bettman/CORBIS/Magma; 88 UN PHOTO 177913/H. Vassal; 90 John Parkin/Associated Press AP/World Wide Photos Inc.; 91 Zo Selsky/Associated Press AP/World Wide Photos Inc.; 92 National Archives of Canada PA-169887; 93 UN PHOTO 183790/E. Kanalstein; 94 UN /DPI Photo by Milton Grant; 95 Donald Stampfli/Associated Press AP; 97 Chuck Stoody/Canadian Press CP; 98 Greg Gibson/Associated Press AP; 100 Paul Chiasson/Canadian Press CP; 101 Bettman/ CORBIS/Magma; 102 U.S. National Achives and Department of Records WW2170; 103 UN Photo 23783 Dcoc WP/Gaval2; 105 top Nick Ut/Associated Press AP, bottom Dennis Cook/

INDEX

head of state, 44
influencing, 64–65
law-making powers, 44
lobby, 64
majority, 61
minority, 62
municipal, 58, 60–61
pressure groups, 65
provincial, 58–59
unitary, 43
United States, 80
values, 116
Governor General, 51–52
Great Depression, 183
social programs, 119
Great Law of Peace, 19
Greenpeace, 177, 178

H

Habitants, 27, 29
Haida, 97
Hammurabi, 7
Hammurabi's Code, 7
Hansard, 57
Harper, Elijah, 157, 158
Hazardous waste, 188
Head of government, 51–52
Head of State, 50, 51
Health care, 58
social programs, 120
Herzegovina, 172
Hiroshima, 91
Hitler, Adolf, 6, 84, 85, 86
Holocaust, 87
Homelands (South Africa), 88–89
House of Commons, 15, 45, 52,
55–57
House of Lords, 15
House of Representatives, 80
Howe, Joseph, 38
Human rights, 96, 101–2, 162
agreements, 171–76
global economy, 186–89
protecting, 103–4
Humphrey, John P., 103

I

Illegal migrants, 166, 167

Immigration, 164–68
Canada, 39, 138
citizens, 165
deportation, 165
points system, 165
policies, 164
voting, 165
In camera, 53
Indian Act, 143
Intellectual property, 183
International Court of Justice, 175
International Covenant on Civil and
Political Rights, 104
International Covenant on
Economic, Social and Cultural
Rights, 104
International Criminal Tribunals,
173, 174
International Land Mines
Treaty, 180
International Military
Tribunal, 101–2
International Monetary
Fund (IMF), 96
International trade, 79
Inuit, 145–147
Iroquois Confederacy, 19, 27

J

James I, 16
James II, 16
Jefferson, Thomas, 18
Judicial branch, 50
United States, 80
Junta, 82
Justinian, 13
Justinian Code, 13

K

Keegstra, James, 128
Kielburger, Craig, 132
King Louis XIV, 8
King, William Lyon Mackenzie,
52, 119, 120
Kitchen compromise, 72
Kosovo, 173
Kristallnacht, 87
Kyoto Protocol, 189

L

Labour disputes, 68
LaFontaine, Louis-Hippolyte, 37,
38
Lambton, John, 36
Language, 155
Charter of Rights and
Freedoms, 73, 155, 156
Laporte, Pierre, 152
Laurier, Wilfrid, 52, 140, 150
Laws
civil, 65–66
courts, 65–66
criminal, 65–66
General Assembly, 98
parliament, 57
power to make, 44
proposed, 57
Rule of, 26
war, 178
League of Nations, 92
Legislation, 26
Legislative branch, 50
United States, 80
Legislature, 26
Lesage, Jean, 151, 155
Lévesque, René, 71, 72, 152, 153,
155
Libel, 128
Liberal Party, 62
Lieutenant-governor, 58
Life, liberty and security, 73, 75
Lincoln, Abraham, 6
Lobby, 64, 65
Lobster wars, 145
Locke, John, 3, 17, 20
Lockout, 70
Lord Durham, 36
Louis XIV, 29
Louis XVI, 20–21
Lower Canada, 31
rebellion of 1837, 32–33
Loyalists, 31

M

Macdonald, John A., 42–45
Mackenzie, William Lyon, 24, 25,
33, 34, 35
Magna Carta, 14, 15, 70
Maîtres chez nous, 151
Majority government, 61
Majority rule, 27